Principles of Argument Structure

Linguistic Inquiry Monographs
Samuel Jay Keyser, general editor

A complete list of books published in the Linguistic Inquiry Monographs series appears at the back of this book.

Principles of Argument Structure
A Merge-Based Approach

Chris Collins

The MIT Press
Cambridge, Massachusetts
London, England

The MIT Press would like to thank the anonymous peer reviewers who provided comments on drafts of this book. The generous work of academic experts is essential for establishing the authority and quality of our publications. We acknowledge with gratitude the contributions of these otherwise uncredited readers.

This book was set in Times New Roman by Westchester Publishing Services. Printed and bound in the United States of America.

Library of Congress Cataloging-in-Publication Data

Names: Collins, Chris, 1963– author.
Title: Principles of argument structure : a merge-based approach / Chris Collins.
Description: Cambridge, Massachusetts : The MIT Press, 2024. | Series: Linguistic inquiry monographs | Includes bibliographical references and index.
Identifiers: LCCN 2023036900 (print) | LCCN 2023036901 (ebook) | ISBN 9780262548274 (paperback) | ISBN 9780262379137 (epub) | ISBN 9780262379120 (pdf)
Subjects: LCSH: English language—Passive voice. | English language—Verb phrase. | English language—Syntax. | Construction grammar.
Classification: LCC PE1285 .C65 2024 (print) | LCC PE1285 (ebook) | DDC 425—dc23/eng/20231206
LC record available at https://lccn.loc.gov/2023036900
LC ebook record available at https://lccn.loc.gov/2023036901

10 9 8 7 6 5 4 3 2

This monograph is dedicated to my three great syntax teachers: Noam Chomsky, Richard Kayne, and Paul Postal. Their influence can be felt on every page.

Contents

Series Foreword

We are pleased to present the eighty-seventh volume in the series *Linguistic Inquiry Monographs*. These monographs present new and original research beyond the scope of the article. We hope they will benefit our field by bringing to it perspectives that will stimulate further research and insight.

Originally published in limited edition, the *Linguistic Inquiry Monographs* are now more widely available. This change is due to the great interest engendered by the series and by the needs of a growing readership. The editors thank the readers for their support and welcome suggestions about future directions for the series.

Samuel Jay Keyser
for the Editorial Board

Acknowledgments

I thank Nikos Angelopoulos, Mark Baker, Adriana Belletti, Guglielmo Cinque, Selikem Gotah, Erich Groat, Anders Holmberg, Richard Kayne, Hilda Koopman, Richard Larson, Olivia Ndapo, Paul Postal, Andrew Radford, Tom Roeper, Abdul-Razak Sulemana, Thomas Stroik, Gary Thoms, and Arhonto Terzi for discussing the issues in this book with me.

My collaboration with Nikos Angelopoulos and Arhonto Terzi on the comparison of Greek and English (Angelopoulos, Collins, and Terzi 2020) was especially valuable in helping me to understand the cross-linguistic scope of the principles involved. My collaboration with Adriana Belletti on the OUP smuggling volume (Belletti and Collins 2020) was useful to me in sharpening my ideas on the dative alternation and smuggling more generally.

Thanks also to the participants of my NYU seminars on argument structure (Fall 2018 and Fall 2021) for their useful feedback on the data and on the developing ideas. The Fall 2018 participants were Omar Agha, Gurprit Bains, Karoliina Lohiniva, Kate Mooney, Yining Nie, Dan Simon, and Hongchen Wu. The Fall 2021 participants were Rachel Christensen, Mica Clausen, Selikem Gotah, Stephanie Harves, Soo-Hwan Lee, John David Storment, and Gary Thoms. I also presented various sections in other syntax courses (including the undergraduate course Grammatical Analysis II, Spring 2018, 2023 and the graduate course Syntax I, Fall 2020, 2022). Thanks to the students of those courses for their feedback.

I benefited from the feedback of members of the audiences at the Brussels Conference on Generative Linguistics (BCGL) (October 6, 2022), NYU Syntax Brown Bag (September 23, 2022), UCONN Department of Linguistics (February 7, 2020), and the University of the Basque Country (February 10, 2022), where I presented various parts of this monograph.

Chapters 5 and 8 incorporate material from the following two published papers, respectively.

Angelopoulos, Nikos, Chris Collins, and Arhonto Terzi. 2020. Greek and English Passives and the Role of *by*-Phrases. *Glossa* 5(1): 90, 1–29.

Collins, Chris. 2020. A Smuggling Approach to the Dative Alternation. In *Smuggling in Syntax*, edited by Adriana Belletti and Chris Collins, 96–107. Oxford: Oxford University Press.

Finally, the monograph has benefited from two rounds of reviewing and five separate reviewers at the MIT Press. I am grateful to the reviewers for their expertise and for their time and effort in providing me with feedback, and to Philip Laughlin (Senior Acquisitions Editor, MIT Press), who shepherded my manuscript through the whole process.

1 A Merge-Based Approach to Argument Structure

1.1 Leading Ideas

This book investigates principles of argument structure in minimalist syntax through an in-depth analysis of certain properties of the English passive construction, illustrated in (1):

(1) a. John wrote the book. (active)
 b. The book was written by John. (passive)
 c. The book was written. (short passive)

The paradigm in (1) raises questions about argument structure. First, is the underlying syntactic position of the determiner phrase (DP) *John* in (1a) the same as or different from the underlying syntactic position of the *by*-phrase in (1b)? Another way to put the question is this: Is the external argument projected in the same way in the active and the passive? Furthermore, what principles of Universal Grammar (UG) determine these positions?

The relation between the passive and active was addressed in Chomsky (1957). His analysis is summarized in (2):

(2) If S_1 is a grammatical sentence of the form
 $NP_1 - Aux - V - NP_2$,
 then the corresponding string of the form
 $NP_2 - Aux + be + en - V - by + NP_1$
 is also a grammatical sentence.
 (pgs. 42–43, 78–81, 112)

In this formulation, the passive is derived from the active, so that (3) is trivially true.

(3) The external argument of the passive is projected in exactly the same way as the external argument of the active.

Chomsky (1957:42–43) gives a famous argument for the transformational rule in (2) based on selectional restrictions: "Finally, note that in elaborating (13) [C.C., a grammar containing only rewrite rules, no transformations] into a full-fledged grammar we will have to place many restrictions on the choice of V in terms of subject and object in order to permit such sentences as: 'John admires sincerity,' 'sincerity frightens John,' 'John plays golf,' 'John drinks wine,' while excluding the 'inverse' non-sentences 'sincerity admires John,' 'John frightens sincerity,' 'golf plays John,' 'wine drinks John.' But this whole network of restrictions fails completely when we choose *be* + *en* as part of the auxiliary verb. In fact, in this case the same selectional dependencies hold, but in the opposite order."

Essentially, Chomsky argues for the transformational rule of the passive in (2) on the basis of selectional restrictions. The passive and the active show the same selectional restrictions, and this fact can be captured if the passive sentence is derived from an active sentence by transformation (which by implicit assumption does not change selectional restrictions).

In this monograph, I will argue for (3) (contra Bruening 2013; Legate 2014; and Alexiadou, Anagnostopoulou, and Schäfer 2015) and show how (3) follows from UG principles (outlined in the next two sections).

The paradigm in (1) also raises the issue of implicit arguments. In (1c) an implicit argument can be detected through entailments. In this case, we have the entailment in (4):

(4) The book was written. ⊨ Somebody or something wrote the book.

If it is true that the book was written, then it is true that somebody or something wrote the book. Because of this entailment, we know that there is an implicit argument in (1c). What is the syntactic and semantic status of that implicit argument? Furthermore, what principles of UG determine the status of implicit arguments?

For Chomsky (1957), the implicit argument in the short passive comes about by ellipsis:

(5) "The sentences of (104) without the parenthetical expression are formed by a second 'elliptical' transformation that converts e.g., 'the boy was seen by John' into 'the boy was seen.'" (pgs. 81, 89–90)

For example, Chomsky (1957:89) discusses the following paradigm:

(6) a. The picture was painted by a new technique.
b. The picture was painted by a real artist.

He comments as follows: "[6b] is the passive of 'a real artist painted the picture.' . . . [6a] is formed from, e.g., 'John painted the picture by a new technique' by a double transformation; first the passive, then the elliptical transformation . . . that drops the 'agent' in the passive." The point of the example is that the two sentences in (6) differ in the transformations that apply to derive them.

In the framework of Chomsky (1957), the only way to get an implicit argument in the passive is through ellipsis. So, the implicit argument must have been syntactically projected (before being elided):

(7) The implicit argument in the passive is syntactically projected.

In this monograph, I will argue for (7) (again contra Bruening 2013; Legate 2014; and Alexiadou, Anagnostopoulou, and Schäfer 2015) and show how it follows from UG principles. As we shall see, (3) and (7) are closely related and follow from the same UG principle: the Argument Criterion/Theta-Criterion, as explained in the next section.

1.2 Argument-Introducing Heads

I adopt an approach to argument structure arising from Larson 1988 (which builds on Barss and Lasnik 1986), which shows that c-command asymmetries in double object constructions can be analyzed in terms of VP shells, where different arguments are introduced in different VP shells. Subsequent work developing that general framework includes Hale and Keyser 1993, 2002, Bowers 1993, Marantz 1993, Chomsky 1995, Collins and Thráinsson 1996, Kratzer 1996, Baker 1997, Travis 2000, Gruber 2001, Harley 2002, 2011, 2013, Borer 2020, Collins 2005a, Pylkkänen 2008a, Ramchand 2008, and many others. The fundamental assumption is that there is a series of verbal projections that introduce arguments, including at least v and Appl. I will call these *argument-introducing heads* (see Pylkkänen 2008a:8 for additional kinds of argument-introducing heads; see Bowers 1993 on PredP).

Even though I focus mostly on v and Appl in this monograph, the results should apply generally to any system that uses such argument-introducing heads. For example, the *Argument Criterion* below would also apply in Ramchand's (2008) system based on Init (initiator), Proc (process), and Res (result) projections (see Ramchand 2008:60). Therefore, any such system (based on argument-introducing heads) would need to adopt the conclusions in this monograph about implicit arguments, KPs, and the role of voice.

The discussion in this monograph focuses mostly on external arguments (e.g., implicit external arguments and *by*-phrases), so I do not say much about internal arguments (e.g., themes, patients). For simplicity, I assume that there is a lexical transitive verb *write* that introduces an argument as a complement: $[_{VP}$ write $[_{DP}$ the book$]]$. This is a huge simplification. Rather, such arguments should also be introduced by various argument-introducing heads in the spirit of Ramchand 2008. I briefly return to this issue at the end of chapter 4 (see section 4.7, "Complement Deletion").

Highly relevant for the issue of internal arguments is Postal's (2010) three-way classification of objects into 2, 3, and 4 objects. In the foreword of Postal 2010, Collins remarks "The challenge, then, is to match up the 2, 3, and 4 objects to positions within the system of VP shells and to show how their syntactic behavior (with respect to passivization, relativization, etc.) can be explained on the basis of this matching." I leave this challenging project to future research.

1.3 Principles of Argument Structure

In this section, I outline the principles relevant to deriving (3) and (7) above. First, I discuss the relationship between Merge and argument structure. *Merge* is defined as follows (see Collins and Stabler 2016 for a formalization):

(8) Merge(A,B) = {A,B}

Chomsky (2005:14; see also Chomsky 2004:111; Chomsky 2021; Chomsky, Gallego, and Ott 2019:242) observes that "External Merge correlates with argument structure, internal Merge with edge properties, scopal or discourse related (new and old information, topic, etc.)." Strengthening Chomsky's observation, I propose that the only way to build argument structure is by external Merge. I call this the *Merge-based theory of argument structure*. The core of this thesis can be formalized as follows.

First, I define what it means for a head to introduce an argument:

(9) A head H introduces an argument A if A externally merges with a projection of H.

The definition in (9) is purely terminological. It just defines what it means for a head to introduce an argument by specifying a particular structural configuration.

As noted above, I am assuming that there is a series of *argument-introducing heads*, including v and Appl (among others). These heads are designated as argument-introducing heads as part of UG. Other heads such as Pl (the plural head), T (the tense head), Asp (the aspect head), and Foc (the focus head) are not argument-introducing heads. Pl takes an NP (not a DP complement), and the specifier of Foc is filled by internal Merge (of the focused constituent) not external Merge.

But (9) does not say anything about whether or not an argument needs to be introduced by an argument-introducing head, or whether or not an argument-introducing head needs to introduce an argument. The following condition answers these questions:

(10) Argument Criterion
  a. Each argument is introduced by a single argument-introducing head.
  b. Each argument-introducing head introduces a single argument.

I take arguments to be nonexpletive DPs (e.g., *John*, *nobody*, *the dog*), pronouns, KPs (e.g., passive *by John* to be discussed in chapter 6 and dative *to John* to be discussed in chapter 8), and some kinds of clauses (e.g., *that John is late*). AdjPs (adjective phrases), NPs, and other kinds of predicative expressions are not arguments. This list is sufficient for the purposes of the monograph, so I do not attempt a formal definition.

(10) is the fundamental thesis of the monograph. While it is simple and seemingly obvious, I will show that it has far-reaching empirical and theoretical consequences and rules out many widely accepted analyses.

The Argument Criterion is closely related to the Theta-Criterion (on a recent revision of the Theta-Criterion, see Chomsky 2021):

(11) Theta-Criterion (First Version)
  Each argument bears one and only one theta-role, and each theta-role is assigned to one and only one argument.
  (Chomsky 1981:36)

But the formulation in (11) raises difficult questions about individuating theta-roles. For example, what is the theta-role of *John* in "John deliberately rolled down the hill"? Is *John* a theme, an agent, or some kind of composite (see Chomsky 1981:139, fn. 14 for discussion). The formulation of the Theta-Criterion in Chomsky 1986 sidesteps this kind of question entirely by focusing on theta-positions, not theta-roles:

(12) Theta-Criterion (Second and Final Version)
  Each argument α appears in a chain containing a unique visible theta-position P, and each theta-position P is visible in a chain containing a unique argument α.
  (Chomsky 1986:97)

This formulation of the Theta-Criterion says nothing about particular theta-roles, or what a theta-role is, or even whether theta-roles exist. It does not presuppose a way to distinguish particular theta-roles (e.g., locations from goals, or themes from patients, or experiencers and causers from agents). Rather, it talks about theta-positions, which are just the external Merge positions of arguments. In other words, (12) forces the external Merge of arguments in certain positions.

The difference between the Argument Criterion (10) and the second version of the Theta-Criterion (12) is that the Argument Criterion focuses on the argument-introducing heads. In effect, the argument-introducing heads define the theta-positions. If the system were formalized (e.g., as in Collins and Stabler 2016), the Argument Criterion would be an axiom (a principle of UG) and the Theta-Criterion would be a theorem (derived from the Argument Criterion and other definitions and principles). I will not give a proof here. In this monograph, I will often discuss the Theta-Criterion since it is already widely referred to in the syntax literature. I will refer to AC/TC (Argument Criterion/Theta-Criterion) where the difference between them is not relevant.

The effect of the Argument Criterion is to force a bijection (one-to-one onto function) between argument-introducing heads and arguments. Therefore, there are four ways to violate it. Case 1: Some argument-introducing head does not introduce an argument. Case 2: Some argument-introducing head introduces two arguments (e.g., in a multiple-specifier configuration). Case 3: Some argument is not introduced by an argument-introducing head. Case 4: Some argument is introduced by two argument-introducing heads.

In this monograph, we focus mostly on case 1. I show that blocking case 1 has concrete implications for the theory of implicit arguments. Case 4 occurs when an argument occupies two theta-positions. I assume this is ruled out, but I do not discuss it in this monograph (see Hornstein 1999).

The AC/TC are closely related to the configurational approach to theta-theory outlined in Chomsky 1995:313 (see also Hale and Keyser 1993:68, 69 for a related conception):

(13) "A theta-role is assigned in a certain structural configuration; β assigns a theta-role only in the sense that it is the head of that configuration."

Chomsky continues in the next paragraph: "theta-relatedness is a property of the position of merger and its (very local) configuration." The configurational approach has the following two properties:

(14) a. There is a syntactic configurational relation between an argument and an argument-introducing head.
b. That relation is unique.

(14a) already follows from the Argument Criterion. But why is (14b) true? Why is the syntactic relation unique? Why couldn't there be several different syntactic relations between little v and DP that would all yield an agentive interpretation? The Argument Criterion says that each argument-introducing head introduces a single argument, but it does not stipulate a unique position for the introduced argument. Curiously, (14b) does follow from the

Theta-Criterion, since the Theta-Criterion is defined in terms of positions. I propose that uniqueness in (14b) follows in part from economy.

Here are some possible syntactic relations (I will return to adjunction structures shortly):

(15) a. DP is the complement of v.
b. DP is the first (inner) specifier of vP.
c. DP is the second specifier of vP.
d. DP is the third specifier of vP.
e. DP is the first specifier of the first specifier of vP.
f. DP is the second specifier of the first specifier of vP.
g. DP is the first specifier of the complement of v.
h. DP asymmetrically c-commands vP in a phase.
i. DP asymmetrically c-commands vP in a phase with no intervening DP.
j. DP asymmetrically c-commands vP in a clause.

In fact, there are an unlimited number of conceivable syntactic configurational relations between v and the external argument DP, so why is only (15b) chosen? The question is even more acute under a theory eliminating labels (Collins 2002) or introducing labels by a labeling algorithm (Chomsky 2013). In that kind of theory, Spec vP is undefined; rather, Spec vP corresponds to the second merged XP:

(16) {DP, {v, VP}}

So why is the DP in (16) the only possible argument position for v? First, I put aside the possibility of {VP, {v, DP}} (VP is the specifier). I assume that this configuration is never allowed. The generalization is the following: in the extended projection of a verb V, the arguments introduced must c-command V. I put aside how this follows from general principles (such as labeling or economy). Second, I propose that the proximity of DP to v and the uniqueness of the position (Spec vP) are both the result of economy considerations. Basically, DP is being merged as close to v as possible (given that v takes a VP complement), and there is only one such closest position (shown in (16)). On external Merge being constrained by economy, see Collins 1997:75–78 and Collins 2022.

A reviewer raises the possibility that the passive *by*-phrase could be an adjunct to vP, formed by Pair-Merge. Applied to *by*-phrases, this would yield the adjunction structure [$_{vP}$ vP [by John]]. An empirical problem with the adjunct analysis is that it yields the wrong c-command facts. If the *by*-phrase is right-adjoined to the vP, this incorrectly predicts that the *by*-phrase will c-command things to the left. But standard c-command tests show this prediction does not hold. This point is already made in Collins 2005a:86, (10). See also chapter 7, example (14).

More generally, adjunction and Pair-Merge play no role at all in the principles of argument structure that I lay out in this chapter. Rather, the theory that I propose is based solidly on (nonpair) set Merge. In fact, for Chomsky (2004), Pair-Merge concerns "predicate composition" and not argument structure, which is built by Merge (see also Chomsky, Gallego, and Ott 2019:249):

(17) "Recall that the strong interface condition (however formulated precisely) requires sufficient diversity at SEM. Possibly richness of expressive power requires an operation of predicate composition: that is not provided by set Merge, which yields the duality of interpretation discussed earlier: argument structure and edge properties. But it is the essential semantic contribution of pair Merge. If the C-I-system imposes this condition, then the existence of a device to yield predicate composition would conform to SMT—a promissory note, given the limitations of understanding of C-I, but not unreasonable."
(Chomsky 2004:118)

According to Chomsky (2004), argument structure is accounted for by (Set) Merge, and predicate composition is accounted for by Pair-Merge. Going even further, Collins (2017:52) notes: "Pair-Merge is a completely different operation from Merge, and would have to be stipulated as an independent operation of UG (going against the SMT as defined in section 1)." Lastly, Sportiche (2017b) argues that "There are no adjuncts, there is no adjunction." If Sportiche is right, *by*-phrases could not be adjuncts since adjuncts don't exist. In summary, for a variety of empirical and theoretical reasons, I reject the proposal that the passive *by*-phrase is an adjunct to vP formed by Pair-Merge.

An alternative way to state the Theta-Criterion might be in terms of features, such as [+D] (requiring a DP argument). In effect, such an account would be treating the Theta-Criterion in terms of c-selection (category-selection). However, I reject this alternative because it would allow different kinds of lexical items that should be excluded. For example, all of the following would be possible feature specifications for an argument-introducing head: [+D], [(+D)], [–D], [+/–D]. Are all these different systems attested? Since the D is a category feature, presumably such an account would also allow any category label as a c-selectional feature (e.g., [+C], [+Adj]). Also, there are other technologies accompanying the use of features (e.g., feature inheritance, feature percolation, Agree, valued versus unvalued features, interpretable versus uninterpretable features, feature deletion) all of which seem completely irrelevant to argument structure.

The only assumption I need is that certain heads are designated as argument-introducing heads as part of UG. Once a head is classified as an argument-introducing head, it then obeys the AC/TC. One can call this property a feature (informally), but there is no reason to say that there is anything like the formal syntactic symbol +AIH ("argument-introducing head") that is a component part of the lexical item. And since the formal syntactic symbol +AIH does not exist as part of lexical items, none of its variants (such as –AIH, +/–AIH, etc.) exists either. Nor is there any reason to suppose that any of the common operations on features (e.g., Agree, inheritance, percolation, deletion, valuation) will be able to take place either.

There are people who deny the existence of the Theta-Criterion (see chapter 10 for a detailed discussion). For example, Bruening (2013:23) gives the following statement (see also Heim and Kratzer 1998:51):

(18) "Because there are no syntactic thematic roles in this system, there is also no θ-Criterion. Elements will either combine semantically, or they will not. If a head is a function that calls for an argument and an argument of the appropriate type combines with it, the semantics will be well-formed. If a predicate calls for an argument and no argument combines with it, it will be ill-formed. If there is an argument that does not serve as the argument of any predicate in the semantics, the result will also be ill-formed. All the work of the θ-Criterion is done by the semantics."

A similar sentiment can be found in Myler and Mali 2021:3 (see also Harley 2011:430):

(19) "Also, the Theta-Criterion has no status in this conception: all that is required is that the structure compose successfully in the semantics (Full Interpretation; see also Baker 1997:121–122; Heim and Kratzer 1998: 53–58)."

Bruening and others try to make the case that the Theta-Criterion can be eliminated and replaced by the assumptions of formal semantics. Nothing more needs to be said. However, I will argue that analyses that do not assume the Theta-Criterion (e.g., the analysis of the passive in Bruening 2013) make the wrong empirical predictions with respect to the distribution of reflexives, reciprocals, pronouns, Helke expressions, and secondary predicates (see chapters 2 and 3). Therefore, the chapters of this monograph can be seen as a direct empirical argument for the Theta-Criterion. I return to a discussion of the tension between the Merge-based approach to argument structure and formal semantics in chapter 10.

A direct consequence of AC/TC is the following (see (7) above):

(20) Implicit arguments are syntactically realized.

Here is the argument that (20) follows from the Argument Criterion in (10). Consider again the passive in (1). In the active in (1a), *John* is externally merged as Spec vP (by assumption). This shows that little v is an argument-introducing head (by (10a)). I assume that little v is also present in the passive (on the basis of semantic entailments and the possibility of a *by*-phrase). Furthermore, there is no special passive flavor of little v. Rather, the same little v is used in the passive and active. Therefore, in the short passive in (1c), little v must introduce an argument (by (10b)). Therefore, in (1c), there must be a syntactically present, but phonologically null, implicit argument.

In the above argument, I have claimed that little v is also present in the passive, based on semantic entailments and the possibility of the *by*-phrase. A version of this assumption is shared by all the analyses considered in this monograph. For example, for Bruening (2013:22), VoiceP introduces the external argument in the active, and this same VoiceP is present in the passive.

Here is the closely parallel argument that (20) follows from the Theta-Criterion. Consider again the passive in (1). In the active in (1a), *John* is externally merged as Spec vP (by assumption). This shows that Spec vP is a theta-position. I assume that little v is also present in the passive (on the basis of semantic entailments and the possibility of a *by*-phrase). Furthermore, there is no special passive flavor of little v. Rather, the same little v is used in the passive and active. Therefore, in the short passive in (1c), Spec vP is also a theta-position. Therefore, in (1c), there must be a syntactically present, but phonologically null, implicit argument occupying Spec vP.

In light of these arguments, consider the sentence "The toy broke." A reviewer notes: "Given how we conceive of the world there must be some cause to the toy breaking, so there is some kind of implicit agent or cause. Yet I do not think there are grounds to conclude that this implicit agent or cause is syntactically represented . . .". The reviewer's example is important. When I say implicit arguments are syntactically projected, what exactly do I mean by "implicit argument"? I agree with the reviewer's judgments and conclude that implications alone are not sufficient to justify the projection of an implicit external argument.

For the reviewer's example ("The toy broke"), I find the following acceptable: "It broke by itself/on its own." This could be said if something about the material or technological composition of the toy was defective, and it just stopped working. But I find a clear contrast with "It was broken by itself/on its own." The latter sentence seems to me to be gibberish, because it is contradictory. In other words, the toy cannot break on its own if somebody breaks it.

So, these considerations show that we need to draw a distinction between an implicature based on real-world knowledge (which can often be canceled), and an entailment based on syntactic structure (in this case, a syntactically projected external argument in the short passive) that cannot be canceled. See also the related discussion of complement deletion in section 4.7.

As I will show in chapter 4, the principle in (20) covers the implicit argument in the short passive, but other cases of implicit arguments as well (see Elbourne 2021 and Bhatt and Pancheva 2017 for surveys). Consider the following examples:

(21) a. Libertarian doctrine never advocates the promotion of oneself at the expense of others.
b. Letters to oneself compose quickly.
(Stroik 1992:129)
c. It was upsetting to see herself in the newspaper.
(See Landau 2010 and Epstein 1984 on control by experiencers.)

The prediction of (20) is that all such implicit arguments are syntactically represented. In (21a), the noun *promotion* has an implicit external argument. We know that the implicit argument is syntactically present since it binds the reflexive *oneself.* Similarly, in (21b), the middle verb *compose* has an implicit external argument whose syntactic presence is felt as the antecedent for the reflexive *oneself.* Lastly, in (21c), *upsetting* has an implicit argument that controls PRO in the infinitival clause.

An important question is whether all such implicit arguments have the same syntactic and semantic properties or whether there are subtypes of implicit arguments. For example, is there a unified theory of licensing for all the implicit arguments in (21)? Are the implicit arguments in (21) syntactically active to the same extent? Do all implicit arguments have the same phi-features? I will return to these and other questions in chapter 4, where I present a new theory of implicit arguments consistent with the AC/TC.

Another consequence of the AC/TC is that passive *by*-phrases are externally merged into Spec vP. More generally, the following principle holds:

(22) KPs are arguments (and hence obey the AC/TC).

A KP is a projection with a semantically vacuous head (e.g., passive *by*, dative *to*, some uses of *of*) that is part of the extended projection of the DP. In the context of the passive, (22) makes the claim that the *by*-phrase is an argument (see (3) above). In the active in (1a), *John* is externally merged as Spec vP (by assumption). This shows that Spec vP is a theta-position. Therefore, in the passive in (1c), Spec vP is also a theta-position. Therefore, in (1c), the *by*-phrase is externally merged into Spec vP (satisfying the AC/TC).

Lastly, this monograph will discuss the relation between voice and argument structure with the following conclusion (contra Kratzer 1996; Pylkkänen 2008a; Bruening 2013; Legate 2014; Alexiadou, Anagnostopoulou, and Schäfer 2015; and Sigurðsson and Wood 2021):

(23) Voice is independent of the projection of arguments.

Although I only discuss passive voice in this monograph, I allow the formulation in (23) to cover all kinds of voice (active, middle, nonactive, antipassive, inverse, etc.). Basically, arguments are projected in exactly the same way in the active and the passive. Based on the empirical evidence I give, it is not the case that the external argument is projected in the active, while remaining unprojected in the passive (contra Bruening 2013). Therefore, voice is independent from the projection of external arguments, and more generally, it is independent from argument structure. Voice and argument structure are two independent but interacting systems. They should not be conflated.

Why is voice independent of argument structure? Why doesn't UG allow for the external argument to be projected in Spec VoiceP (allowing for many different kinds of interactions between voice and the projection of the external argument)? I argue that the AC/TC severely limits the way in which arguments can be projected. The kinds of analyses proposed in the literature involving VoiceP projecting an external argument violate the AC/TC. I return to a detailed discussion in chapter 8.

See chapter 11 for a more detailed exposition of the principles of argument structure argued for in this monograph.

1.4 Overview of Monograph

In chapter 2, I investigate the phi-features of the implicit argument in the short passive in English, using the distribution of reflexives (Principle A), pronouns (Principle B), and bound pronouns (Helke expressions) as diagnostics. I show that there are three cases: (a) null versions of generic *one* and *you* (dubbed pro_{gen}), (b) a null existentially bound pro with no-phi features (dubbed pro_{un} where *un* stands for unspecified), and (c) a null definite pro with any combination of phi-features (dubbed pro_{def}). This chapter supports the claim that the implicit argument in the short passive is syntactically projected (contra Alexiadou, Anagnostopoulou, and Schäfer 2015; Bruening 2013; Legate 2014; and Pylkkänen 2008a).

In chapter 3, I discuss the distribution of secondary predicates in the short passive. Based on a systematic discussion of the existing literature, and new data from the Internet, I establish that secondary predicates can modify the implicit argument in the short passive (contra Pylkkänen 2008a). Chapters 2 and 3 together show that many different tests (the distribution of reflexives, reciprocals, pronouns, Helke expressions, and secondary predicates) converge on the same result: there is a syntactically projected implicit external argument in the short passive in English.

In chapter 4, I embed the results of chapters 2 and 3 in a general theory of implicit arguments. I argue that implicit arguments are syntactically projected, including implicit arguments with evaluative predicates, middles, nominalizations, and passives. I propose that implicit arguments are covert pronominals (pro) lacking a structural Case feature. Using the wedge argument, I argue that syntactically projected implicit arguments are made available by UG.

In chapter 5, I provide cross-linguistic support for the theory of implicit arguments from three African languages: Buli (Sulemana 2022), Oshiwambo (Ndapo 2022), and Ewe (Gotah 2022). Reporting on recent work, I discuss how in the short passive in Buli and Oshiwambo, and in the Ewe middle, the implicit external argument must be syntactically projected.

In chapter 6, I discuss the *by*-phrase in the passive. A common position taken in recent literature on the passive is that *by*-phrases are adjuncts (Bruening 2013; Legate 2014). Chapter 6 shows that passive *by*-phrases differ from adjuncts in terms of binding phenomena. From these facts, I conclude that *by*-phrases are not adjuncts, but rather arguments. I briefly report on data from Angelopoulos, Collins, and Terzi 2020 on modern Greek that reach the same conclusion. These conclusions dovetail with the conclusions of chapters 2–5 by showing that the passive always has a syntactically projected external argument (whether or not a *by*-phrase is present).

Chapter 7 combines the results of the preceding chapters and gives full derivations of several passive sentences, stating clearly all the technical assumptions and discussing several differences from Collins 2005a.

In chapter 8, I compare two distinct conceptions of VoiceP. In one conception, the external argument is projected (externally merged) into Spec VoiceP (Kratzer 1996, and much related work). In the other conception, VoiceP plays no role in the projection of arguments, but determines how the arguments are realized in various A-positions. I dub these two theories the projection theory and the realization theory, respectively. I present several empirical reasons for preferring the realization theory. Basically, since the external argument is projected in the same way in the active and the passive, there is no reason to assume that the external argument is externally merged in Spec VoiceP (where its occurrence would naturally depend on the particular kind of voice head). Furthermore, I show that the projection theory is inconsistent with the AC/TC.

In chapter 9, I give an analysis of the dative alternation, which I analyze as a kind of "inner passive." On the basis of traditional c-command tests, I show that the prepositional dative is derived from an underlying structure where the goal is projected higher than the theme. Just as with the passive, I motivate a smuggling analysis, where a VP containing the theme is moved over the goal. I present additional evidence for this analysis from Hallman 2015.

In chapter 10, I discuss the tension between the Merge-based theory of argument structure and a theory of argument structure constrained only by formal semantics. First, I respond to Heim and Kratzer's (1998) critique of the Theta-Criterion and point out some problems with their arguments. Second, I discuss a range of cases in the syntax/semantics literature where people have relied heavily on formal semantics to explain argument structure phenomena. Third, I discuss the status of UTAH in the Merge-based framework. Lastly, I outline the main conceptual problems with adopting formal semantics as the sole basis for a theory of argument structure.

In chapter 11, I summarize the principles discussed throughout this monograph.

2 The Phi-Features of the Implicit Argument

2.1 Introduction

It has been claimed in the generative syntax literature that the implicit argument of a short passive can bind a reflexive pronoun. Some cases follow:

(1) a. Such privileges should be kept to oneself.
(Baker, Johnson, and Roberts 1989:228; Roberts 1987:162)
b. Damaging testimony is always given about oneself in secret trials.
(Roberts 1987:162)

Because reflexive pronouns are subject to Principle A of the Binding Theory, these examples suggest that the implicit argument of the short passive is syntactically present. In this account, the implicit argument of the passive verb *kept* binds the reflexive *oneself*.

Principles A and B of the Binding Theory are stated for convenience below. I use the standard formulation from Sportiche, Koopman, and Stabler 2014:

(2) a. Principle A: An anaphor must be bound in its domain.
b. Principle B: A pronoun cannot be bound in its domain.

Such a conclusion about the sentences in (1) is contrary to recent claims by Bruening (2013); Legate (2014); and Alexiadou, Anagnostopoulou, and Schäfer (2015) that there is no syntactically represented implicit argument in the short passive. Rather, in these theories, the implicit argument is not syntactically projected, but is semantically existentially closed.

Some quotes illustrating these claims follow:

(3) "I propose that passive is a head (Pass) that selects a projection of Voice that has not yet projected its external argument."
(Bruening 2013:22)

(4) "In chapter 2, I argued for a new analysis of the implicit initiator in passives: this is present on the Voice head, both as a T-role, introduced but not assigned to any DP, and as features restricting this T-position." (Legate 2014:141)

But the data in (1) are incompatible with such analyses. Because a reflexive pronoun requires a syntactic antecedent, the passive verbs in (1a,b) need syntactically present external arguments. For example, in (1a), *oneself* is bound by the implicit external argument, which is syntactically projected as pro (see chapter 4 on the general theory of implicit arguments).

Alexiadou, Anagnostopoulou, and Schäfer (2015:131) suggest for data like (1) that the reflexive is a logophor (see also Reed 2011; Schäfer 2012:214, fn. 2):

(5) "the English data might also find a quite different explanation, as they could arguably involve a logophor instead of an ordinary reflexive pronoun."

In section 2.8, I argue against the claim that the reflexives in (1a,b) can be analyzed as logophors. For the moment, I point out that the reflexive in (1a) is an inherent reflexive and so cannot be analyzed as a logophor or exempt anaphor (see Büring 2005:22 for a discussion of inherent reflexives). The expression *to keep privileges to* requires that the complement of the preposition *to* be coindexed with the external argument. Because of this requirement, the only possible complement of *to* is a reflexive pronoun. For example, substituting a nonreflexive pronoun would meet the coindexation requirement, but would violate Principle B, as shown in (6b). Substituting an R-expression for the reflexive, as in (6c), would violate the coindexation requirement.

(6) a. John_1 keeps such privileges to himself_1.
b. *John_1 keeps such privileges to him_1.
c. *John_1 keeps such privileges to Mary_2.

The binding of the reflexive pronoun is entirely parallel in (1a) and (6a). In (1a) and (6a), the reflexive must be locally bound by the external argument (because it is an inherent reflexive): it is not a logophoric or an exempt anaphor. In (1a) (as in (6a)) requirements of both the reflexive pronoun (subject to Principle A) and the expression *to keep privileges to* (requiring coindexation) are satisfied if there is a syntactically projected implicit external argument binding the reflexive pronoun.

But the presence of a syntactically present implicit argument in short passives raises the question of what the possible phi-features of that implicit argument are. In this chapter, I sort through the various possibilities and show that there are three cases: (a) null pro versions of generic *one/you* (pro_{gen}), (b) a null pro lacking phi-features (pro_{un}), and (c) a null definite pro with any combination of phi-features (pro_{def}).

The rest of the chapter is structured as follows. Section 2.2 gives further generic examples, such as those involving the reflexive *oneself.* I dub the generic implicit argument pro_{gen}. Section 2.3 discusses existential implicit arguments. The main claim in this section is that the existential implicit argument is a null pronoun pro that lacks phi-features, which I dub pro_{un} (for unspecified). Section 2.4 discusses a new class of cases that has not, to my knowledge, been previously discussed, where the implicit argument is a definite pronoun, which I dub pro_{def}. Section 2.5 shows the implicit argument in the passive can bind reciprocals. Section 2.6 argues that the implicit argument of the passive can be bound. Section 2.7 addresses the issue of whether there are any animacy restrictions on the implicit argument of the passive and concludes that there are no such restrictions. Section 2.8 gives five arguments against analyzing the reflexives in (1a,b) as exempt anaphors with a logophoric interpretation. Section 2.9 is the conclusion.

2.2 Generic *pro*

It is relatively easy to find examples involving *oneself* like (1a,b) on the Internet. A few such examples follow (on the general methodology of using the Internet for syntactic research, see the appendix):

(7) Increased privacy and individuality result in more time spent on oneself.
(https://www.sciencedirect.com/science/article/pii/S2452315116000035)

(8) Anything done for another is done for oneself.
(https://en.wikiquote.org/wiki/Talk:Pope_John_Paul_II)

(9) Depression is anger turned against oneself.
(https://www.slideshare.net/saita1991/mood-disorders-48816847)

(10) An e-mail sent to oneself as a "memo to file" is considered a university record if it documents university business.
(http://ipo.info.yorku.ca/tool-and-tips/tip-sheet-5-email-management/)

(11) We know that, in general, humor aimed at oneself is well received by others.
(https://www.humormatters.com/articles/crisis.htm)

(12) Therefore, certain private matters must be kept to oneself and remain untouched.
(https://dokumen.pub/the-zaza-kurds-of-turkey-a-middle-eastern-minority-in-a-globalised-society-9780755609376-9781845118754.html)

(13) If feelings and emotions and fears and frustrations are to be kept inside oneself, those emotions are often also kept away from God.
(https://books.google.com/books?isbn=1929626177)

(14) and when that feeling overflows and cannot be kept inside oneself anymore
(https://livinginsentences.tumblr.com/)

These examples are all acceptable to me. And in each case, the antecedent of the reflexive is clearly the implicit argument of the short passive, as indicated by the interpretation. For example, in (10) the sender (the implicit argument) and the receiver (*oneself*) are the same person. The sheer number of such examples, and the ease with which they are found on the Internet, makes it impossible to claim that (1a,b) are infrequent fixed expressions (and hence ignorable when constructing a theory of UG). Rather, the examples in (7–14) suggest that principles of UG must make it possible for the implicit argument in the passive to bind a reflexive.

Some of the previous examples are reduced relatives modifying nouns. A reviewer suggests that the use of such examples may give rise to complications. Commenting on (9), the reviewer points out: "it is not out of the question that the head noun has a covert possessor argument, something like 'pro's depression is pro's anger turned against oneself', with the covert possessor binding the anaphor *oneself*, rather than a null nominal in Spec vP, as the author assumes." Because I give examples of both regular passives (e.g., (8)) and reduced relatives, I don't think there is a problem with the data. Also, in some cases it is easy to paraphrase without a reduced relative ("If an e-mail is sent to oneself as a memo file").

What phi-features are involved in these kinds of examples? First, *oneself* is singular (as indicated by the use of the form *oneself*, rather than *oneselves*). Second, it is third person (with a semantic connection to the speaker, as described in Moltmann 2006). Third, it is human and animate. Fourth, it has a feature [+generic] (following Moltmann 2006:262; see also Rizzi 1986:512), which I will analyze as a kind of phi-feature (because it determines the form of the pronoun *one*). Moltmann claims that "formally this means that generic *one* as well as arbitrary PRO should carry the feature [+gn] as a formal agreement feature which will require those pronominal elements to be bound by a generic operator carrying that feature as well (but as an interpretable feature)." I follow Moltmann in all these assumptions.

According to Moltmann (2006:260): "Generic *one*, we can thus say, acts as a variable ranging over individuals, a variable bound not by a universal quantifier, but rather by a generic quantifier that allows for exceptions and has itself modal force. Without going into any further detail about the nature of that quantifier, let us simply say it is the generic quantifier Gn as commonly used in the linguistic semantic literature on generic sentences (cf. Krifka et al. 1995)."

Putting these ideas together, I assume that the implicit argument in the short passive in these cases is a null version of the pronoun *one*, which I will call pro_{gen} (on null generic pronouns, see Rizzi 1986; on "pronouns with arbitrary reference," see Chomsky 1986:117; on the syntax and semantics of impersonal pronouns cross-linguistically, see Fenger 2018). In interpretation, this null pronoun is very closely related to PRO_{arb} (*arb* stands for arbitrary) from the syntax literature on nonobligatory control.

(15) Generic Implicit Argument (pro_{gen})

a. pro_{gen} is a DP.

b. Phi-features: third person, singular, human, animate, generic

c. Intepretation: pro_{gen} is of type <e> and is bound by a generic operator Gen.

A partial tree diagram for examples like those in (1a) is shown below:

(16)

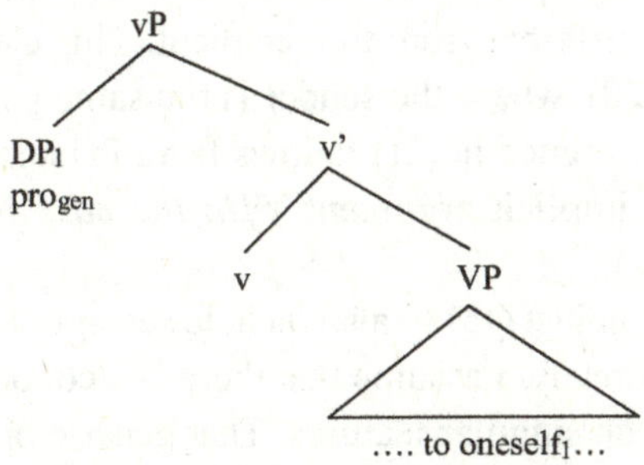

Crucially, the reflexive and the implicit argument agree in phi-features. I assume that this agreement is governed by the Pronominal Agreement Condition (PAC):

(17) The Pronominal Agreement Condition

An anaphor agrees in phi-features with its antecedent.

(See Collins and Postal 2012:92; Sportiche, Koopman, and Stabler 2014:168.)

The reflexive *oneself* in (16) is locally bound and agrees in phi-features with its antecedent. That is why (1a) is grammatical. See Collins and Postal (2012) for discussion of apparent counterexamples to (17).

The second-person singular pronoun *you* occurs in generic contexts as a colloquial substitute for *one*. There are examples that correspond to those in (7–14) using second-person reflexives:

(18) Time spent on yourself is time well spent.

(https://carsontate.com/work-life-balance-how-to-balance-your-life-like-the-four-seasons/)

(19) Some things are better kept to yourself.
(https://www.morningcoach.com/blog/what-you-should-keep-to-yourself)

(20) In the case of an e-mail sent to yourself, it decides to show it in Inbox, even if its true location is in Sent Mail.
(https://github.com/nylas/nylas-mail/issues/2456)

Like earlier *one* examples, these reflexives cannot be analyzed as exempt anaphors. First, example (19) involves the fixed expression *keep x to self* that does not allow a logophoric or exempt anaphor (see the discussion of (6)).

Second, replacing the reflexive with a nonreflexive pronoun yields a different interpretation, which would not be predicted if the reflexives were exempt anaphors. Consider the result of replacing *yourself* by *you* in example (20) (see also (49)):

(21) In the case of an e-mail sent to you

In (21) the sender of the e-mail is different from the recipient. This clearly contrasts with the interpretation of (20), where the sender is the same person that *yourself* refers to. The disjoint reference in (21) follows from Principle B if there is a syntactically projected implicit argument: **[In the case of an e-mail sent pro$_1$ to you$_1$].*

Because of these examples, we can adjust (15) to also include second-person singular generic pronouns. More concretely, I assume that there is a colloquial generic operator that has second-person singular features. That generic operator binds an implicit argument with second-person singular features.

2.3 Existential pro

Now consider the following nongeneric examples of passives:

(22) a. The proposal was criticized at the meeting.
b. The package was sent this morning.
c. John was killed this morning.

Example (22a) can be true if either a man or a woman criticized the proposal. Furthermore, it can also be true if either one person or more than one person criticized the proposal. Similarly, I can say (22b) to my boss if I myself have sent the package (with my boss understanding that nobody but me could have sent the package). So (22b) does not exclude the speaker from being the sender (see also Bianchi 2015:6). Sentence (22c) is consistent either with a report of a murder (animate agent) or death by a natural force (inanimate causer). These sentences show that the existential implicit argument is either ambiguous in its feature specifications for phi-features—person, number, gender, and animacy—or unspecified for those feature values. In this section, I will argue that the existential implicit argument is unspecified for phi-feature values.

These observations are consistent with McCawley's (1988:82) remarks about implicit arguments in passives:

(23) "If reduced passives are to be analyzed as having underlying subjects, the underlying subject must be something more indefinite than any expression of English is: it must be neutral with regard to whether it refers to human or non-human entities, and with regard to whether its referent is the same as or different from other individuals mentioned in the discourse. I will invoke a deux ex machina at this point and simply assume that such an element, hereby christened UNSPEC, is available, and will set up deep structures having UNSPEC as subject in the case of reduced passives."

I will call the existential implicit argument in short passives pro_{un} (for unspecified) (partly following Johnson and Postal (1980)).

As Grinder (1971:186) points out, there is a striking difference between the implicit argument of a passive and an overt indefinite. The following sentences are based on his examples:

(24) a. $Someone_1$ stole the painting, and he_1 left his fingerprints on the wall.
b. The painting was stolen by $someone_1$, and he_1 left his fingerprints on the wall.
c. The painting was stolen, and he left his fingerprints on the wall.

Although *someone* can be the antecedent of *he* in (24a,b), it is much more difficult for the implicit argument in the passive to be the antecedent of *he* in (24c). Grinder (1971) explains this difference in terms of his Chaining Constraint, which informally says that if an indefinite is the antecedent of a pronoun, then the indefinite cannot undergo deletion (where implicit arguments are assumed to be indefinites that undergo deletion).

The contrast can be replicated with intrasentential anaphora:

(25) a. If $somebody_1$ sends an e-mail to his_1 mother, how long does it take to arrive?
b. If an e-mail is sent to his mother, how long does it take to arrive?

Example (25b) cannot have the same interpretation as (25a), suggesting that the implicit argument of the passive cannot bind the possessive pronoun *his* in (25b).

What accounts for the constraint illustrated in (24) and (25)?

Koenig (1998), Koenig and Mauner (2000), and Creissels (2008) (see also Kayne 1975:196, fn. 154 on intraclausal anaphora) notice a similar constraint on the impersonal pronoun *on* when it is used existentially in French. In fact,

Koenig (1998:243) himself makes this connection: "I close this section by pointing out the strong similarities between French ultra-indefinite *on* and (prototypical) short passives." It is possible that the explanation I give for (24) and (25) in terms of the PAC in (17) can be carried over to the anaphoric possibilities with French *on*.

I suggest that the facts in (24) and (25) can be explained in terms of the PAC in (17) on the assumption that pro_{un}, the existential implicit argument in the short passive, does not have any phi-features (see Bianchi 2015:8, which reaches the conclusion that the implicit argument of the passive is not specified for participant features). The relevant part of the structure of (25b) will be the following (I assume pro_{un} linearly follows the participle, just as an overt *by*-phrase would):

(26) *If an e-mail is sent pro_1 to his_1 mother

But because pro_{un} does not have phi-features, (26) violates (17), requiring phi-feature agreement between the possessive pronoun *his* (third-person masculine singular) and its antecedent pro_{un}.

I assume that pro_{un}'s lack of phi-features is the reason that it can be used in such a wide variety of situations, as described in (22, 23). pro_{un} lacks phi-features because it is bound by an unrestricted existential operator (on the exact implementation of these ideas, see section 4.5). The assumptions about pro_{un} are summarized here:

(27) Existential Implicit Argument (pro_{un}):
a. pro_{un} is a DP.
b. Phi-features: none
c. Interpretation: pro_{un} is of type <e> and is bound by an existential operator.

See Fenger 2018, which claims that impersonal pronouns in Germanic that can take an existential interpretation do not have phi-features. See Holmberg and Phimsawat 2017 for the claim that there is a generic null subject pronoun without phi-features.

An alternative theory of the existential interpretation of the passive is that there is no syntactically realized implicit argument at all. I will call this the nonprojection theory. In this case, Spec vP is empty, but it is existentially closed. Such a theory would automatically account for Grinder's (1971) generalization. Because Spec vP is empty, there is no antecedent for a pronoun. I reject this analysis because it is not compatible with the other cases discussed in sections 4.2 (generic implicit arguments) and 4.4 (definite implicit arguments). In my analysis, in all cases there is a syntactically projected DP as the implicit argument.

Another reason to reject the nonprojection theory is that pro_{un} plays a role in obligatory control:

(28) Once it had been decided to build a walled enclosure, new possibilities opened up.
(www.paulgough.org/places_of_peace/sites.htm)

In this example, the implicit external argument of *decided* controls PRO of the infinitival complement of *decided.* Furthermore, the implicit argument seems to be existential (as opposed to generic or definite). If obligatory control is a syntactic phenomenon, then this example argues against the nonprojection theory of implicit arguments. See section 4.7 for more on control by implicit arguments.

2.4 Definite pro

Helke (1973) investigates a class of possessor pronouns that have the requirement of being bound locally. Consider the following examples of the idiomatic expression *to lose one's mind* (see Helke 1973:11):

(29) a. *The lady hopes that the gentleman won't lose her mind.
b. *The man who found the girl lost her mind.
c. *The girl's father lost her mind.
d. *The girl and the boy lost her mind.

Example (29a) shows that there is a locality (clausemate) constraint on the relation between *her* and its antecedent *the lady.* Examples (29b,c,d) show that there is a c-command condition. For example, in (29c), the possessor DP *the girl* does not c-command *her,* and the example is unacceptable. I will call such pronouns bound possessor pronouns.

From this point of view, consider the expression *on my own* in the following examples:

(30) a. I did the homework on my own.
b. *I did the homework on John's own.
c. *Mary said I did the homework on her own.
d. *John's mother did the homework on his own.
e. *Somebody did the homework on my own.
f. *It rained on my own.

Example (30a) shows the use of *on my own.* Example (30b) shows that the possessor must be a pronoun bound by the subject. Example (30c) shows a locality effect: (30c) is only acceptable if *on her own* modifies the matrix VP, not the embedded VP. Example (30d) illustrates a c-command effect: *his* is not c-commanded by *John*, and so the sentence is unacceptable. In (30e,f), there is no possible local antecedent for the possessor.

So, the following syntactic generalization holds:

(31) In the expression *on X's own*, X is a locally bound pronominal possessor.

Given this condition, consider the following example:

(32) A: Did you get help on this assignment?
B: No, it was done on my own.

While B's response might be a bit awkward, it is grammatical. It may improve if certain modifiers such as *completely* or *all* are added before *on my own*. In an informal Facebook survey, out of eight native speakers of English, four said it was fine, and four others rejected it to varying degrees (ranging from ? to *). Furthermore, such examples are easy to find on the Internet. These facts suggest that there are people for whom (32B) is completely acceptable. However, there is definitely some variation that would be worth investigating.

Assuming that (32B) is acceptable, given condition (31), there must be an implicit argument binding the possessor *my*. Therefore, by condition (17), that implicit argument must be a first-person singular pronoun.

Such examples do not seem any worse with other person-number combinations:

(33) a. It was done on your own, right?
b. It was done on his own, right?
c. Homework done on one's own is never easy.

Here are related examples from the Internet, all of which I find acceptable:

(34) I'm not even going to lie, but the solo has been the hardest to create and perform as everything was done on my own.
(https://www.mandy.com/aa/news/dancer-yukiko-masui-interview-hip-hop-contemporary)

(35) This was done on my own time and with no reimbursement for my gasoline.
(https://books.google.com/books?isbn=311097391X)

(36) Occasionally, he was able to study formally with an accomplished artist, but much of his training was done on his own.
(https://helpinghandhomeschool.com/vincent-van-gogh-artist-study-activities/)

(37) This work was written on my own during the summer and fall of 1963.
(www.smcq.qc.ca/smcq/en/oeuvres/216/87.php)

(38) First, the research framework was created on my own.
(https://aaltodoc.aalto.fi/bitstream/handle/123456789/634/hse_ethesis_12502.pdf?isAllowed=y&sequence=1)

The distribution of bound possessor pronouns in the short passive shows that there is another kind of implicit argument, described in (39). I use the term *definite* to distinguish these cases from the generic and existential implicit arguments discussed in sections 2.2 and 2.3.

(39) Definite Implicit Argument (pro_{def}):
a. pro_{def} is a DP.
b. Phi-features: any non-null combination of phi-features (other than [+generic])
c. Interpretation: pro_{def} is of type <e>.

But if such definite pronominal implicit arguments are possible, can they bind reflexive pronouns? Consider first the following examples involving first- and second-person reflexives:

(40) E-mails sent to myself go to my junk folder.
(https://forums.xfinity.com/conversations/email/emails-sent-to-myself-go-to-my-junk-folder/6196a96663ac0d5bf9faee94)

(41) Finding ways to balance time spent on myself and time spent on others is hard.
(https://www.trainerroad.com/forum/t/explaining-to-the-mrs-mr/22423/17)

(42) Most of this blog is self-deprecating humor aimed at myself as much as others.
(http://eveoganda.blogspot.com/2016/01/rixx-in-local.html)

(43) Please understand that my family does not excuse her mistakes. She knows she made them, and she knows that she should not have gotten pregnant so young. I would really appreciate it if any negative feelings you have toward teen mothers were kept to yourselves.
(https://www.disboards.com/threads/the-multi-reason-special-family-wdw-trip.1800085/)

It is also possible to find third-person reflexives bound by the implicit argument of the passive:

(44) In a blistering farewell e-mail sent to himself, Jones defended his stance against further cuts.
(http://www.notthelatimes.com/fired.html)

(45) He is so self-involved he could not even think of a title for a song dedicated to himself other than his own name.
(https://www.thequiz.com/finish-the-lyrics-disney-edition/)

(46) Gore delivered the message with a mix of seriousness, humor aimed at himself, and measured alarm.
(https://newspaperarchive.com/santa-ana-evening-blade-aug-28-1996-p-13/)

(47) Rumor has it that Mike Tyson bought over 200 cars throughout his career, totaling $4.5 million. Many were bought for himself and others as gifts for his friends and family.
(https://gazettereview.com/2016/06/mike-tyson-net-worth/)

(48) His interest in hockey, soccer, and chess was never displayed and was kept to himself.
(www.biography.co.in/justin-bieber-biohraphy.html)

I did an informal survey of seven people on these sentences. I asked them to rate the sentences from 1 (acceptable) to 5 (unacceptable). Every sentence had an average less than 2: ((40): 1.7), ((41): 1.7), ((42): 1), ((43): 1), ((44): 1.4), ((45): 1), ((46): 1.1), ((47): 1), and ((48): 1.1). Furthermore, for every sentence and every speaker, the most natural interpretation was that the implicit argument binds the reflexive.

The implicit argument in the passive also gives rise to Principle B effects. For example, consider the following example (see also (21)):

(49) In a blistering farewell e-mail sent to him (compare to (44))

In (49), the most natural interpretation is that the sender (the implicit argument) is not the recipient (*him*). This is exactly the expected interpretation if there is an implicit argument giving rise to a Principle B effect:

(50) *In a blistering farewell e-mail sent pro_1 to him_1

Note that in these cases it is not possible to describe the reflexive argument as logophoric. For example, in (47) the implicit argument is not describing the thoughts of Mike Tyson. Rather, the sentence describes the thoughts of the narrator discussing Mike Tyson. Consider also example (48), which once again uses the fixed expression *keep x to self.* This expression does not allow a logophoric or exempt use (see the discussion of (6)). Furthermore, the Helke expression *on my own* does not seem to allow any long-distance binding at all (unlike reflexives).

A similar test for the implicit argument can be found in the following examples from Stroik 2000:148, example (15):

(51) a. $John_1$'s first novel was translated into Polish by $himself_1$.
b. Pat_1 told me that her_1 father was fired by $herself_1$.
c. Such things are to be done by yourself.

Stroik argues convincingly that the *by*-phrases here are what he calls agent-related manner adverbials that you find in nonpassive examples like those in (52). The presence of *all* in the examples in (52) is an important test distinguishing the manner adverbial from the passive *by*-phrase:

(52) a. I did it (all) by myself.
b. Mary translated the book into Polish (all) by herself.

As Stroik shows, the reflexive in these agent-related manner adverbials obeys Principle A of the Binding Theory (see page 151, example (22)):

(53) a. *John did it (all) by myself.
b. I_1 did it (all) by $myself_1$.
c. *Mary wrote it (all) by yourself.
d. You_1 wrote it (all) by $yourself_1$.
e. *Mary's father translated the book (all) by herself.
f. $Mary_1$ translated the book all by $herself_1$.
(151, example (22))

In (53a,c) there is a mismatch in phi-features between the pronoun and its antecedent. And the reason that (53e) is ungrammatical is that the reflexive does not have a c-commanding antecedent. In this explanation, I employ the standard Binding Theory, in contrast to Stroik, who makes reference to Reinhart and Reuland 1993. The difference does not matter for the points that I am raising.

Stroik goes on to argue that the reflexives in (51) take the implicit argument in the passive as their antecedent, with the following representations:

(54) a. John's first novel was translated into Polish PRO by himself.
b. She told me her father was fired PRO by herself.
c. Such things are to be done PRO by yourself.
(155, example (24))

Crucially, Stroik's conclusions only hold if the implicit argument of the passive is like a definite pronoun with the phi-feature sets third-person masculine singular (see (51a)) and third-person feminine singular (see (51b)). In principle, the second-person singular phi-features in (51c) are ambiguous between an indexical use and a colloquial generic use. Stroik's paradigm in (51), based on agent-related manner adverbials, strongly supports the conclusions based on the other tests discussed in this chapter.

Putting together the results from Helke expressions, from reflexives and pronouns, and from agent-oriented manner adverbials, I conclude that the implicit argument in this case can be a null pro with any non-null combination of phi-features (except [+generic]). A partial syntactic tree for an example like (44) would be

(55)

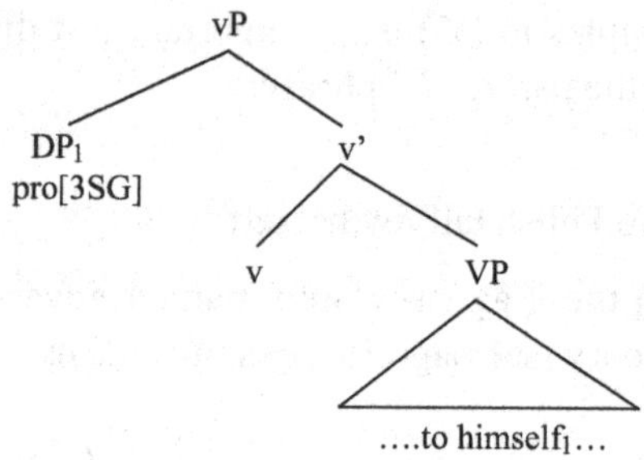

Putting together the results of section 2.3 and the current section, the prediction about the interpretation of these reflexive pronouns is the following:

(56) a. An existential implicit argument cannot bind a reflexive, or equivalently:
b. If a reflexive is bound by an implicit argument, the implicit argument is interpreted as generic (bound by a generic operator) or definite.

Recall that the existential implicit argument has no phi-features (27), and so it cannot be the antecedent of a pronoun that has phi-features.

It is clear in all of these cases that the implicit argument is not understood existentially. For example, in (47), *himself* refers to the buyer, who is Mike Tyson.

2.5 Reciprocals

It is easy to find examples similar to the examples already presented, where the implicit argument binds a reciprocal:

(57) Unfortunately, the extra work of parenting a child with ADHD can use up parents' time and energy that could otherwise be spent on each other. (https://impactparents.com/blog/adhd/adhd-makes-sex-even-more-important-four-big-ideas/)

(58) Enjoy shared experiences which excite you both. Shared experiences go a long way in bolstering relationships. That could be a reasonable dinner at a meaningful place or going to a museum or play which you both enjoy. Or, maybe it's a glass of wine after putting the kids to bed.

Remember the point is to be together, because time spent on each other is a valuable gift in and of itself. (https://www.carinekeenanmft.com/blog)

(59) My friend recently showed me a WhatsApp conversation between her and a friend of hers. It was essentially a series of voice notes sent to each other at disparate times of the day. (https://medium.com/atta-girl/4-reasons-why-switching-over-to-voice-notes-is-a-must-9467e94cd7ce)

In all three examples, the implicit argument binds the reciprocal, satisfying Principle A of the Binding Theory.

In all three examples, the implicit argument pro seems to be definite with a particular combination of nongeneric phi-features. In (57), the implicit argument is null pro whose antecedent is *parents* (third-person plural). In (58), the implicit argument takes the DP *you both* (second-person plural) as an antecedent. In (59), the implicit argument seems to take the DP *her and a friend of hers* (third-person plural) as antecedent.

The fact that reciprocals can be bound by the implicit argument provides further evidence for the hypothesis that the implicit argument in the passive is syntactically projected.

2.6 Binding the Implicit Argument

In the preceding sections, I investigated the kinds of pronouns that an implicit argument can bind. A related question is whether the implicit argument can be bound. Consider the following example (see Baker, Johnson, and Roberts 1989:226 for an analysis of similar facts based on the definition of chains):

(60) John was killed.
  a. "John was killed by somebody."
  b. Not: "John killed himself."

Because (60) is not a generic sentence, the implicit argument could only be pro_{un} or pro_{def}. But pro_{un} would yield the interpretation in (60a), not the bound interpretation in (60b).

Now consider the possibility of pro_{def} (once again, the implicit argument is placed linearly in the same position as a *by*-phrase would be):

(61) $John_1$ was killed pro_1.

While this representation yields the interpretation in (60b), it violates Principle B of the Binding Theory because *John*$_1$ binds pro_1 in its domain (the finite TP). So, it follows that (60a) and not (60b) is the right interpretation of (60).

Williams (1987:155) claims that the implicit argument in the passive is never bound (see also Bruening 2013:19; Bhatt and Pancheva 2017:16). Consider the following sentence:

(62) John wants Mary to be seen.

About (62), Williams says:

(63) "When an implicit argument is existentially quantified, it acts like an R expression, in that it is disjoint from c-commanding NPs. . . . The unassigned Agent is understood as disjoint from John, or at least is vague on that point in the same way that John wants Mary to be seen by somebody is; neither means John wants to see Mary."

This result is perplexing when compared to the results of section 2.4. Example (64a) with pro_{def} (with the interpretation of (64b)) should be a possible representation of (62):

(64) a. $John_1$ wants Mary to be seen pro_1.
b. $John_1$ wants Mary to be seen by him_1.

But (62) does not seem to have the interpretation in (64). Rather, (62) seems to have the same interpretation as

(65) John wants Mary to be seen by somebody.

But there are other cases in which sentences similar to (62) have an interpretation where the implicit argument is taken to be identical to the matrix subject. Consider the following sentences:

(66) a. I set myself some health-related goals and I want those goals to be met by the new year.
b. I plan on going on vacation to Jamaica this summer, so I want all revisions to be made on my thesis before then.

In these cases, the implicit argument is taken to be identical with the matrix subject. No other interpretation makes sense. How could I want somebody else to meet my health goals? However, (66) could still be consistent with Williams's claim in that what is expressed could be that the speaker wants somebody to meet those goals, and the only person who could possibly meet them is the speaker.

More convincingly, there are embedded passive sentences involving reflexives and bound possessor pronouns that do allow the matrix subject to bind the implicit argument of the passive:

(67) He reveals to Skyler in the end that everything was done for himself, as it made him feel alive.
(villians.wikia.com/wiki/Walter_White)

(68) He is so self-involved he could not even think of a title for a song dedicated to himself other than his own name.
(https://www.thequiz.com/finish-the-lyrics-disney-edition/)

(69) a. $John_1$ thought that a friendly e-mail sent to $himself_1$ would cheer him_1 up.
b. Every corporate manager has been advised that e-mails sent to himself can be used as incriminating evidence.

In (69a), the antecedent of *himself* is the implicit argument of *send*, and that implicit argument takes *John* as an antecedent, a clear counterexample to Williams's generalization in (62) (see also Roeper 2022 for a different set of data that are problematic for Williams's generalization). In fact, example (69b) shows that the implicit argument can have a quantificational antecedent, and so it is interpreted as a bound variable (which in turn binds the reflexive).

Our results in this section seem to conflict with Müller's (2019:60) conclusion that the implicit argument in the German passive cannot be bound by a quantifier in the higher clause. The next step would be to look at sentences like (67–69) in German.

How then can we account for Williams's observations about the interpretation of (62)? I suggest that the definite interpretation of the implicit argument is made clear when the implicit argument binds a reflexive or a pronoun. So, in (69), the implicit argument is pro[3SG] and it binds the reflexive pronoun *himself*. In Williams's example (62), the implicit argument does not bind a reflexive or a pronoun, so the existential interpretation is preferred.

Now consider again the contrast in (25), repeated here as (70):

(70) a. If $somebody_1$ sends an e-mail to his_1 mother, how long does it take to arrive?
b. If an e-mail is sent to his mother, how long does it take to arrive?

Recall that (70b) lacks the interpretation of (70a). I accounted for this by claiming that the implicit argument in (70b) is pro_{un}. But now there is an alternative representation involving pro_{def}:

(71) If an e-mail is sent pro_1 to his_1 mother,

Nothing rules out representation (71). The possessor *his* could agree in phi-features with its null pro antecedent. And I believe that in the right context (70b) has this interpretation. But for (70b), presented with no linguistic context and especially in comparison with (70a), the most natural interpretation is the one where the implicit argument is existentially bound, that is, pro_{un}. And in that case, (70b) (with the interpretation of (70a)) is unacceptable (because it violates the PAC in (17)).

2.7 The Inanimacy Gap

Can the null definite pro be an inanimate pronoun? It is difficult to find relevant examples. One way to try would be to first look for examples with an inanimate *by*-phrase binding a reflexive and then drop the *by*-phrase. Consider the following Internet examples (from Angelopoulos, Collins, and Terzi 2020):

(72) You find yourself rising and being pulled by the sun toward itself. (pg. 12, (39))

(73) The most direct way to determine it is to examine the far distant behavior of the magnetic field generated by the black hole around itself. (pg. 12, (40))

(74) More recently oxytocin has been found to be released by the brain into itself. (pg. 12, (42))

(75) But soon also this will be sucked up by the earth into itself. (pg. 12, (43))

(76) For that which is decidedly thick and earthy in nature, and has entirely escaped alteration in the liver, is drawn by the spleen into itself. (pg. 12, (46))

Dropping the *by*-phrase in these examples yields unacceptable results. And it is perhaps impossible to find the relevant acceptable examples on the Internet.

(77) *You find yourself rising and being pulled toward itself.

(78) *The most direct way to determine it is to examine the far distant behavior of the magnetic field generated around itself.

(79) *More recently oxytocin has been found to be released into itself.

(80) *But soon also this will be sucked up into itself.

(81) *For that which is decidedly thick and earthy in nature, and has entirely escaped alteration in the liver, is drawn into itself.

Examples (77–81) are unacceptable when the reflexive is bound by the implicit external argument. I put aside the reading of the reflexive bound by the subject (e.g., in (79) *itself* is bound by *oxytocin*). The question is how to explain the unacceptability of (77–81). There are three cases to consider: (a) null generic pro_{gen}, (b) null existential pro_{un}, and (c) null definite pro_{def}. Only the last case is relevant. The null generic must be human, and the null existential has no phi-features. So, the question is what rules out the following representation where pro_{def} is (3SG, inanimate):

(82) *The magnetic field generated pro_1 around $itself_1$.

I am not entirely convinced that this representation is ungrammatical. It may just be hard to interpret for a confluence of reasons. First, the existential interpretations are more accessible than the null definite pro interpretations (see the discussion following (69)). Second, the inanimate *itself* also has the inanimate subject as a possible antecedent, making the choice of the implicit argument as the antecedent difficult. For example, in (80), a possible antecedent of *itself* is the subject *this*. Third, in examples (77–81), there is no antecedent for the implicit arguments.

If there is an overt antecedent present for the implicit argument, the examples become better:

(83) a. A black $hole_1$ can be measured if one examines the far distant behavior of the magnetic field generated pro_1 around $itself_1$.
b. A black $hole_1$ can be measured if one examines the far distant behavior of the magnetic field generated pro_2 around it_1.
(Gary Thoms, personal communication)

As these examples show, both reflexive and nonreflexive pronouns are possible. But the difference may be correlated with different implicit arguments. In (80a), the black hole generates the magnetic field. In (80b), something else (not the black hole) generates the magnetic field. This difference is confirmed in the following example:

(84) A black $hole_1$ can be measured if one examines the far distant behavior of the magnetic field generated by the simulation program around it_1/*$itself_1$.
(Gary Thoms, personal communication)

When there is an explicit *by*-phrase, the nonreflexive pronoun is acceptable, and the reflexive is worse (because the reflexive pronoun cannot be bound by *the simulation program*).

2.8 Logophoricity

Given the discussions in this chapter, I return to (1a,b) and discuss whether they can be analyzed as exempt anaphors with a logophoric interpretation:

(85) a. Such privileges should be kept to oneself.
(Baker, Johnson, and Roberts 1989:228; Roberts 1987:162)
b. Damaging testimony is always given about oneself in secret trials.
(Roberts 1987:162)

I have analyzed the reflexives in examples like (85a,b) (and many others throughout the chapter) as cases of locally bound reflexives, bound by the syntactically projected implicit external argument of the passive. An alternative is that in these kinds of examples, there is no syntactically projected implicit external argument, but rather that the reflexives are exempt anaphors (not subject to Principle A), and they are interpreted as logophoric, referring back to an individual whose thoughts (or perspective) are being reported. Under this analysis, the reflexive pronouns in (1a,b) would be similar to morphologically logophoric pronouns in the West African language Ewe. See Charnavel and Zlogar 2015 and Charnavel and Bryant 2022 for recent discussions of logophoric interpretations of reflexives in English.

In this section, I will give five reasons for not adopting the logophoric analysis (in addition to the issues surrounding inherent reflexives outlined in section 2.1).

First, exempt anaphors do not show Principle B effects with their antecedents (see Lebeaux 1984:346; Charnavel and Bryant 2022:fn. 31):

(86) a. Bill_1 said that the rain had damaged pictures of $\text{himself}_1/\text{him}_1$.
b. In her_1 opinion, physicists like $\text{herself}_1/\text{her}_1$ are rare.
c. Max_1 boasted that the Queen invited Lucie and $\text{himself}_1/\text{him}_1$ for a drink.

For example, in (86a), either the reflexive *himself* or the pronoun *him* can take *Bill* as an antecedent. The reason for this is that Bill is not in the same local domain as the pronoun in (86a), and so no Principle B effect is triggered. A similar account holds for (86c). But as I have shown a number of times in this chapter (see (21) and (49)), the implicit external argument of a passive can give rise to Principle B effects. This makes sense if the implicit external argument of the passive is syntactically present and can locally bind a reflexive (satisfying Principle A) or a pronoun (violating Principle B). In other words, a pronoun whose antecedent is the implicit argument in the passive shows Principle B effects with its antecedent, but a pronoun replacing a logophoric reflexive does not show Principle B effects with its antecedent (as shown in (86a,c)). This is a very clear generalization that is absolutely devasting for any view seeking to explain away the data ((1a,b) = (85a,b)) in terms of logophoricity.

Second, many of the examples involving reflexives in this chapter do not express the thoughts or perspectives of the individual referred to by the reflexive, as already pointed out for example (47).

Third, we have seen in this chapter that the bound pronoun in Helke expressions can be bound by the implicit external argument in the passive. But unlike reflexives in English, there are no exempt or logophoric uses of Helke expressions. Putting aside passives, when a Helke expression is used, the pronoun is always bound by a local syntactically present antecedent. Therefore, if the bound pronoun in a Helke expression can be bound by the implicit argument in the passive, there is no reason why a reflexive pronoun should not be able to be bound in the same way. In chapter 3, I will show that the implicit argument in the passive is also visible to secondary predicates.

Fourth, I have shown that even inanimate implicit external arguments can bind reflexives. But as stressed by Charnavel and Zlogar (2015) and Charnavel and Bryant (2022), inanimate DPs cannot be the antecedent of exempt anaphors interpreted logophorically, because inanimates do not denote objects with thoughts or perspectives.

Fifth, from a cross-linguistic perspective, Gotah (2022:16) shows that the implicit argument in the Ewe middle can be the antecedent of a reflexive pronoun. But the interesting thing about reflexive pronouns in Ewe is that they have no exempt or logophoric uses, as Gotah notes. Rather, in Ewe there is a dedicated logophoric pronoun (completely independent from reflexives). If implicit arguments in Ewe can bind reflexives, there is no reason why that possibility should not exist in English. The Ewe data provide striking support for the analysis of implicit arguments in this chapter, and therefore for the whole Merge-based framework. A similar argument can be run for Buli (see Sulemana 2022). See chapter 5 for more discussion of these cases.

Even though the reflexives in this chapter cannot be analyzed as exempt anaphors with a logophoric interpretation, there are related examples that do seem to involve exempt anaphors with logophoric interpretations:

(87) Wrong done to oneself by others is hard to forget.
(Andrew Radford, personal communication)

(88) One should not seek revenge for the harm done to oneself by others.
(https://jainqq.org/explore/001520/92)

In these examples, *oneself* does not refer to the doer (*others*), but to a different individual. In this case, it seems reasonable to suppose that *oneself* refers to a generic individual whose thoughts or perspective are being expressed by the sentence. In other words, in these examples the reflexive does seem to be logophoric.

I have not investigated this type of sentence extensively. In my dialect of English, the examples (87–88) are not completely acceptable. Here is a near minimal pair comparing the two different interpretations of the reflexive (that is, locally bound by an implicit argument versus logophoric):

(89) a. A book of stories written about oneself should be brief and honest.
b. ?A book of stories appearing about oneself should be brief and honest.

The most natural interpretation of (89a) is that the reflexive is bound by the implicit external argument (the writer). No such interpretation is possible in (89b), so it has to have the logophoric interpretation. For the speakers of American English that I have consulted, (89a) is perfect, but (89b) is marginal.

Such examples in (87–89) do not contradict the general claims of this chapter. They just show that reflexives in passives can have two different uses, either as locally bound reflexives bound by the syntactically projected implicit external argument or as exempt anaphors with a logophoric interpretation. A similar situation arises for picture noun phrases (as discussed recently by Charnavel and Bryant 2022), where the reflexive in a picture noun can either be locally bound by the possessor or have a logophoric interpretation, depending on the antecedent (see Charnavel and Bryant 2022:153, ciii).

What remains to be done is to show that (87–88) can be fit into a general theory of exempt anaphora (see Reinhart and Reuland 1993 for a well-known theory). That is, which syntactic contexts allow exempt anaphora, and which do not? I leave this large and ambitious topic for future work.

2.9 Conclusion

In this chapter, I have shown that there are three possibilities for the phi-features of the implicit argument of the short passive. I summarize the results here. See section 4.5 for some additional discussion of (90b).

(90) a. Generic Implicit Argument (pro_{gen}):
i. pro_{gen} is a DP.
ii. Phi-features: third person, singular, human, animate, generic
iii. Intepretation: pro_{gen} is of type <e> and is bound by a generic operator Gen.
b. Existential Implicit Argument (pro_{un}):
i. pro_{un} is a DP.
ii. Phi-features: none
iii. Interpretation: pro_{un} is of type <e> and is bound by an existential operator.
c. Definite Implicit Argument (pro_{def}):
i. pro_{def} is a DP.
ii. Phi-features: any non-null combination of phi-features (other than [+generic])
iii. Interpretation: pro_{def} is of type <e>.

These three cases divide up perfectly the possible phi-feature sets of the implicit argument:

(91) Implicit Arguments

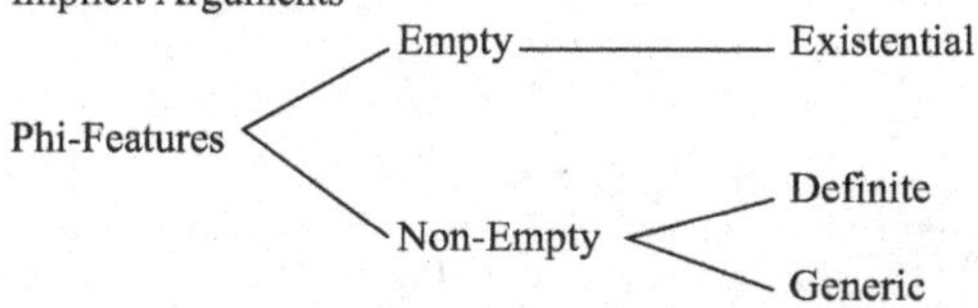

In each case, I showed the existence of the implicit argument using a variety of different diagnostics (e.g., Principle A, Principle B, Helke expressions). The trickiest case is (81b). Because the existential pro_{un} lacks phi-features, one cannot use the Binding Theory or Helke expressions to diagnose its existence. However, such implicit arguments can still be controllers and they can be modified by a depictive secondary predicate (see chapter 3). Therefore, I claim that even in (90b) there is a syntactically present implicit argument.

The typology raises the question of why the existential interpretation requires a pro that does not have any phi-features. I return to this issue in chapter 4.

A consequence of this work is that English has pro. English is not a null subject language, in the sense of Italian, Spanish, and other well-known languages, but there are certain contexts where pro can appear. For example, the implicit argument of the passive is pro. Another such case is the implicit dative argument described by Epstein (1984), Landau (2010), and Rizzi (1986:550). If English has pro, then why isn't it a null subject language? In other words, if pro can be an implicit argument, then why can't it be a null subject (in the sense of Italian and Spanish)? In chapter 4, I will return to this question and place the empirical results of this chapter in the larger context of a theory of implicit arguments.

In this chapter, I have shown that implicit arguments are syntactically projected, using Principles A and B and the distribution of Helke expressions as diagnostics. All of these topics need to be looked at from a cross-linguistic perspective. See Gotah 2022, Ndapo 2022, and Sulemana 2022 for some preliminary studies (see chapter 5). Müller (2019:58) claims that the implicit argument in the passive can bind reflexives and reciprocals in German. Shäfer 2012 is a rich source of cross-linguistic data on reflexives in both impersonal and personal passives. However, he gives a nonsyntactic account based on the assumption that "a variable can be reconstructed on conceptual grounds" (pg. 244). It is unclear how such an approach would extend to reciprocals, Principle B effects, and Helke expressions. Also, Shäfer's analysis ends up giving two completely different ways that reflexives can be bound, either by Agree (pg. 238) or on "conceptual grounds" (pg. 244). In the theory presented here, nonlogophoric reflexives are always locally bound by a c-commanding antecedent.

3 Secondary Predicates and the Implicit Argument

3.1 Introduction

The fundamental question that this monograph addresses is how external arguments are represented in passive constructions. Collins (2005a) argues that the external argument in the passive is merged in the same way as it is in the active, namely in Spec vP (following the spirit of Chomsky 1957). Consider (1a,b):

(1) a. John wrote the book.
    b. The book was written by John.

The proposal in Collins 2005a has the consequence that the DP *John* is merged into Spec vP in (1b) in the same way as it is in (1a). Another consequence of the proposal in Collins 2005a is that the short passive has a syntactically present null external argument, analyzed there as arbitrary PRO (but see chapter 4 for a discussion of implicit arguments as PRO versus pro).

The structure of (2a) is then either (2b) or (2c), depending on the position of PRO. The precise position of the null implicit argument in the short passive is a tricky issue, since it is covert, and is not relevant for the points made in this chapter.

(2) a. The book was written.
    b. The book was [PRO written].
    c. The book was [written PRO].

One important piece of evidence in Collins 2005a:101 for this analysis of short passives is based on the distribution of depictive secondary predicates:

(3) At the commune, breakfast is usually eaten nude.

(3) shows that the implicit argument in a passive can license a depictive secondary predicate, just like the overt subject argument in an active can:

(4) At the commune, the campers usually eat breakfast nude.

On the assumption that secondary predicates need to be licensed by a local c-commanding DP, it follows that in (3) there must be a syntactically present null argument. Surprisingly, a number of authors have claimed that depictive secondary predicates cannot modify the implicit argument of the short passive (including Williams 1985, Chomsky 1986, Pylkkänen 2008a, Landau 2010). Most of this chapter attempts to establish the following generalization:

(5) Depictive secondary predicates can modify the implicit argument of the short passive.

The rest of the chapter is structured as follows. In section 3.2, I present all the cases of depictive secondary predicates found in short passives that I can find in the syntax literature. I augment this list with naturally occurring examples found on the Internet. Section 3.3 reviews the syntax literature that rejects (5). Section 3.4 presents a formal analysis of depictive secondary predicates and shows how to account for the generalization in (5). Section 3.5 shows that there is an important difference between passives and unaccusatives with respect to the distribution of secondary predicates. Since unaccusatives do not have an implicit argument (unlike the short passive), they do not permit secondary predicates. Section 3.6 is the conclusion.

3.2 Secondary Depictive Predicates in the Short Passive

In this section, I present data concerning secondary depictive predicates in short passives. First, I review the examples given in the linguistics literature. Then I present some naturally occurring examples from the Internet.

A number of examples are given in Roeper 1987:297:

(6) The game was played drunk/nude/sober/angry.

Baker (1988:318) gives the following examples:

(7) a. This song must not be sung drunk.
b. Such petitions should not be presented kneeling.

Collins (2005a:101) adds the following example:

(8) At the commune, breakfast is usually eaten nude.

Meltzer-Asscher (2012:281) adds the following examples:

(9) a. Traditionally, the koto was played seated on the floor.
b. The hula is danced barefoot.

Stroik (1992:132, fn. 7) adds the following examples:

(10) a. The painting was painted blindfolded.
b. I can tell that this letter was written in a good mood.
c. This bank-job wasn't done alone.

Naturally occurring examples can easily be found on the Internet (see also Müller 2008 for additional English examples found on the Internet). See the appendix of this monograph on the general methodology of using Internet searches for syntactic research.

First, I present a list of generic examples, then a list of episodic examples. All the following examples are completely acceptable for me (a native speaker of English). The following examples are all generic, describing an activity that is usually done in a certain way (or should be done in a certain way):

(11) If beach volleyball was played nude, I would never leave my house.
(http://imgur.com/gallery/fPIhe)

(12) So here's looking at top 15 sports that should be played nude.
(http://www.thesportster.com/entertainment/top-15-sports-that-should-be-played-nude/)

(13) Originally the game was played naked in the burning sun.
(https://en.uncyclopedia.co/wiki/Australia)

(14) Musical chairs must be played fully clothed.
(https://www.thingsinsquares.com/letter/rules-years-office-christmas-party/)

(15) At the refugee camp, soccer was played barefoot,
(https://www.socceramerica.com/publications/article/23353/the-soccer-life-soccer-smoothes-the-path.html)

(16) Next the procession headed for the Chapel of the Burning Bush, which was entered barefoot.
(https://www.degruyter.com/document/doi/10.7312/char13230-013/pdf)

(17) Coffee will be served topless.
(https://www.robertcookofnorthbucks.com/hate-male-2-2/)

(18) It really should be sung drunk, or not at all.
(https://twitter.com/stephenkb/status/781142776570339328)

(19) Our album is meant to be listened to stoned.
(http://www.nme.com/news/music/warpaint-61-1293400)

(20) Morning prayer was sung together at 6:55 a.m. before going to work.
(http://www.walsinghamcommunity.org/about-us/history/the-cornerstone-community)

(21) Dinner was eaten together.
(http://www.huffingtonpost.com/entry/a-different-kind-of-dinnertime-grace_us_58f51c4fe4b04cae050dc9df)

(22) A duet can't be sung alone.
(http://archiveofourown.org/works/11051532/chapters/24638334)

(23) Completion of the hike must be done unassisted.
(http://www.margarita-adventures.com/faq/)

Simpson (2005:89) notes that depictive predicates in passives are often improved by modality and negation:

(24) a. ?The song was sung drunk.
b. This song can't be sung drunk.

Simpson proposes that in the case of (24b), there is a higher ModalP, and that the secondary predicate is adjoined to that ModalP as a "conditional attribute." Even if the syntactic position of the secondary predicate in (24b) is different from that in (24a), it is still able to pick out the implicit external argument of the passivized verb, which is the fact that needs to be accounted for.

In fact, Demonte (1986:58) claims for Spanish that secondary predication of implicit arguments in the passive is acceptable in sentences with a modal and unacceptable without one. As the following examples show, no such constraint exists for English.

The following examples are all episodic.

(25) At one place in one year, everything I saw was performed nude—a double bill of Baal and Woyzek, cabaret and improvisational dance.
(https://www.timeshighereducation.com/news/marks-for-the-nude-artists-and-beer-glass-hurler/163984.article)

(26) The field was crowded onto a relatively clear stretch of sand, the game was played barefoot, . . .
(https://rosethomson.wordpress.com/tag/spirit-circles/)

(27) All of this very important work was done shirtless (natch), giving Zac plenty of opportunity to show off his newly acquired six-pack.
(http://www.huffingtonpost.co.uk/entry/zac-efron-body-chest-shirtless-pictures-baywatch_uk_56dfffd2e4b05c52666e6558)

(28) Minaj admitted that the lapdance was completely choreographed, and was performed drunk.
(https://uinterview.com/news/nicki-minaj-twerks-and-gives-drake-a-lap-dance-in-anaconda-video/)

(29) . . . and I'm pretty sure most of the part of Benjy in The Sound and the Fury was written drunk.
(https://arstechnica.com/civis/viewtopic.php?f=23&t=710318)

(30) The majority was written sober. Some of it was written drunk.
(https://www.glamourmagazine.co.uk/article/aiden-grimshaw-interview-misty-eye-2012)

(31) It seems appropriate that this one was done stoned; going into alternate mindstates is a large part of the trade of the mystic.
(https://silicon-dawn.livejournal.com/1906.html)

(32) Everything was written sober. Everything was performed sober.
(https://wmmr.com/2019/07/15/brent-smith-relapsing-before-latest-shinedown-album/)

(33) The first verse was sung alone, with instrumental accompaniments, then gradually the choir joined in.
(http://libera-historicaltimelinepart7.blogspot.com/2013_12_01_archive.html)

(34) It was done BLINDFOLDED, and this is one of the hardest Chopin etudes.
(https://www.youtube.com/watch?v=zW5Y1Cx4zQw)

(35) However, Carlsen won the second encounter, which was played blindfolded.
(https://anmachriel817.amebaownd.com/posts/30746523/)

(36) All this was done unarmed!
(https://afrolegends.com/2009/12/03/the-forgotten-angel-of-rwanda-capt-mbaye-diagne/)

(37) Almost all the lifting was done unassisted.
(https://www.cdc.gov/niosh/nioshtic-2/00231105.html)

(38) Seven of his "buzzer beating" shots were made unassisted.
(https://stepienrules.com/most-buzzer-beaters-nba/)

(39) It was done unprepared and with hardly any script at all.
(https://blog.ivercy.com/page/3/)

For the purposes of this chapter, I have limited attention to adjectival secondary depictive predicates (including adjectival passives). I have yet to investigate examples with prepositional phrases (PPs) (e.g., *in a good mood, in shorts*) and *-ing* participles (e.g., *singing, standing, sitting*) as secondary predicates.

A number of generalizations can be drawn about the data above. First, using depictive predicates in the short passive seems to be a productive process. A wide range of adjectives are permitted, in both generic and episodic contexts. The adjectives found in the examples above are naturally grouped into various categories: state of clothing (*nude, naked, fully clothed, barefoot, topless, shirtless*), state of intoxication (*drunk, stoned, sober*), number (*alone, together*), and adjectival passives (*unassisted, blindfolded, unarmed, unprepared*). The examples do not seem to be idiomatic or fixed expressions.

I was unable to find a comprehensive list of adjectival secondary predicates for English. Most syntax papers that deal with the issue repeat the same handful of examples (e.g., using *nude* and *drunk*). Therefore, it is not possible to know at this point if there are systematic gaps between the kinds of secondary predicates that can modify the subject in active sentences and those that can modify the implicit argument in passive sentences. A large-scale corpus study of this issue would be quite useful.

Second, all the above examples also admit a *by*-phrase. In the following example, *the campers* are nude.

(40) a. Breakfast is usually eaten nude by the campers.
b. Breakfast is usually eaten by the campers nude.

Third, all of the examples work in the active:

(41) The campers usually eat breakfast nude.

Fourth, if a secondary depictive predicate is not possible in the active, then it will not be possible in the passive either. For example, as Simpson (2005:93) notes: "Adjectives that can appear as depictives or resultatives are those that denote a transitory, bounded, temporally-restricted state, so-called stage-level predicates." (42a) below is from Simpson and (42b) is the passive variant. As predicted, both are unacceptable:

(42) a. He read the book *intelligent/*knowing/*knowledgeable.
b. The book was read *intelligent/*knowing/*knowledgeable.

In the next section, I address a number of cases from the literature in which it has been claimed that a depictive secondary predicate is possible in the active, but not the passive.

3.3 Some Counterproposals

The data in section 2 show that depictive secondary predicates can modify the implicit argument of a passive. Despite this, there are numerous claims in the syntax literature that deny this possibility.

Williams (1985:308) considers the following example, attributed to Roeper:

(43) The game was played nude.

Williams proposes that "rather than saying that the adjective *nude* modifies the implicit agent of *played* we might say that it modifies the (overt) subject *game*, since one may call a game nude if it is played by nude people."

In response to this argument, Bhatt and Pancheva (2006:585, fn. 11) note: "We find *The movie was watched nude* . . . acceptable. However, it seems a much greater stretch to refer to a movie that is watched nude as a nude movie." Similarly, considering (29) above, saying that the part of Benjy is drunk seems nonsensical (see also Roeper 1993:213 for a similar point).

Williams (1985:309) also gives the following sentence (but see Roeper 2020:301):

(44) *The game was played mad at Bill.

He explains that (44) is odd because one cannot say "The game was mad at Bill." I find this sentence strained as well, and I have been unable to find Internet examples with *mad* used as a secondary predicate in short passives. Meltzer-Asscher (2012:282) claims that the unacceptability of (44) is due to semantic or pragmatic factors: "Whether the players are mad at Bill has, in most contexts, no relevance to their playing the game."

Alternatively, it may be that various classes of adjectives are not acceptable for modifying the implicit argument of the passive for independent reasons. For example, it is difficult to find naturally occurring depictive adjectives that assign an experiencer theta-role to their argument (*mad, angry, happy*).

Note, however, that Roeper (1987) uses *angry* in the example in (6), which assigns an experiencer theta-role. Furthermore, while (44) does seem to be degraded, Mica Clausen (personal communication, September 2021) has found examples involving experiencer adjectives, which I find acceptable:

(45) a. A game played angry isn't as fun.
b. Apparently, revenge is a dish best served angry.
(torontosun.com/2014/09/28/matthew-stafford-stellar-for-detroit-lions)

The contrast between Williams's unacceptable example and Clausen's acceptable examples raises the general issue of when experiencer adjectives make good secondary predicates. I will not pursue that issue here.

Chomsky (1986:121) gives the following example (see also Jaeggli 1986:614, which provides similar data based on *leave* and endorses Chomsky's conclusion):

(46) a. They expected [PRO to leave the room angry].
b. *The room was left angry.
c. *The book sank angry.

He states: “The adjective phrase *angry* is predicated of PRO, not *they*, and only a syntactically present element can be its subject.”

There are a few things to say about (46b). Passivizing this use of *leave* is marginal for some people (even without the secondary predicate):

(47) a. ?The room was left by everybody.
 b. ?The room needs to be left early.

Second, in hearing (46b), one wonders *who* is angry. The interpretation that immediately comes to mind is that the room itself is somehow angry. So, the interpretation would be parallel to the construction in (48a), which passivizes easily, as shown in (48b):

(48) a. I left the room messy.
 b. The room was left messy.

But even if example (46b) is fixed to avoid these issues, it is still difficult to find examples on the Internet of experiencer adjectives like *angry* modifying the implicit argument of the short passive. As noted above, an independent constraint might be at work.

In a footnote, Chomsky (1986:211) discusses Roeper's data:

(49) “Roeper (1984) notes such examples as ‘the game was played barefoot (nude),’ which seems to violate the paradigm illustrated. Luigi Rizzi suggests that ‘nude’ may actually be adverbial, not adjectival, despite the morphology, as in some other languages.”

Chomsky does not say what criteria are used here to classify *nude* as adverbial. There seem to be clear differences in meaning between secondary predicates and adverbs. Consider the following examples from Roeper 1993:192:

(50) a. The game was played drunk.
 b. The game was played drunkenly.

(50a) means that at the time the game was played, the players were drunk. (50b) can imply (50a), but has a meaning related to the manner in which the game was played (e.g., screaming, yelling, exaggerated movements, lack of respect for the rules, slurred speech). Or to put it another way, (50b) does not entail that the players were drunk while playing the game (see also Aarts 1995:90 and Schultze-Berndt and Himmelmann 2004:61 for related discussion).

Another possibility for construing *nude* as an adverb in (49) is to suppose that it applies to an event: an event can be characterized as nude if the agent of the event is nude. This idea is different from Williams's proposal in that it relates the secondary predicate to the event described by the verb, and not to the derived subject. Also, even though *nude* would be an event predicate, it would not describe the manner of that event. Formally, this could be presented as follows. O is a type shifter, which takes the semantic value of an adjective and shifts it to a function that takes event arguments.

(51) For all e, if e is in the domain of Agent, then O(P)(e) iff P(Agent(e)).

So, in (49) above, the type shifter applies to *nude*, and the resulting predicate applies to the event described by the passive verb *played.* Such an analysis of secondary predicates makes no reference to a syntactically projected implicit argument.

The prediction of this account is that in general DPs describing events (event descriptions) should be possible as the arguments of adjectives that describe the agent of the event. Generally, the examples are understandable, but marginal or ungrammatical:

(52) a. *The game/race/World Cup/competition was nude/naked.
  b. *The first verse/performance/song/race was alone/together.
  c. *The final piece/first movement/concert was blindfolded.

But note that such event descriptions can appear with predicates (like *take an hour*) that take events as arguments (this is similar for other predicates such as *started at 6:00, involved many participants, took place last year*).

(53) a. The game/race/World Cup/competition took one hour.
  b. The first verse/performance/song/race took one hour.
  c. The final piece/first movement/concert took one hour.

Under the theory in (51), it is unclear what would account for the clear difference in grammaticality between the sentences in (52) and the sentences in (53).

Lappin and Shlonsky (1993:10) claim that for English (but not for German) "The passive morpheme is –TRB [cc. theta-role bearer], and so it cannot serve as the external argument of a circumstantial predicate." They give the following examples:

(54) a. *The concert was played formally dressed.
  b. *The lecture will be given naked.

While (54a) does seem a bit strained (as does the active variant), (54b) is acceptable, or at least not any worse than its active variant. I presented acceptable Internet examples involving *naked* above.

Pylkkänen (2008a:22) characterizes the distribution of depictive secondary predicates as follows:

(55) "This state can be predicated of either an internal or an external argument, although if the external argument is implicit, as in a passive, it cannot be modified by a depictive."

She provides the following example:

(56) *This letter was written drunk.

For me, this sentence is a bit strained, but not ungrammatical. Gary Thoms and Andrew Radford state that it is acceptable (personal communication). Richard Kayne suggests that (56) improves if one adds *it is obvious*, or *obviously*. I gave numerous Internet examples with *drunk* above, all of which are grammatical. The Internet examples provide a linguistic context, which tends to ameliorate the acceptability of the secondary predicate.

Citing Chomsky's (1986) discussion, Landau (2010:359) makes a distinction between two types of implicit arguments (see also Landau 2013:72, 180, 185, 228). Then in (57) he stipulates that secondary predicates cannot modify weak implicit arguments:

(57) a. Strong Implicit Arguments (SIA): PRO, pro
b. Weak Implicit Arguments (WIA): passive agent, implicit object

(58) An implicit argument must be strong to license a secondary predicate.

Landau (2010:360) provides the following two sentences to illustrate his claims:

(59) a. *The issue was decided unassisted.
b. *The game was played shoeless.

First, these sentences are both a bit strained, but not unacceptable for me. Second, (59a) without a secondary predicate is not completely felicitous out of the blue ("The issue was decided."). Third, an episodic sentence with *unassisted* is given in (37) above. Fourth, (59b) gets better if one uses *barefoot* instead of *shoeless*; see the example in (26).

Landau notes in a footnote "See Roeper 1987:297–298 for a different view." In addition to Roeper 1987, evidence contrary to (58) had already been presented by Baker (1988), Roeper (1993), Collins (2005a), Bhatt and Pancheva (2006) and Müller (2008). See chapter 4 for more discussion of Landau 2010.

This section has discussed all the cases in the syntax literature (that I know of) that purport to show that an implicit argument in the passive cannot be modified by a secondary predicate. In all cases, the conclusion is unwarranted. Rather, the discussion in this section supports the conclusion in (5): depictive secondary predicates can modify the implicit argument of the short passive.

3.4 Analysis

So far, the following generalization has been established:

(60) A depictive secondary predicate can modify the implicit argument of a short passive.

In this section, I lay out the assumptions about depictive secondary predicates and the passive that allow us to explain (60).

Based on binding, agreement, and other data, Legendre (1997) convincingly argues that depictive secondary predicates are small clauses with a PRO subject (Dep is defined below in (64b)):

(61) $They_1$ played the game [Dep [PRO_1 nude]].

Exactly what the internal structure of [PRO nude] is, and what the label of the small clause is, are beyond the scope of this chapter (see Bowers 1997 for an analysis of resultative secondary predicates based on PredP). There is no evidence that depictive secondary predicates are nonobligatory control structures (e.g., long distance control, PROarb interpretations). Therefore, I assume that the relationship between *they* and PRO in (61) is obligatory control. This assumption entails three properties commonly ascribed to obligatory control (see Hornstein 1999 for an overview of properties of obligatory control; Bowers 1993:628 on the MDP and *promise*; and Landau 2013: section 5.1.3 for arguments against (62c)):

(62) a. PRO_1 requires a controller DP_1.
  b. The controller DP_1 c-commands PRO_1.
  c. Minimal Distance Principle: no DP can intervene between the controller DP_1 and PRO_1.

In (62c), intervention is defined in terms of asymmetric c-command: A intervenes between B and C iff B asymmetrically c-commands A, and A asymmetrically c-commands C.

The properties are illustrated below:

(63) a. *It rained [PRO sad].
  b. John's $mother_1$ wrote the book [PRO_1 drunk].
  c. [John and $Mary]_1$ wrote the book [PRO_1 drunk].
  d. John said that $Bill_1$ left [PRO_1 angry].

In (63a), PRO has no antecedent, so the example is unacceptable. In (63b), the only antecedent of PRO is *John's mother*, not *John*. *John* cannot be the antecedent of PRO because *John* does not c-command PRO. Similarly, in (63c), both John and Mary have to be drunk, not just John. In (63d), if *angry* is in the embedded clause (when Bill left, somebody was angry), then its antecedent must be *Bill*, not *John*. In other words, (63d) cannot mean "John said Bill left while he (John) was angry."

In addition to these assumptions, the temporal dependence of the secondary predicate on the main verb needs to be captured. Following Pylkkänen (2008a:23), I assume that there is a head Dep that introduces the depictive (and that binds its situation variable). Pylkkänen notes that depictive predicates get essive case in Finnish and assumes that it is assigned by the Dep head. The semantic values of the adjective and the Dep head are given below:

(64) a. $[\![\text{nude}]\!] = \lambda x.\lambda s.\text{nude}(s,x)$
b. $[\![\text{Dep}]\!] = \lambda P.\lambda e.\ \exists s.P(s) \text{ and } e°s$

The raised circle symbol in (64b) is the temporal overlap relation, "employed to capture the fact that the depictive describes a state that holds during an event." When the two morphemes are combined, we get the following (suppose that PRO denotes John):

(65) $[\![\text{DEP}]\!]\ ([\![[\text{PRO nude}]]\!]) = \lambda e.\exists s.[\text{nude}(s, \text{John}) \wedge e°s]$

This expression is a predicate of events, such that the event overlaps with a state where John is nude. I also assume the following syntactic condition, motivated by the semantic value in (65) (see Andrews 1982 and Roberts 1988 for syntactic tests indicating the position of depictive secondary predicates). In this definition, *verbal projection* refers to any projection of V, v, ApplP, PartP (participle phrase), or VoiceP (any projection in the extended projection of the VP).

(66) DepP is the sister of a verbal projection.

Given these assumptions, and assuming Collins's (2005a) theory of the passive, a partial representation of the sentence in (67) is given in (68):

(67) The game was played nude.

(68)

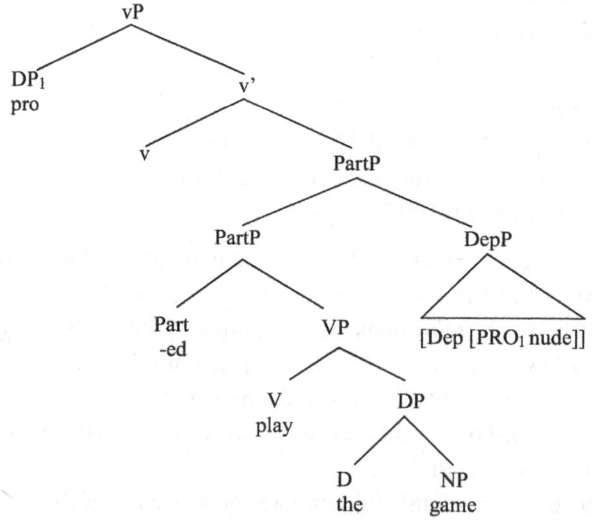

This structure is the underlying structure for the passive in the theory of Collins 2005a. As in Collins 2005a, I assume that the external argument (in this case pro) is projected in the same place in the passive as in the active, Spec vP. In chapter 4, I give a general theory of implicit arguments, where I analyze them as instances of pro.

Later operations move PartP to Spec VoiceP (not shown in the diagram), and the object DP to Spec TP (VoiceP and TP are not shown in (68); see Collins 2005a and chapter 7 for details). I have represented the DepP as right-adjoined to PartP, although other positions are possible (e.g., adjoined to VP).

Consider how all the requirements of the depictive predicate are satisfied. First, PRO has a c-commanding controller, satisfying (62a,b). Second, no other DP intervenes between the implicit argument and PRO, satisfying (62c). Third, DepP is a sister of PartP, satisfying (66). So, all conditions on depictive predicates are satisfied, and (67) is acceptable.

Other uses of adjectives should be distinguished from depictive secondary predicates:

(69) a. Drunk, the world is beautiful.
b. If one is/you are drunk, the world is beautiful.

(69a) could be paraphrased as in (69b). One difference between (69a) and the examples of depictive predicates is that it involves an extra semantic relation between the adjective and the rest of the clause (indicated by the translation as a conditional). I assume that (69a) involves ghosting in the sense of Collins and Postal 2012, and that the syntactic structure is similar to the sentence (69b), except the string <if one is/you are> has been deleted.

3.5 Unaccusatives

Since unaccusatives lack an implicit external argument, the above theory of secondary predicates makes the prediction that unaccusatives should not license secondary predicates in the same way as short passives. The following examples show that there is a difference between passives and unaccusatives in the distribution of secondary predicates:

(70) a. The toy truck was rolled across the sand barefoot.
b. *The toy truck rolled across the sand barefoot.

(71) a. The tree was chopped down naked.
b. *The tree fell naked.

(72) a. The tires must have been rotated stoned.
b. *The tires must have rotated stoned.

There is a clear difference in acceptability between the (a) and (b) examples above. In an out-of-the-blue context, the (a) examples may be a little awkward, but the (b) examples are gibberish. For example, the only way to make sense out of (70b) is if the toy truck itself is barefoot. Similarly, for (71b), the tree itself would have to be somehow naked (e.g., stripped of leaves and bark).

These examples show that as opposed to passives, unaccusatives have no syntactically projected implicit external argument. From this I conclude that unaccusatives lack an argument-introducing head for external arguments. I leave it to further research to explore the argument structure of unaccusatives within the Merge-based framework.

3.6 Conclusion

I have demonstrated the following generalization:

(73) A depictive secondary predicate can modify the implicit argument of the short passive.

I then proposed a theory of secondary predicates and passives that allowed one to account for this generalization. Briefly, secondary predicates are small clause structures (e.g., [PRO nude]) where the subject PRO is controlled by either the subject or the object. In the passive, the implicit argument is syntactically projected, and so is able to control PRO. The data in this section converge in a striking fashion with the data adduced in chapter 2 based on reflexives, reciprocals, pronouns, and Helke expressions. In all cases, the diagnostics show that there is a syntactically projected implicit external argument in the passive.

An important question for future work is what the cross-linguistic scope of the generalization in (73) is. Müller (2019:57) reports that secondary predicates can modify the external argument in the passive in German (DP_{ext} is the implicit argument):

(74) Die Daten wurden DP_{ext1} [PRO_1 nackt] analysiert.
the data were naked analyzed
'The data were analyzed by someone who was naked.'

For similar results, see Sulemana 2022 for Buli and Gotah 2022 for Ewe. Angelopoulos et al. (2023) report a more complicated set of facts for Greek, where only nonagreeing secondary predicates can modify the external argument of the passive.

4 A Theory of Implicit Arguments

The purpose of this chapter is to provide a general theory of implicit arguments consistent with the empirical results of chapters 2 and 3. In particular, in those chapters I showed that the implicit argument of the passive is a syntactically active argument (for secondary predicates, Principle A, Principle B, and Helke expressions). From this, I concluded that the implicit argument is syntactically projected. In this conclusion, I differ from researchers who claim that implicit arguments are not syntactically projected, including Williams (1987:151): "implicit arguments, which we will take to be simply unassigned theta-roles."

First, I explain which principles of UG force implicit arguments to be projected syntactically. Then, I discuss formal licensing and interpretation. Lastly, I survey various kinds of implicit arguments in English and demonstrate how the general theory applies in each case.

The strength of the theory proposed here is that it covers not only the passive, but also other cases of implicit arguments in English, including implicit arguments found with evaluative predicates, dative controllers, middles, and nominalizations. Furthermore, as I explain below (using the wedge argument), implicit arguments are made available by UG, and should be syntactically projected in a wide variety of constructions across all languages.

Chapter 5 discusses some cross-linguistic evidence based on several African languages for the theory of implicit arguments presented here.

The rest of the chapter is structured as follows. Section 4.1 compares the semantic account of implicit arguments in Bruening 2013 with the Merge-based theory. Sections 4.2 and 4.3 present the general theory of implicit arguments, including an account of licensing and interpretation. The key claim here is that implicit arguments are pro, and that they lack a uCase (unvalued Case) feature. Section 4.4 surveys various implicit arguments found in English, including analyses of evaluative adjectives, implicit datives, middles, and nominalizations. Section 4.5 revisits the existential interpretation of the implicit argument in the short passive and shows how it fits into the general theory. Section 4.6 presents the wedge argument, which extends the conclusions about implicit arguments from the passive in English to a wide variety of constructions cross-linguistically. Section 4.7 discusses the tricky case of complement deletion in English (e.g., *John ate*), and evaluates it in terms of the general theory of implicit arguments. Section 4.8 is the conclusion.

4.1 Principles of UG and Implicit Arguments

What principles of UG force implicit arguments to be syntactically projected? The answer was presented briefly in the introduction of the monograph, but I will give a more detailed version here in terms of the Theta-Criterion.

In an active sentence, the external argument is projected in Spec vP, as shown below:

(1)

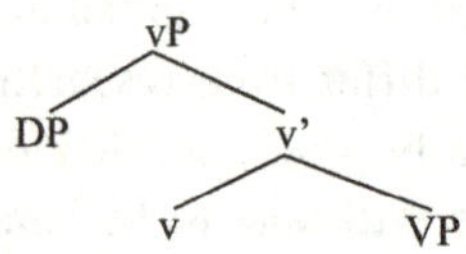

From this we know that Spec vP is a theta-position. We know this because that position is occupied by an argument, and by the Theta-Criterion, arguments must occupy (be externally merged into) theta-positions.

From this point of view, consider the passive in the examples below:

(2) a. The book was written by John. (long passive)
   b. The book was written. (short passive)

I assume that both forms of the passive (with or without the *by*-phrase) involve vP. After all, in (2a) the external argument is realized as a *by*-phrase, and in (2b) the external argument is detectable through entailments (e.g., *the book was written iff somebody or something wrote the book*). If there were no vP in (2a,b), then there would be no evidence for the presence of an external argument (e.g., no *by*-phrase and no entailments).

But if (2a) and (2b) involve vP, then an argument must fill Spec vP by the Theta-Criterion (because Spec vP is a theta-position). Therefore, both forms of the passive in (2) will involve a syntactically projected external argument. But this means that the implicit argument in (2b) will be syntactically projected. As noted in chapter 1, a parallel argument can be given based on the Argument Criterion. We will return to *by*-phrases in chapter 6 and show that a similar argument holds for projecting them in Spec vP.

To clarify these issues, compare the analysis outlined above with the account of implicit arguments in Bruening 2013. Bruening gives the following structure for implicit arguments (modified slightly):

(3)

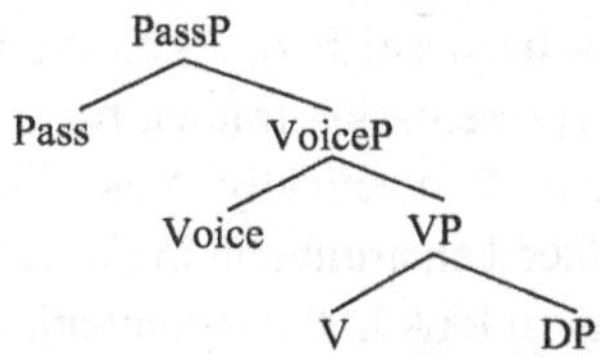

About this structure, he proposes "that passive is a head (Pass) that selects a projection of Voice that has not yet projected its external argument" (pg. 22). He elaborates on how the structure is interpreted as follows: "Although Pass syntactically selects an unsaturated Voice projection, it has the property of requiring that all of the arguments be saturated. This means that if the external argument of Voice has not been saturated, Pass will have to saturate it. It does this by existentially binding it. As stated earlier, all the evidence indicates that the external argument of a short passive is existentially quantified" (pg. 23).

Sigurðsson and Wood (2021:584), who adopt a very similar system, put this as follows: "In both the active and the passive structures, there is a Voice head that introduces agentive semantics. In actives, the agent is projected syntactically in Spec, VoiceP. In passives, the agent remains part of the semantics of Voice, but is not projected syntactically." In fact, they characterize this view as the "standard view": "the standard view is that in languages like English (with periphrastic, participle-based passives), a Passive head attaches outside of a specifierless VoiceP" (pg. 602). As with Bruening (2013), Legate (2014), and Pylkkänen (2008a), Sigurðsson and Wood (2021) fail to discuss the well-known Binding Theory data discussed in example (1), chapter 2.

The structure in (3) is a violation of the Theta-Criterion. In Bruening's system, the external argument in the active is merged into Spec VoiceP, therefore Spec VoiceP is a theta-position. But in (3), Spec VoiceP is not projected. Therefore, the Theta-Criterion is incompatible with such representations.

Bruening's generalization that the external argument of the short passive is existentially quantified is found fairly frequently in the literature (e.g., Williams 1987:155). However, as shown in chapter 2, the claim is not correct. There are in fact three different cases of implicit arguments in the passive: generic, existential, and definite.

Putting aside this issue of interpretation, consider the semantic values that Bruening gives for Pass (passive), PassP, and Voice (for the example "The senator was bribed.").

(4) a. ⟦Voice⟧ = $\lambda f \lambda x \lambda e.f(e)$ & Initiator(e,x)
b. ⟦Pass⟧ = $\lambda f \lambda e.\exists x{:}f(e,x)$
c. ⟦PassP⟧ = $\lambda e.\exists x$:bribing(e,the senator) & Initiator(e,x)

Notice that in (4c) the argument of *Initiator* has been satisfied, yet no external argument has been merged into the syntactic representation (rather, the argument of Initiator has been existentially closed). Syntactically, Voice is an argument-introducing head, but it has not introduced an argument in (3), violating the Argument Criterion. This is another way to look at the incompatibility of Bruening's theory with the Merge-based theory of argument structure.

To summarize the discussion, we have the following two theories and their properties:

(5) **Collins 2005a** (see also Angelopoulos, Collins, and Terzi 2020):
a. Principles: Argument Criterion/Theta-Criterion
b. Prediction: Implicit arguments *are* syntactically projected.
c. Empirical support: distribution of reflexives, reciprocals, pronouns, Helke expressions, and secondary predicates in the short passive in English

(6) **Bruening 2013** (see also Legate 2014 and Alexiadou, Anagnostopoulou, and Schäfer 2015):
a. Principles: no Argument Criterion/Theta-Criterion, only formal semantics
b. Prediction: Implicit arguments *are not* syntactically projected.
c. Empirical problems: distribution of reflexives, reciprocals, pronouns, Helke expressions, and secondary predicates in the short passive in English

4.2 Licensing Implicit Arguments

Following Rizzi (1986:518), a general theory of any kind of empty element will have to specify (a) how they are formally licensed, and (b) how they are interpreted. Rizzi puts it this way: "The minimal contribution that is to be expected from a theory of a null element is that it should specify (a) the conditions that formally license the null element (the conditions that allow it to occur in a given environment) and (b) the way in which the content of the null element (minimally, its phi-features) is determined or 'recovered', from the phonetically realized environment."

As explained in the discussion of the Merge-based theory of argument structure above, implicit arguments are syntactically projected elements.

Therefore, in formulating a theory of implicit arguments, we need to address the following three questions:

(7) a. What kind of empty element is an implicit argument?
    b. How is it licensed syntactically?
    c. How is it interpreted?

As for (7a), it is clear that implicit arguments are pronominal in nature. They can be understood indexically to be first- or second-person pronouns, or they can have antecedents or they can be bound by a quantifier phrase. So, the choice is between the two pronominal empty categories: small pro and big PRO. Prototypical cases of PRO are licensed in the specifier of an infinitival TP, unlike all of the cases of implicit arguments discussed in this chapter. Furthermore, although implicit arguments can be bound, they are never obligatorily controlled (unlike PRO). And if Hornstein 1999 is on the right track, obligatory control (OC) PRO reduces to a copy left by A-movement. Therefore, I will analyze implicit arguments as pro, not PRO (see also Borer 2020 for relevant discussion of this issue), contra Collins 2005a:104, keeping in mind that the distinction is subtle.

Implicit arguments are similar to nonobligatory control (NOC) PRO. Hornstein (1999:91) notes: "I have said very little about NOC PRO. I have silently assumed that it is identical to pro, the null pronominal found in various Romance and East Asian languages. This pro can be interpreted as a pronoun, either definite (hence similar to *he*, *they*, *she*, etc.) or indefinite (like English *one*). The latter underlies the so-called arbitrary reading. This requires assuming that pro can be licensed in English in NOC configurations."

It may be that NOC PRO has the same analysis as the implicit arguments discussed in this chapter, and that a unified theory of both—that is, implicit arguments and NOC PRO—can be formulated. I will leave a more detailed comparison of implicit arguments and NOC PRO to future work.

What is the syntactic category of an implicit argument? Is it DP or NP or something else? I assume that arguments are DPs (see Gambarage and Matthewson 2022), and that pronouns are arguments. Therefore, pronouns in general (whether overt or covert) are DPs. Since implicit arguments are covert pronouns, they are also DPs. Empirically, implicit arguments can take DP antecedents, bind reflexives and pronouns (which are DPs), and have definite interpretations (e.g., as indexicals), so it makes sense to analyze them as DPs. I will take the strong position that all three types of implicit arguments (generic, existential, and definite) are DPs.

As for licensing, I propose that implicit arguments are caseless. In minimalist syntax, being caseless comes down to lacking an uninterpretable structural Case feature [uCase] (for a precursor, see Epstein 1984:503, fn. 8, which gives the filter *[pro + Case]; see also Borer 1998:81, Borer 2020:127).

(8) Implicit argument pro lacks a structural Case feature [uCase].

Nothing special needs to be said about UG or particular I-languages (on I-languages, see Chomsky 1986) to allow (8). Pronouns are defined by various sets of features (person, number, gender, case). (8) specifies just one of the possible ways of defining a pronoun in terms of features. In other words, the existence of a pronoun lacking [uCase] is an immediate consequence of a UG that allows for pronouns defined by various sets of features. A particular I-language could only exclude implicit arguments defined as in (8) if there was some way for a child to learn that there were no syntactically projected implicit arguments, which seems highly unlikely. Therefore, I speculate that implicit arguments exist in all I-languages, and in each I-language they are characterized by (8) (see the wedge argument in section 4.6 below).

From the assumption in (8), I draw the following conclusions about implicit argument pro (but not about the pro found in null subject languages, like Spanish or Italian for Finnish):

(9) a. Implicit arguments are null.
    b. Implicit arguments cannot be the goal for Agree.
    c. Implicit arguments are always in situ.
    d. When the implicit argument alternates with an overt argument, the overt argument is a PP or a KP, not a DP.

Overt DPs such as *John* or *the dog* all bear Case. In fact, the Case Filter is often stated with a proviso about phonetic overtness (see Chomsky 1995:111 for a discussion of this):

(10) Every phonetically realized NP must be assigned (abstract) Case.

Putting aside the issue of the distribution of PRO, and assuming (10) to be at least descriptively accurate, it follows that implicit arguments will never be overtly realized, because they do not have a structural Case feature. This statement might seem like a tautology, because "implicit" means "not overly realized." However, the point is that the null arguments of the passive (and other constructions, such as nominalizations) will not alternate with overt pronouns, precisely because they lack Case and so cannot be realized overtly. In this property, implicit arguments differ from pro in null subject languages, which do have a uCase feature (see Holmberg 2010:97, 99).

If we assume that Agree needs an unchecked Case feature (the Activity Condition), then it follows that an implicit argument will never be the goal for

Agree. Therefore, an implicit argument will never agree with T (the tense head). In this way, implicit arguments are very different from the null subjects found in Italian and Spanish, which do agree with T (see Holmberg 2010:97). So, even though English has implicit arguments, it does not count as a null subject language in the classical sense.

Furthermore, if we assume that A-movement requires Agree, then no A-movement will be possible. From this, it follows that implicit arguments never appear in positions normally associated with the structural Cases: nominative, accusative, or genitive. Rather, implicit arguments are forced to remain in situ in their theta-position (externally merged position). For example, in the passive, the implicit argument pro remains in Spec vP.

Could an implicit argument undergo A'-movement? I assume that this is impossible, perhaps because implicit arguments lack any kind of [uWH] (unvalued WH) feature that would allow them to be active for A'-movement (assuming an Activity Condition for A'-movement). See Müller 2019:61 for compelling evidence that the implicit argument in the passive cannot undergo A'-movement to Spec CP (giving rise to V/2).

Most of the examples of implicit arguments surveyed below have the property that they alternate with PPs or KPs of various kinds (on KPs, see chapters 6 and 9 for examples). For example, the implicit argument in the passive alternates with a *by*-phrase. The dative implicit argument alternates with a *to*-phrase (see section 4.4.2 below). Since these PPs and KPs lack structural Case, it is not surprising to find them alternating with implicit argument pro, which also lacks Case. This shows that there are two ways for an argument in Spec vP to lack a structural Case feature: either Spec vP is the DP pro lacking Case, or it is a KP with a DP complement (a *by*-phrase).

A related theory would be that all implicit arguments are actually accompanied by a null K. For example, in the passive the implicit argument would be $[_{KP}$ by pro], where *by* is unpronounced. This theory (the covert KP theory) has the benefit of making implicit arguments completely parallel to overtly occurring arguments (*by*-phrases) in the passive and other constructions. It also does not need to assume that pro lacks a structural Case feature, since pro is the complement of *by*, which can presumably check/value/assign structural Case. It also explains why implicit arguments appear in non-Case positions, because they are KPs that by assumption do not have a Case feature. However, the covert KP theory needs to explain how the preposition comes to be null (see Collins 2007 for a discussion of the licensing conditions of null prepositions). While this theory is an interesting approach, I will not pursue it here.

4.3 Interpreting Implicit Arguments

Setting aside the existential interpretation of the implicit argument in the passive (see section 4.5 below for discussion), implicit arguments can be interpreted in the same way as any other pronoun (including small pro). They may be understood indexically (referring to the speaker or hearer). They may be understood by virtue of an antecedent (either in the same sentence or in earlier sentences). Lastly, they may be understood as bound variables. A special case of the bound variable interpretation is the generic interpretation (binding by a null generic operator Gen). These interpretations are the following:

(11) a. indexical interpretations
  b. coreferential with antecedent
  c. bound variable
  d. generic

Other than the existential interpretation, these seem to be the same interpretations found in null subject languages with small pro. In particular, in a string of papers Holmberg and his colleagues have documented that in so-called "partial null subject languages" (e.g., Finnish); the small pro subject can have a generic interpretation (see Holmberg 2005, 2010; Holmberg, Nayudu and Sheehan 2009; Holmberg and Phimsawat 2017).

Holmberg (2010:93) claims that "Null existential indefinites do not exist in active clauses in any language that I have encountered, and there is some reason to believe that they do not exist at all." This is a sharp contrast to implicit arguments, which can be understood as bound by an existential operator in the short passive. I speculate that this gap is related (at least in part) to agreement. Subject pro agrees with T in languages like Italian and Finish, but I have argued that the existential implicit argument has no phi-features, making agreement impossible.

The only type of interpretation that implicit arguments lack (but overt pronouns possess) seems to be the deictic pointing interpretation illustrated here:

(12) HE is guilty! (pointing to the criminal)

The constraint can be illustrated with the passive:

(13) a. John was seen. (pointing to the person who saw John)
  b. John was seen by HIM. (pointing to the person who saw John)

While (13b) is acceptable in a pointing context, (13a) is not. This shows that implicit arguments cannot be used in a deictic pointing context.

This prohibition seems to be closely related to another property of implicit arguments:

(14) Implicit arguments cannot be focused.

This property of implicit arguments follows from the assumption that focus requires an intonational contour realized by an overt DP. In other words, (14) is part of a larger generalization prohibiting covert arguments from being focused (including all kinds of pro and PRO).

4.4 A Survey of Implicit Arguments in English

The assumptions (8–11) above constitute a general theory of implicit arguments. In this section, I discuss a range of constructions having implicit arguments and show how the assumptions given in (8–11) apply in each case. I will discuss evaluative adjectives, implicit datives, middles, and nominalizations.

4.4.1 Evaluative Adjectives

Evaluative adjectives provide a prominent example of implicit arguments in English (see also Kimball 1971; Roeper 1987:275; Bhatt and Pancheva 2017):

(15) a. It is fun to play baseball.
b. ($\forall$x) if x plays baseball, it is fun for x.

As Epstein (1984) argues, the interpretation of (15a) is given in (15b). In other words, (15) involves an implicit argument pro of *fun*, which controls the PRO subject of the embedded infinitival clause. Epstein proposes that pro is a universal quantifier: "in the correct S-structure representation of the sentence, so-called PRO is controlled by (obligatorily controlled with) a base-generated quantificational empty category, namely, pro, occupying the governed complement NP position to the adjective" (pg. 502).

However, it is clear that evaluative predicates do not always involve universal quantification, as in the following example:

(16) a. It was fun to promote myself at the conference.
b. It was fun pro_1 [PRO_1 to promote myself at the conference.]
c. John said it was fun to promote himself at the conference.
d. $John_1$ said it was fun pro_1 [PRO_1 to promote himself at the conference].

I assume that pro in (16b) occupies a theta-position of the adjective phrase headed by *fun*, and so appears in situ in a caseless position, alternating with a *for*-phrase. In (16b), in order to account for the first-person singular form of the reflexive, we must analyze pro_1 as an indexical referring to the speaker and controlling PRO. In (16d), the implicit argument is bound by its antecedent *John*.

It is also possible for the implicit argument to be bound by a quantifier:

(17) a. Every boy said it would be fun to promote himself.
b. [Every boy]$_1$ said it would be fun pro$_1$ [PRO$_1$ to promote himself].

In (17b), the implicit argument is bound by the quantifier phrase *every boy*, and receives a bound variable interpretation.

Therefore, I claim that in (15a) the implicit argument is just a pronoun (and not a universal quantifier, contra Epstein 1984), and it can be interpreted in the same way as other pronouns. When there is a universal reading, there is a generic null operator Gen in the sentence binding pro (just as the implicit argument of the passive can be bound by a null generic operator; see chapter 2). This approach seems more plausible (and uniform across the various examples in (16) and (17)) than Epstein's approach, where he assumes that "This element (pro) receives a universal quantifier interpretation in English only if it is antecedentless" (pg. 502, fn. 6). (See also Bhatt and Pancheva 2017:24, which also invokes a generic operator for evaluative predicates.)

As shown above, the implicit argument for evaluative predicates can receive a generic, definite, or bound variable interpretation. Can it be understood existentially? In their overview, Bhatt and Pancheva (2017:25) conclude that "Existentially quantifying the implicit argument results in a meaning that is too weak." Consider the following example:

(18) Context: We are all going out to a bar, but we need to choose a designated driver for the way home. I say one of the following to our group:
a. It is important to not drink tonight.
b. For one of us, it is important to not drink tonight.

(18b) fits the context, but not (18a). Rather, (18a) uttered in the given context implies that the speaker or people in general should not drink tonight. In other words, (18a) does not seem to be existentially interpreted; rather, it seems stronger (in that it entails an existential interpretation).

The examples in (18) are in the present tense. But a similar lack of existential interpretation also arises for evaluative predicates in past tense sentences:

(19) Context: Yesterday, I went to a baseball game. When a batter hit a home run in the fourth inning, a fan seated high up in the bleachers caught it. The next day, I report what happened as follows:
a. Yesterday, it was great to catch that home run in the fourth inning.
b. Yesterday, for somebody or the other, it was great to catch that home run in the fourth inning.

Although (19b) seems OK in context, (19a) does not seem to fit the context. Rather, (19a) uttered in the given context implies that the speaker or addressee caught the home run. (19a) does not seem to have an interpretation involving existential interpretation. To get the existential interpretation, an explicit phrase such as *somebody or the other* in (19b) needs to be added.

Another example of a past tense sentence is given below (thanks to Friederike Moltmann for discussing this issue):

(20) Context: There was an exercise class. Some people are in shape and had an easy time. Others are out of shape and had a difficult time.
a. Yesterday it was easy to do the workout, and it was difficult to do it.
b. Yesterday, for some, it was easy to do the workout, for others it was difficult.

(20b) reports on the situation accurately, but (20a) seems to be reporting on contradictory opinions of a single person (e.g., the speaker). In other words, (20a) does not seem to have the interpretation in (20b); rather, (20a) means something like "In some respects, it was easy to do the workout and in some respects it was difficult to do it."

The generalization seems to be that the implicit argument of evaluative adjectives cannot be an existentially bound variable. If true, such facts suggest that the existential interpretation of an implicit argument is not possible across all constructions. Rather, where it exists, it must be licensed by some particular morpheme that denotes an existential operator. No such morpheme is present with evaluative predicates. I return to the existential interpretation of implicit arguments in the passive in section 4.5 below.

4.4.2 Implicit Datives

A similar case occurs with the dative argument of verbs of saying (for discussion see Landau 2010; Rizzi 1986):

(21) a. John signaled (to Mary) to leave.
b. John whispered (to Mary) to leave.
c. John said (to Mary) to leave.

In these cases, the implicit dative argument obligatorily controls PRO in the embedded infinitival clause. Consider the following example from Landau 2010:367:

(22) a. Mary hated it when we said to behave herself.
b. Mary_1 hated it when we said pro_1 [PRO_1 to behave herself].

In (22b), *Mary* binds the implicit dative argument of *say*, which in turn controls PRO. This analysis makes the prediction that if the implicit argument of *say* is replaced by an overt argument, control by *Mary* should be blocked:

(23) *Mary$_1$ hated it when we said to Jim [PRO$_1$ to behave herself].

About control by an implicit argument, I agree with Landau (2010:357), who argues: "Although they participate in control relations, implicit arguments are standardly viewed as unprojected theta-roles, absent from the syntax. I challenge this view and argue that implicit arguments are syntactically represented."

However, the theory developed in this chapter (as well as other theories in this monograph) differs from Landau's. In particular, Landau claims that there are two types of implicit arguments, weak implicit arguments and strong implicit arguments. Furthermore, he claims that the implicit argument in the passive is a WIA and cannot be modified by a secondary predicate. But chapter 3 showed the implicit argument in the passive can be modified by a secondary predicate. So, I reject Landau's classification of the implicit argument in the passive as a WIA, and correspondingly I reject his division between WIAs and SIAs. In my theory, there is only one type of implicit argument governed by the assumptions in (8–11).

The example in (22) shows that implicit dative arguments can be interpreted as definite. Can they also be existential and generic? I have not yet investigated this issue.

4.4.3 Middles

Stroik (1992, 1995, 1999, 2000, 2005, 2006) (see also Hoekstra and Roberts 1993; Postal 2010) argues that the external argument in the middle is syntactically realized as PRO (but see Newman 2020 for a very rich empirical discussion that assumes that the external argument is not projected). The example below is from Stroik 1992:134, (20):

(24) a Bureaucrats bribe easily.

b. [$_{IP}$ bureaucrats [$_{I'}$I [$_{VP}$ [$_{VP}$ bribe easily] PRO]]]

The arguments that Stroik gives for a syntactically present external argument involve Principle A of the Binding Theory and control of PRO in adjunct clauses. For example, consider the following example involving a reflexive pronoun contained in the subject (from Stroik 1992:129):

(25) Letters to oneself compose quickly.

According to Stroik the DP *letters to oneself* starts out in object position and moves to subject position. When in object position, the reflexive is bound by the implicit argument.

We can strengthen this argument by looking at Principle B effects:

(26) a. Letters to yourself compose more quickly than letters to other people.
b. Letters to you compose more quickly than letters to other people.

My intuition about these examples is that *yourself* refers to the composer in (26a), but *you* does not refer to the composer in (26b), just exactly as would be predicted by Principle B if there were an implicit external argument referring to the composer in both. If the reflexive pronoun was a logophor in (26a), there is no reason it would show a Principle B effect (see section 2.8 for discussion of logophoric interpretations).

Stroik (1995:168) also shows that control into adjunct clauses is possible with middles (see also Vinet 1987). Stroik analyzes these cases as control of PRO by the implicit argument of the middle:

(27) a. Most physics books read poorly even after reading them several times.
b. Bureaucrats bribe easily after doing them a favor or two.

Stroik argues that the implicit argument is PRO, which occupies an adjunct position (adjoined to VP). I reject this part of Stroik's analysis, and propose instead that the implicit argument is caseless pro, which is merged into Spec vP, as with all external arguments. In other words, the external argument in the middle is projected exactly in the same way as in the active.

I do not take up the interpretation of the implicit argument in middles. For some discussion, see Ackema and Schoorlemer 2017:10: "A type I middle expresses a generic modal reading that can be roughly paraphrased as 'anyone could V (Adv)'. For example, *this meat cuts easily* can be paraphrased as 'anyone could cut this meat with ease'." Their paraphrase of the middle suggests that middles are always interpreted generically. From our perspective, the issue is whether the implicit argument in middles has existential, generic, and definite interpretations, just like the implicit argument in the passive. I have not yet investigated this issue.

4.4.4 Nominalizations

The examples in (28) show that the implicit argument in nominalizations is syntactically active (for control, binding, and secondary predicates) (see also Borer 2020 on the implicit argument of nominalizations).

(28) a. The attempt to leave (Williams 1987:51)
b. Respect for oneself is important. (Williams 1987:51)
c. Discussion of these issues stoned (Safir 1987:582)

In the theory I am developing, the representation of these examples is as follows:

(29) a. The pro_1 attempt [PRO_1 to leave]
b. [pro_1 respect for $oneself_1$] is important.
c. [pro_1 discussion of these issues [$_{AdjP}$ PRO_1 stoned]]

In (29a), the implicit argument controls PRO of the embedded infinitival clause. In (29b), the implicit argument binds the reflexive *oneself.* In (29c), the implicit argument is modified by a secondary predicate internal to the nominalization.

A famous contrast by Ross (1969:195) gives further support for implicit arguments in nominalizations (see also Sichel 2009 on Principle C effects in nominalizations):

(30) a. *The knowledge that $Fred_1$ will be unpopular doesn't bother him_1.
b. The knowledge that he_1 will be unpopular doesn't bother $Fred_1$.

(31) a. The possibility that $Fred_1$ will be unpopular doesn't bother him_1.
b. The possibility that he_1 will be unpopular doesn't bother $Fred_1$.

In (30a), the implicit argument of *knowledge* gives rise to a Principle C effect. Since *possibility* does not have an implicit external argument, there is no similar Principle C effect in (31a). This is another illustration of the syntactic activity of implicit arguments. The representation of (30a) is as follows:

(32) *The pro_1 knowledge that $Fred_1$ will be unpopular doesn't bother him_1.

Williams does not accept that implicit arguments are syntactically projected, but he does this at the cost of having to radically modify the Binding Theory: "I will explore here the possibility that the binding theory (plus control) applies not to NPs, but to the theta roles that are assigned to the NPs" (1987:151). In this monograph, I adopt a standard version of the Binding Theory (not involving theta-roles).

The structure of (29a) is given in (33) (leaving out irrelevant details; see Bruening 2018 and Fu, Borer, and Roeper 2001 for related proposals):

(33)

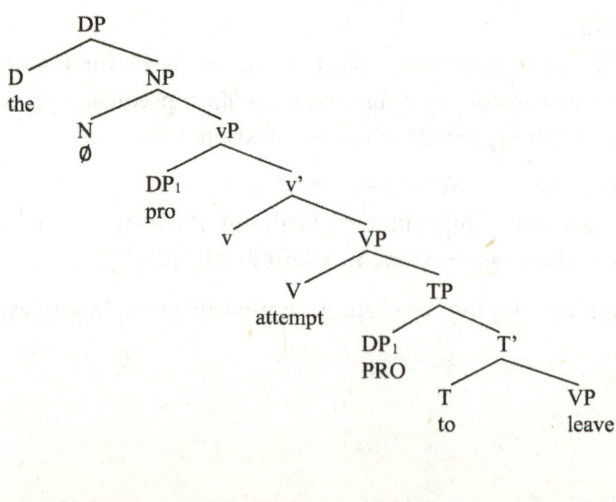

In (33), the implicit argument pro is in situ in Spec vP, a caseless position—that is, it does not have genitive Case).

Depending on the determiner and linguistic context, the implicit argument can be interpreted as definite (34a), bound variable (34b), generic (34c,d), or existential (34e):

(34) a. The constant promotion of himself at conferences hurt John's career.
  b. Every player was involved in the promotion of himself at matches.
  c. Any attempt to promote oneself is met with opposition.
  d. The exclusion of girls from school entails the denial of education. (Borer 2020:117)
  e. There was an attempt to breach the fence this morning. (I don't know by whom).

In (34a), the antecedent of *himself* is the definite implicit argument of *promotion*. This is the same in (34b), but in this case the implicit argument is bound by the quantifier phrase and gets a bound variable interpretation. In (34c), the antecedent of the reflexive *oneself* is the generic pro (equivalent to generic *one*; see chapter 2 on the passive). The most natural interpretation of the implicit arguments in (34d) also seems to be generic *pro* ("One's exclusion of girls from school . . ."). Lastly, the implicit argument in (34e) is existential, as shown clearly by the continuation.

On the existential and generic interpretations of implicit arguments in nominalizations, see Borer 2020. Borer argues that nominalizations lacking an overtly expressed external argument (short argument structure nominals) are actually nominalizations of verbal passives. If so, the existential interpretations of implicit arguments in nominalizations could have the same analysis as the existential interpretations arising in the passive.

Borer (2020:116–117, 128) does not seem to recognize definite interpretations for the implicit argument in passives or nominalizations. But chapter 2 showed that definite interpretations are possible for the passive, and (34a) shows a definite interpretation for the implicit argument in a nominalization.

Much more work is needed on the syntactic mechanisms giving rise to these interpretations (generic, existential, definite), the contexts that bring them out, and the syntactic diagnostics (e.g., pronoun binding) that distinguish them.

4.5 Revisiting the Passive

Consider again the passive, discussed in chapters 2 and 3:

(35) That book was written in 1784.

Out of the blue, the most obvious interpretation of (35) is that the external argument is existentially quantified:

(36) Somebody wrote that book in 1784.

The question is how the existential interpretation arises in the theory of implicit arguments laid out in the preceding sections. So far, in chapter 2, I have been assuming that in this case there is a null pronoun (pro_{un}) that is bound by an existential operator. The purpose of this section is to revisit this assumption in more detail.

First, note that overt pronouns do not generally have an existential interpretation. In other words, the sentence "He left" does not have the existential interpretation that somebody left (unlike definite and generic interpretations, which overt pronouns have). So how does the implicit argument in the passive come to be interpreted existentially?

In line with the Merge-based approach to argument structure, I assume that the existential interpretation is not the result of some purely semantic rule (see chapter 10 for a discussion of the tension between the Merge-based approach and formal semantics). Rather, I assume the following:

(37) In the existential interpretation of the passive, there is a morpheme in the syntactic representation that denotes an existential quantifier.

Given this general background assumption, we can divide the possibilities for capturing the existential interpretation in the passive into the following:

(38) (a) The external argument is not projected.
(Bruening 2013; Legate 2014; Alexiadou, Anagnostopoulou, and Schäfer 2015; Pylkkänen 2008a)
(b) The external argument is projected as a null pronoun.
(Collins 2005a; Borer 2020)
(c) The external argument is projected as a null quantifier expression.

This monograph argues extensively against (38a). See the beginning of this chapter for a critical discussion of Bruening 2013, for example. So, here I will just consider (37) combined with either (38b) or (38c). As it turns out, both are consistent with the Merge-based approach.

Consider first (38b), which is consistent with the general theory of implicit arguments that treats them as caseless pro. There are two possibilities consistent with the assumptions in (37) and (38b). First, there could be a null operator (similar to the generic operator Gen in chapter 2, following Moltmann 2006) that unselectively binds the implicit argument pro. Second, there could be a head (similar to Bruening's Pass and Pylkkänen's $Voice_{Pass}$; see also

Borer 2020:127), that unselectively binds the syntactically projected implicit argument pro.

Under either approach, I assume that the existential quantifier is unrestricted, accounting for (a) the wide-ranging domain of quantification (see McCawley's remarks in (23)), and (b) the lack of phi-features of an existentially bound implicit argument.

Consider the possibility that there is an existential operator OP unselectively binding the implicit argument pro. The structure is given below:

(39)

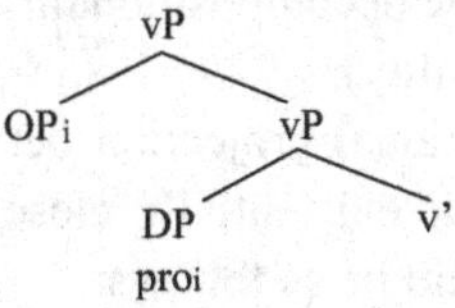

The model for this kind of analysis could be Diesing's (1992:6) analysis of indefinites (see also Zimmermann 2007): "Here the variable introduced by the indefinite is bound by an implicit existential quantifier that 'existentially' closes off the nuclear scope, preventing the occurrence of unbound variables." Crucially, Diesing (1992) does not link such an existential interpretation to the passive, but rather to the indefinite arguments dominated by VP: "existential closure applies to nuclear scopes (or VPs) only, as implied by the tree-splitting algorithm" (pg. 57). For an application of existential closure in Diesing's sense to the implicit argument in the passive, see Murphy 2015.

One question this approach raises is what determines the syntactic distribution of the existential OP. Can it adjoin to any maximal projection? Or is it restricted to VPs only? A closely related question is whether existential interpretations are available for implicit arguments in general (no matter what construction they appear in). If the existential interpretation were freely available, tied only to the presence of existential OP adjoined to XP, it is not clear why an existential interpretation is missing for evaluative predicates (as discussed earlier in this chapter). Another question is whether it is ever possible for a single existential operator to unselectively bind two implicit arguments at the same time.

Consider now the possibility that there is a functional head introducing the existential quantifier. One possibility is that Voice (in the sense of Collins 2005a) itself introduces the existential interpretation. So, in the structure $[_{\text{VoiceP}}$ Voice $[_{\text{vP}}$ pro v']], Voice would be an unselective existential quantifier binding the implicit argument pro. But not all passives involve an existential interpretation. For example, when the *by*-phrase is present, there is no existential interpretation (unless the *by*-phrase itself contains an existential quantifier phrase). Also, as shown in chapter 2, sometimes short passives are interpreted with a generic or definite external argument. So, there would have to be two different Voice heads: one that unselectively binds a variable, and the other that does not. Alternatively, there would have to be a Voice head with an optional existential quantifier feature. This analysis raises the question of which functional heads could have an optional existential quantifier feature. It also involves an instance of syntactic bundling of two very different syntactic functions onto one syntactic head: Voice plus existential quantification (see the discussion in section 8.6 on semantic decompositionality, and Kayne 2005:212 on the Principle of Decompositionality).

An alternative is to optionally generate a functional projection between Voice (in the sense of Collins 2005a) and vP that existentially closes the implicit argument of the passive. The structure would be as follows:

(40)

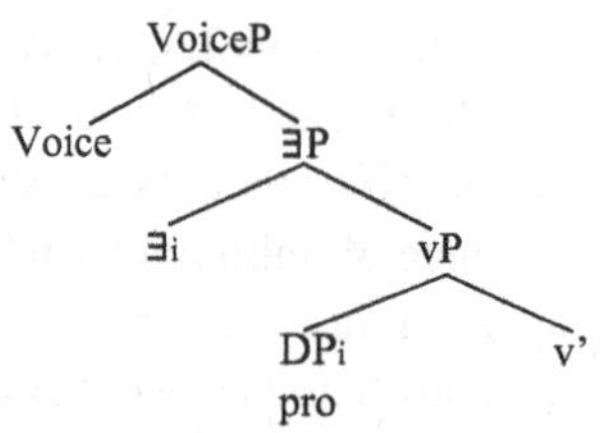

The two issues that need to be addressed in such an analysis are: (a) What is the syntactic distribution of ∃P? Is it limited to the passive, or is it more widely available? Can it appear with any vP (as the discussion in Diesing 1992 seems to suggest)? (b) Why is the existential quantifier the head of a clausal functional projection in (40), whereas it seems to head a QP (quantifier phrase) in other uses (e.g., *some boys*)?

Let us now consider possibility (38c): the implicit external argument in the passive is a null quantifier expression. For convenience, let's call this expression UN, which stands for unspecified quantifier. English has a variety of contexts that permit null existential quantifiers. For example, Collins and Postal (2014) analyze negative existentials such as *no boy* as having the structure [[NEG SOME] boy], where *some* is a covert existential quantifier. The claim of (38c) is that the implicit argument of the passive can also be a null existential quantifier.

Furthermore, I assume that UN is unrestricted (there is no domain restriction), accounting for (a) the wide-ranging domain of quantification (see McCawley's remarks in (23)), and (b) the lack of phi-features of the implicit argument.

The problem with this approach is that if UN is available for the passive, why is it not available for all the implicit argument constructions? I pointed out above that evaluative adjective constructions are not interpreted existentially. If UN is possible, then why isn't the following representation possible?

(41) It was fun UN_1 [PRO_1 to swim].
Intended: "For somebody, it was fun to swim."

I propose that the existential reading of the passive is given by UN (a kind of null argument), but that UN itself is only licensed in Spec vP. In section 6.7, I propose that *by*-phrases are constrained to Spec vP because they have the c-selectional feature [__vP]. The simplest assumption for UN is that it has the same syntactic c-selectional feature.

In summary, I have proposed two possible sources for the existential interpretation of the implicit argument in the passive.

(42) a. Existential quantifier binding pro
b. Existential quantifier argument (UN) in Spec vP

I assume that both (42a,b) are consistent with the general Merge-based framework I outline in this monograph. They also happen to be very closely related. In both cases, an unrestricted existential quantifier with no phi-features binds a variable. The only difference is whether the variable is a null pro (pro_{un}) or a trace/copy left by QR (quantifier raising) of UN. I leave it to other linguists to articulate the different predictions of these two possibilities. For example, there is the issue of how these various possibilities dovetail with theories of narrow scope indefinites (bare plurals) and wide scope indefinites (see Heim 2011 for discussion of these topics).

4.6 The Wedge

In proposing a general theory of implicit arguments, it could be argued that I am overgeneralizing. Even though the implicit argument in the English passive is syntactically projected (as demonstrated by the diagnostics in chapters 2 and 3), perhaps there may be many other kinds of implicit arguments that are not syntactically projected. Perhaps there are other languages different from English where implicit arguments are not projected syntactically at all (even in passives and nominalizations, for which the evidence in English is very strong). To find out, one would need to look at constructions and languages on a case-by-case basis and apply the tests available in each language. However, I want to take the strongest possible position (and therefore, the most easily falsifiable) and claim that all implicit arguments in all languages are syntactically projected.

In chapters 2 and 3, I argued that the implicit argument in the passive is syntactically projected on the basis of the distribution of reflexives, reciprocals, pronouns, Helke expressions, and secondary predicates. I will now argue that all implicit arguments (across different constructions and different languages) are syntactically projected, whether or not any syntactic data actually support that conclusion for a particular construction in a particular language. I will call this argument *the wedge*, because of its far-ranging consequences. The metaphor is that the generalizations about the English passive help to pry open a much larger generalization concerning implicit arguments cross-linguistically.

At least in the case of the passive, it is far from clear that a child would have adequate access to the relevant data to actually learn that the implicit arguments are syntactically projected. Consider the well-known sentences discussed in chapter 2, repeated below:

(43) a. Such privileges should be kept to oneself.
(Baker, Johnson, and Roberts 1989:228; Roberts 1987:162)
b. Damaging testimony is always given about oneself in secret trials.
(Roberts 1987:162)

Exactly when would a child have access to this kind of data (involving a passive, a verb with a PP argument, and the reflexive *oneself*), which seem to be rather complex sentence types? And if somehow the child did hear these kinds of sentences, would they understand them in context? And if they understood them in context, would they parse them correctly? And if they parsed them correctly, would they thereby draw the conclusion that the implicit argument is syntactically projected (or would they chalk the data up to exempt anaphora)? Although I have not done a corpus study, my suspicion is that the relevant data are vanishingly rare, especially in child-directed speech.

Rather, it is more plausible to assume that the child does not have to learn anything at all about implicit arguments. Suppose the child hears an example of the passive, even a very simple one such as (44):

(44) These peas have not been eaten.

If the child understands that the external argument is involved—that is, somebody has not eaten the peas—then given the AC/TC from chapter 1, they automatically assume that there is a syntactically projected implicit argument. So, instead of being guided by empirical phenomena related to whether or not implicit arguments are syntactically projected, the child is guided by principles of UG.

In other words, data from implicit arguments support a classical poverty of stimulus argument for a principle of UG. Principle P (implicit arguments in the passive are syntactically projected) is not learnable from the primary linguistic data, therefore P must be a principle of UG or must follow from principles of UG (in this case the AC/TC).

But if the AC/TC holds, it entails that implicit arguments are syntactically projected. Therefore, it follows that across different kinds of constructions (e.g., evaluative adjectives, implicit datives, middles, nominalizations) and different languages (e.g., English, Italian, Greek, Ewe, Buli, Oshiwambo) implicit arguments are always syntactically projected.

Here is the wedge argument laid out step-by-step:

(45) a. The distribution of reflexives, reciprocals, pronouns, Helke expressions, and secondary predicates shows that the implicit argument in the English short passive is syntactically projected.
b. The child does not have access to the relevant data. That is, the child does not have access to the data that require a syntactically represented external argument (i.e., the distribution of reflexives, reciprocals, pronouns, Helke expressions, and secondary predicates).
c. Therefore, there is a principle of UG (AC/TC) forcing implicit arguments to project syntactically in the passive in English.
d. Principles of UG are not specific to the passive, or any other construction (because particular constructions are not part of UG).
e. Principles of UG hold for all I-languages.
f. Therefore, implicit arguments are syntactically projected in a wide variety of constructions across all I-languages.

This argument goes from particular facts about the English passive to a general cross-linguistic theory of implicit arguments.

4.7 Complement Deletion

Consider the case of the verb *eat* (and related verbs such as *bake* and *read*; see Levin 1993:33 for a list of additional verbs):

(46) a. John ate.
b. John ate something.
c. John ate *(it) raw.

It seems as if (46a) entails (46b), in the sense that whenever (46a) is true, so is (46b). Therefore, on the basis of this entailment, one may want to say that (46a) has a syntactically projected implicit theme argument (i.e., the thing eaten). However, the ungrammaticality of (46c) without the pronoun casts doubt on that conclusion. If there were a syntactically present implicit argument in (46a), then it should be able to be modified by the object-oriented secondary predicate (see chapter 3, where it is shown that the implicit argument in the passive can be modified by a secondary predicate). But (46c) is completely unacceptable without the pronoun, suggesting that there is no syntactically projected implicit argument in (46a).

An alternative, which I will not pursue, is that there is a syntactically projected implicit argument in (46a), but it is somehow inaccessible to secondary predicates and control. I leave this kind of analysis to others.

Rather, I propose that (46a) has no implicit argument at all, syntactically or semantically. And furthermore, the truth conditions of (46a,b) are as in (47a,b):

(47) a. ⟦John ate.⟧ = $\exists e[\text{eat}(e) \wedge \text{Agent}(e,\text{John})]$
b. ⟦John ate something.⟧ = $\exists e \exists x[\text{eat}(e) \wedge \text{Agent}(e,\text{John}) \wedge \text{Theme}(e,x)]$

In other words, in (46a) there is neither a syntactic nor semantic implicit theme. But then how can one account for the entailment relation between (46a) and (46b)? I suggest that it is a matter of real-world knowledge that when one eats, something needs to be eaten. But this information is not reflected in any way in the syntactic representation or in the semantic values of the intransitive verb. My approach is similar to that of Fodor and Fodor (1980:760), who account for the entailment in terms of meaning postulates: "the entailments of verbs are handled not by lexical rules which associate quantificational structure with syntactic form, but rather by rules of logical inference." (See also Williams 2015:106 for relevant discussion.)

Some support for this analysis comes from the following examples (on the use of resultatives with *unspecified object verbs*, see Levin and Rappaport Hovav 1995:37–39):

(48) a. He ate his way across the buffet table.
b. *He ate rice his way across the buffet table.

(49) a. He ate himself sick.
b. *He ate meat himself sick.

(50) a. He ate us out of house and home.
b. *He ate our food us out of house and home.

There are lots of uses of *eat*, which seem to retain the core meaning of *eat* but are impossible with any kind of expressed theme (the object being eaten). I suggest that these uses of *eat* have no syntactic or semantic theme whatsoever.

Consider also the fact that the understood argument of *eat* can never be realized with any kind of KP or PP (unlike *by*-phrases in passives). This fact would be explained if there were no syntactic argument to project in the first place.

(51) a. *I ate by the food.
b. *I ate with the food.
c. *I ate to the food.

d. *I ate for the food.
e. *I ate of the food.
Intended: "I ate the food."

The proposal that intransitive *eat* has the semantic value in (47a) supports an approach to internal arguments where they are introduced by argument-introducing heads separate from the lexical verb (see Ramchand 2008 for a concrete proposal). In other words, in (46b) the internal argument *something* is introduced by an argument-introducing verbal head v_{THEME} or v_{IA} (IA = internal argument). This head is syntactically and semantically distinct from the external argument little v and also from Appl. When v_{IA}P is present, there is a syntactically projected internal argument, and the interpretation is (47b). When v_{IA}P is absent, there is no syntactically projected internal argument, and the interpretation is (47a).

The analysis is illustrated below:

(52) John ate the rice.

(53)

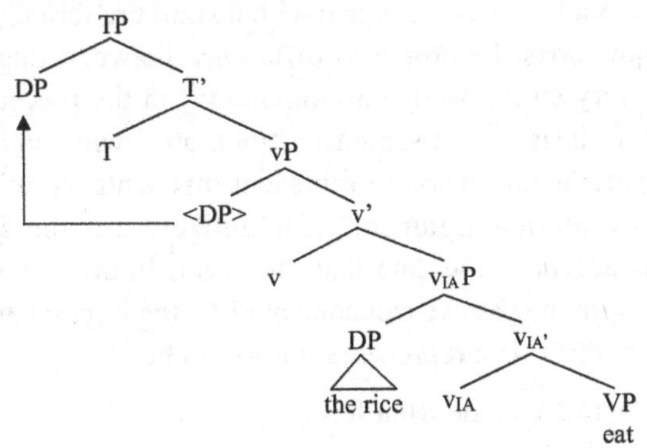

Similar remarks hold for Rizzi's (1986:503) discussion of the following English cases:

(54) a. This leads people to the following conclusion.
b. This leads to the following conclusion.
c. This leads people [PRO to conclude what follows].
d. *This leads [PRO to conclude what follows].

The example in (54d) is important in that it shows that obligatory control is syntactic. Even if there were a pragmatic inference from (54b) to the proposition that somebody was led to a certain conclusion, such a pragmatic inference is not sufficient to license control of PRO in (54d). In other words, whenever there is obligatory control, we can be certain that the antecedent in that obligatory control relation is a syntactically projected DP.

Why are sentences parallel to (54d) acceptable in Italian (see Rizzi 1986:503, example (8))? I assume that Italian has a null direct object form of the generic pronoun *one*, which English lacks. It is unclear to me what accounts for this difference, although it is plausibly related to the fact that Italian independently has null subjects, which are pro with a uCase feature. A cross-linguistic survey of the relationship between null subjects and null objects is needed.

The difference between Italian (presence of syntactically projected implicit theme) and English (absence of syntactically projected implicit theme) might correspond to the difference noted by Baker (2015:203) between Shipibo and Godoberi in the licensing of ergative case. In Shipibo, "A pro object triggers ergative case on the subject." Crucially, this generalization also holds for "an indefinite, existentially bound null object of a verb like 'eat'" (see also Baker 2014:350). In contrast, in Godoberi, "optionally transitive verbs with agentive subjects have subjects in absolutive case when they are used intransitively" (204). Although much more work is needed on implicit arguments in these languages, one way to think of this contrast is that Shibipo is like Italian, with null pro for objects, while Godoberi is like English with no null pro for objects.

To tie up loose ends, how does the proposed difference between English and Italian fit in with the very strong wedge argument (45) in the preceding section? More concretely, in hearing the sentence, "John ate," why isn't the child compelled (by semantic entailments) to represent this sentence with a syntactically projected null internal argument? It is unlikely that the child notices that (46c) above is absent in the data that they hear. In other words, just as the implicit argument in the passive can control PRO, the implicit argument in (54d) would control PRO. The representation would be:

(55) *This leads pro_1 [PRO_1 to conclude what follows].

Note here that the object of *lead* is a Case position. It alternates with an accusative marked DP pronoun, for example. Therefore, pro in (55) does not qualify as an implicit argument according to the assumption in (8), since the pro in (55) does not lack a structural Case feature [uCase]. In general, English does not have structurally Case-marked pro.

The direct object position of a verb is different from Spec vP (the position for the implicit argument in the passive), in that it is a Case position (it gets its accusative Case from v). But this property prevents the implicit argument pro (available as part of UG) from appearing there. In order for a language to license null objects, there must be some independent system of licensing null objects (like the null generic object in Italian, or like the indefinite object drop in Spanish; see Campos 1986). If a child hears "John eats" in a language L and there is no independent evidence for null objects in L, then (since implicit object pro is impossible) they will simply assume that the argument-introducing head v_{IA} is absent, yielding a language like English.

4.8 Conclusion

In this chapter I presented a general theory of implicit arguments: an implicit argument is pro without a [uCase] feature. As such, it cannot appear in any position associated with Case assignment (Spec of finite TP, Spec DP). As a pronoun, it can be interpreted as (a) indexical, (b) coreferential with an antecedent, or as (b) a bound variable. Although I have only discussed English in this chapter, I put forth the strongest possible hypothesis that such an analysis of implicit arguments holds as part of UG, hence for all human languages. If this is true, then all languages have null pro. This means that the terms *null subject language* and *pro-drop parameter* need to be taken as applying specifically to languages that have pro bearing an uninterpretable Case feature (e.g., Italian, Spanish).

In this chapter, I have not discussed intransitive verbs with definite implicit arguments (e.g., *notice*, *join in*, *approve*, *watch*, *apply*). Fodor and Fodor (1980) describe this class of verbs as follows: "The sentence *John ate* (or, at least, *John is eating*) can be used to initiate a discourse, but the sentence *John noticed* cannot; it needs some suitable prior context, such as *Bill was nervously biting his nails*, or *The audience was quietly creeping out of the emergency exit*. A natural way to describe this would be to say that *John noticed* entails not *John noticed something* but *John noticed it*; that is, that the entailed object of a *notice*-class verb is definite." Fillmore (1986) calls these cases *definite null complements*.

It is unclear how this class of verbs fits into the theory outlined in this chapter. Much further work is needed. For example, does the possibility of having a definite null complement need to be lexically specified? What kinds of thematic roles can such null complements have? What kinds of syntactic categories can be null complements (DPs, PPs, CPs, etc.)? How does their interpretation differ from that of an overt definite pronoun? Do they pass any diagnostics for being syntactically active? For further discussion, see Fillmore 1986, Fodor and Fodor 1980. See also Williams 2015: chapter 5 for a detailed discussion of possible analyses.

5 Out of Africa

So far in this monograph, I have focused entirely on English. I have shown that the implicit argument in the passive is syntactically realized, because it licenses secondary predicates and Helke expressions and it gives rise to Principle A and B effects.

Recall the wedge argument from chapter 4. The conclusion of that argument was

(1) Implicit arguments are syntactically projected in a wide variety of constructions across all I-languages.

The purpose of this chapter is to start to give some empirical evidence for this conclusion. I will present cross-linguistic evidence from three African languages: Buli (Gur: Northern Ghana) from Sulemana 2022, Oshiwambo (Bantu: Angola, Namibia) from Ndapo 2022, and Ewe (Kwa: Ghana, Togo, Benin) from Gotah 2022. Each of these three languages provides striking support for (1). I limit the discussion below to diagnostics for implicit arguments.

For preliminary work showing how the framework works for Indo-European languages, see Storment 2022 for Spanish and Angelopoulos et al. 2023 for Greek. For similar conclusions about the implicit argument in the German passive, see Müller 2019.

5.1 Buli

Sulemana (2022) notices the following alternation (tonal morphology plays no role in Sulemana's account, so I leave out tone marking):

(2) a. Asibi bɔni lammu.
Asibi chop meat.DEF
'Asibi chopped the meat.'
b. Lammu bɔni.
meat.DEF chop
'The meat was chopped.'

Sulemana argues that (2b) is the short passive, and not a middle. Furthermore, he shows that it is impossible in (2b) to project the external argument overtly. For example, no *by*-phrase is allowed. So, Buli only has a short passive (with no *by*-phrase), but no long passive.

Sulemana uses a wide range of diagnostics to show that even though the external argument does not appear overtly in (2b), there is a syntactically projected implicit argument. The diagnostics he makes use of are the following:

(3) a. entailments,
 b. Principles A,B of the Binding Theory,
 c. the distribution of "for X's own sake,"
 d. control into purpose clauses, and
 e. the distribution of secondary predicates.

I will illustrate just one of them here.

Consider the distribution of the phrase "for X's own sake":

(4) Asibi$_1$ bɔni lammu wa$_1$-dek-nyiŋ.
 Asibi chop meat.DEF 3SG-SELF-body
 'Asibi chopped the meat for his own sake.'

Sulemana carefully shows that the 3SG pronoun *wa* in *wa-dek-nyiŋ* can only be bound by a local c-commanding antecedent. Given that constraint, consider the passive. The context for the following sentence is that I saw Asibi chopping some meat in the kitchen, and I asked my friend if he was helping his mother cook. My friend responds:

(5) Lammu bɔni wa$_1$-dek-nyiŋ.
 meat.DEF chop 3SG-SELF-body
 'The meat was chopped for his own sake.'

The only possible interpretation of this sentence is that the antecedent of third-person singular *wa* is the chopper. This fact strongly suggests a syntactic representation in which the implicit argument is syntactically projected, binding the pronoun.

Sulemana shows that when a verb lacks an external argument (overt or covert), "for X's own sake" is not licensed:

(6) *Li:ka mɔbi wa$_1$-dek-nyiŋ.
 pot.DEF break 3SG-SELF-BODY
 Intended: 'The pot broke for his own sake.'

In English, just as in Buli, the pronoun in "for X's own sake" can be bound by an implicit argument, as shown in (7).

(7) A second inadequate (I think) interpretation has it that by helping friends and country, you *are* helping yourself. The problem with this is that it makes helping others something that would be done *for one's own sake.* (http://faculty.smcm.edu/mstaber/ne-8&9.htm)

In this example, the pronoun *one* in *for one's own sake* is bound by the implicit argument pro_{gen} of the passive *be done.* Such examples can be found on the Internet, and they are acceptable.

So, this adds another test to the tests already developed in chapters 2 and 3 for the presence of a syntactically projected implicit argument in the short passive in English.

5.2 Oshiwambo

Ndapo (2022) discusses the passive construction in the Oshingandjera dialect of Oshiwambo. Unlike Buli, Oshiwambo allows an overt *by*-phrase. The active, short passive, and long passive are illustrated below:

(8) a. Ndapewa o-kw-a-lesh-a e-mbo. (active)
Ndapewa AFF-SM1-PST-read-FV CL5-book
'Ndapewa read the book.'
b. E-mbo o-ly-a-lesh-w-a. (short passive)
CL5-book AFF-SM5-PST-read-PASS-FV
'The book was read.'
c. E-mbo o-ly-a-lesh-w-a ku-Ndapewa.
CL5-book AFF-SM5-PST-read-PASS-FV by-Ndapewa
'The book was read by Ndapewa.'

The *ku-* in the passive *by*-phrase in (8c) is morphologically the class-17 locative marker.

Ndapo considers two diagnostics for the syntactic status of the implicit argument in the short passive:

(9) a. the expression "on X's own," and
b. reciprocals.

I will illustrate (9a) here.

Consider the distribution of the phrase "on X's own" in Oshiwambo:

(10) Ngame o-nd-a-lesh-a e-mbo (ku-)ngame-mwene.
1SG AFF-1SG-PST-read-FV CL5-book CL17-1SG-own
'I read the book on my own.'

Notice that in (10) the *ku-* is optional, unlike the *ku-* found in the passive *by*-phrase. The optionality of *ku-* in (10) clearly distinguishes "on X's own" phrases from passive *by*-phrases. Ndapo carefully shows that the pronoun in "on X's own" can only be bound by a local c-commanding antecedent.

Given that constraint, consider the passive in the following context: the teacher sees a student's assignment and is amazed by it. She asks, "Who helped you with the assignment?" The student replies:

(11) O-shi-thigilwa o-sh-a-ning-w-a (ku-)ngame-mwene.
AUG-7-assignment AFF-SM7-PST-do-PASS-FV CL17-1SG-own
'The assignment was done on my own.'

In this sentence, the 1SG pronoun *ngame* is bound by the implicit argument, which represents the doer of the assignment. And note that the *ku-* is optional in (11) because it is not a passive *by*-phrase.

When a verb does not have an external argument, it is impossible for "on X's own" to refer back to the implicit argument:

(12) a. O-mbiga o-y-a-tanduk-a.
CL9-pot AFF-SM9-PST-break-FV
'The pot broke.'

b. *O-mbiga o-y-a-tanduk-a (ku-)ngame-mwene.
CL9-pot AFF-SM9-PST-break-FV CL17-1SG-own
Intended: 'The pot broke on my own.'

5.3 Ewe

Gotah (2022) discusses the middle construction in Tongugbe, a dialect of Ewe. The construction is illustrated in (13). Tonal morphology plays no role in Gotah's account, so I leave out tone marking:

(13) a. Kofi ɖa-a mɔlu.
Kofi cook-HAB rice
'Kofi cooks rice.'

b. Mɔlu nya ɖa-a.
rice NYA cook-HAB
'Rice cooks easily.'

c. Mɔlu nya ɖa-a ne Kofi.
rice NYA cook-HAB for Kofi
'Rice cooks easily for Kofi.'

Gotah (2022) argues that (13b,c) are middles that are derived by A-movement of the internal argument to Spec TP. In (13b) the external argument is not overtly realized. In (13c) the external argument is overtly realized by the *for*-phrase *ne Kofi* (on a related analysis of middles, see Stroik 1992, 1995, 1999).

Gotah (2022) argues that the implicit agent argument in (13b) is syntactically projected. The diagnostics he makes use of are the following:

(14) a. Principles A,B of the Binding Theory,
b. control into *without*-adjuncts, and
c. the distribution of secondary predicates.

I will illustrate reflexive binding. Consider the following sentence:

(15) Kofi$_1$ gblɔ be awu nya *f*le-ɛ ne ye-ɖokoe$_1$.
Kofi say that shirt NYA buy-HAB for LOG-self
'Kofi said that he enjoys buying clothes for himself.'

In this example, the implicit external argument of *buy* is binding the reflexive *ye-ɖokoe*. This fact provides strong support for a syntactically projected implicit argument (in Spec vP), allowing the reflexive to satisfy Principle A of the Binding Theory. Interestingly, the implicit argument must be a null logophoric pronoun here, because of the form of the reflexive (LOG-*self*).

6 *By*-Phrases

6.1 Introduction

Some recent works on the passive have claimed that the *by*-phrase is an adjunct. A few quotes illustrate this claim. Consider first the following quote by Legate (2014:2):

(1) "The 'by'-phrase in the passive is an adjunct in which 'by' assigns an initiator T-role to its DP complement, and this initiator is tied semantically to the initiator T-role introduced by Voice."

Although most of Legate's book is about Achenese, it is clear that she maintains an adjunct analysis for English *by*-phrases as well (see pg. 82).

Bruening (2013:24) maintains a similar position (see also Hallman 2015:396 for an adjunct analysis of *by*-phrases similar to that of Bruening):

(2) "As detailed earlier, *by* phrases, instrumentals, and comitatives all require the category Voice. I take this to mean that, although they are adjuncts, they strictly select the syntactic category of the phrase they adjoin to."

These conclusions are familiar from the Principles and Parameters literature that also largely analyzes the *by*-phrase in the passive as an adjunct (see for example, Carnie 2013:334). For a historical overview of analyses of the *by*-phrase in generative grammar, see Collins 2018.

The novelty of the positions in (1) and (2) is that they are tied to an explicit treatment of the semantics of *by* (see Bruening 2013:25 and Legate 2014:41 for a related proposal):

(3) a. $[\![\text{by}]\!] \quad = \quad \lambda x \lambda f_{<e,st>} \lambda e.f(e,x)$
    b. $[\![\text{by the lobbyist}]\!] \quad = \quad \lambda f_{<e,st>} \lambda e.f(e,\text{the lobbyist})$

In (3b), the phrase *by the lobbyist* denotes a function that takes the denotation of a Voice phrase as an argument (so *by the lobbyist* denotes a function of a function).

This chapter will argue against the assumption made by Bruening and Legate that the *by*-phrase is an adjunct based on evidence from the Binding Theory. The evidence clearly shows that *by*-phrases behave very differently from adjuncts for the Binding Theory.

The rest of the chapter is structured as follows. Section 6.2 lays out the consequences of the Argument Criterion/Theta-Criterion for the analysis of the *by*-phrase. Section 6.3 provides empirical support for the conclusions of section 6.2, by showing that *by*-phrases behave very differently from adjuncts with respect to the Binding Theory. Section 6.4 discusses inanimate *by*-phrases. Section 6.5 presents a preliminary analysis of the Binding Theory data in the framework of Collins 2005a. Section 6.6 discusses the differences between Collins 2005a and the current proposals about the passive. Section 6.7 explains why *by*-phrases are limited to being externally merged in Spec vP. Section 6.8 shows that other diagnostics parallel the Binding Theory with respect to the analysis of *by*-phrases (such as Helke expressions, argument control, adjunct control, and secondary predicates). Section 6.9 presents strikingly convergent data from Greek (from Angelopoulos, Collins, and Terzi 2020), suggesting that the results of sections 6.1–6.8 are the results of principles of UG. Section 6.10 shows that Bruening's (2013) analysis of the *by*-phrase cannot capture the Binding Theory data. Section 6.11 shows how the analysis of *by*-phrases and implicit arguments are closely related. Section 6.12 discusses the issue of the optionality of *by*-phrases, and shows that optionality is not an argument that *by*-phrases are adjuncts. Section 6.13 discusses languages that only have a short passive. Section 6.14 is the conclusion.

6.2 Theta-Criterion

In this section, I will show that Bruening's analysis is inconsistent with the Merge-based theory introduced in chapter 1. The question is which principles of UG rule out such an analysis. I suggest that the relevant principle is the AC/TC. The Theta-Criterion is repeated below:

(4) Theta-Criterion
Each argument α appears in a chain containing a unique visible theta-position P, and each theta-position P is visible in a chain containing a unique argument α.
(Chomsky 1986:97)

In light of the Theta-Criterion, consider Bruening's structures. According to Bruening, the external argument in the active is projected in Spec VoiceP, as follows (based on Bruening 2013:21):

(5)

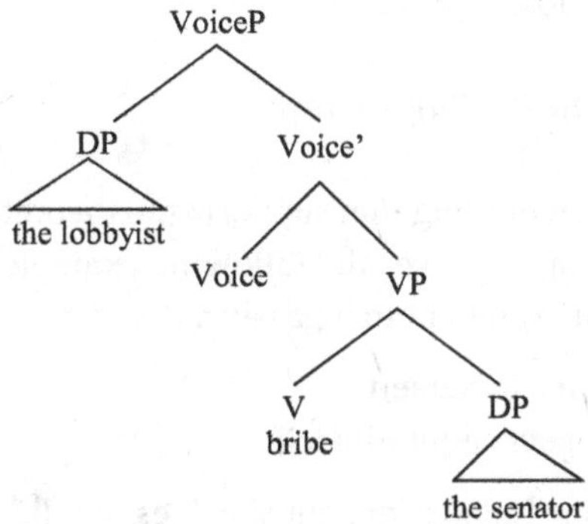

Bruening argues that in the passive, when there is a *by*-phrase, it is adjoined to VoiceP (24):

(6)

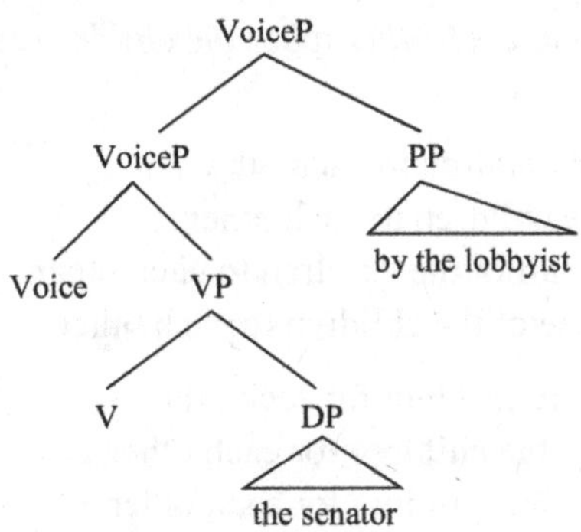

(5) shows that Spec VoiceP is a theta-position in the active, since it is filled by an argument. Therefore, as a theta-position, Spec VoiceP needs to be filled in the passive as well, but as shown in (6), Spec VoiceP is not filled in the passive. Therefore, (6) violates the Theta-Criterion.

Consider now the Argument Criterion. (5) shows that Voice is an argument-introducing head in the active. Therefore, it must introduce an argument in the passive as well. But no argument is introduced in (6). Recall that according to Bruening (2013), the PP *by the lobbyist* is not an argument, but rather a predicate taking a function as an argument. Therefore, (6) violates the Argument Criterion.

Another way to see the inconsistency between the Merge-based theory and the adjunct theory is in terms of the semantic value of *by*. For Bruening, the external argument is satisfied when the *by*-phrase combines with VoiceP and applies the semantic value of VoiceP to *the lobbyist*. But in the Merge-based theory, the only way to build argument structure is by merging arguments together with argument-introducing heads.

6.3 Adjuncts versus *By*-Phrases and the Binding Theory

In this section, I will give evidence from binding that supports the theoretical conclusion in section 6.2. Collins (2005a:111) gives the following examples of a reflexive being bound by the external argument in a passive:

(7) a. The magazines were sent by Mary to herself.
    b. Testimony was given by the suspect about himself.

Legate (2014:71) gives similar data for Indonesian, but she does not discuss its significance.

Building on this data, consider the following contrasts between *by*-phrases and adjuncts with respect to the binding of reciprocals. In the following sentences, the relevant interpretation is where *each other* takes *the children* as an antecedent.

(8) a. The packages were sent by the children to each other.
    b. *The packages were sent for the children to each other.
    c. *The packages were sent on behalf of the children to each other.
    d. *The packages were sent because of the children to each other.

(9) a. The pictures were painted by the children for each other.
    b. *The pictures were painted with the children for each other.
    c. *The pictures were painted near the children for each other.
    d. *The pictures were painted in spite of the children for each other.

Reflexives give rise to a similar paradigm:

(10) a. The packages were sent by the children to themselves.
     b. *The packages were sent for the children to themselves.
     c. *The packages were sent on behalf of the children to themselves.
     d. *The packages were sent because of the children to themselves.

(11) a. The pictures were painted by the children for themselves.
     b. *The pictures were painted with the children for themselves.
     c. *The pictures were painted near the children for themselves.
     d. *The pictures were painted in spite of the children for themselves.

From this data we can make the following generalizations:

(12) a. The DP of the *by*-phrase in a passive can bind a following clause-mate anaphor.
b. The DP of an adjunct PP in a passive cannot bind a following clause-mate anaphor.

The generalization in (12a) already appears in Collins 2005a:111. The generalization in (12) may be part of a larger generalization formulated by Postal (2010:274) that "If A is a reflexive arc, then A has a Term neighbor that arc-antecedes A." This can be translated roughly into lingua franca as follows (thanks to Paul Postal for the translation): "If X is a reflexive form, then there is an antecedent Y which is a clause-mate of X and which is either a subject, direct object, or indirect object." For the purposes of this exposition, we will focus on the generalization in (12).

The data in (8–11) clearly distinguish adjuncts (from which binding is never allowed) and passive *by*-phrases (from which binding of anaphors is allowed). Such a distinction argues against the claims in section 6.1 that *by*-phrases are adjuncts, because if *by*-phrases were adjuncts, they should behave like adjuncts with respect to the binding data.

The following data are controls, showing that the problem with the examples above is the binding of a reflexive or a reciprocal. A pronominal possessor does not give rise to the same contrasts.

(13) a. The packages were sent by the children to their mothers.
b. The packages were sent for the children to their mothers.
c. The packages were sent on behalf of the children to their mothers.
d. The packages were sent because of the children to their mothers.

(14) a. The pictures were painted by the children for their mothers.
b. The pictures were painted with the children for their mothers.
c. The pictures were painted near the children for their mothers.
d. The pictures were painted in spite of the children for their mothers.

6.4 Inanimate *By*-Phrases

Angelopoulos, Collins, and Terzi (2020) show that the above paradigm extends to inanimate *by*-phrases. All the data in this section are from their paper.

(15) a. The magnet$_1$ attracted the metallic objects towards itself$_1$.
b. The metallic objects were attracted by the magnet$_1$ towards itself$_1$.

(16) a. The black hole$_1$ drew the planets into itself$_1$.
b. The planets were drawn by the black hole$_1$ into itself$_1$.

(17) a. The tornado$_1$ sucked the houses up into itself$_1$.
b. The houses were sucked up by the tornado$_1$ into itself$_1$.

(18) a. The magnet$_1$ repelled the pieces of metal away from itself$_1$.
b. The pieces of metal were repelled by the magnet$_1$ away from itself$_1$.

Such examples are also easy to find on the Internet:

(19) You find yourself rising and being pulled by the sun$_1$ toward itself$_1$.
(https://www.do-meditation.com/power-chakra-guided-meditation.html)

(20) The most direct way to determine it is to examine the far distant behavior of the magnetic field generated by the black hole$_1$ around itself$_1$.
(https://slideheaven.com/black-holes-in-our-universe.html)

(21) which is thus an external demagnetising field applied by the magnet$_1$ to itself$_1$
(https://e-magnetsuk.com/alnico-magnets/characteristics-of-alnico-magnets/)

(22) More recently oxytocin has been found to be released by the brain$_1$ into itself$_1$ during sexual intercourse.
(https://books.google.com/books?isbn=9814488372)

(23) But soon also this will be sucked up by the earth$_1$ into itself$_1$.
(https://gottfriedbennpoems.com/the-poems/)

(24) The investment made by the country$_1$ into itself$_1$ has paid back hundreds of times over, and will keep paying back.
(https://www.entrepreneur.com/article/298127)

(25) The objects presenting themselves, in so far as they are sources of pleasure, are absorbed by the ego$_1$ into itself$_1$.
(https://books.google.com/books?isbn=1416573593)

(26) For that which is decidedly thick and earthy in nature, and has entirely escaped alteration in the liver, is drawn by the spleen$_1$ into itself$_1$.
(https://faculty.humanities.uci.edu/bjbecker/PlaguesandPeople/week2j.html)

(27) These are income benefits or resources earned or generated by the organization$_1$ from itself$_1$.
(https://iproject.com.ng/accounting/accounting-as-an-inevitable-tool . . . /index.html)

As pointed out by Angelopoulos, Collins, and Terzi (2020:11), the data involving inanimate *by*-phrases provide an argument that the reflexives that are bound by *by*-phrases are not logophoric pronouns: "Inanimates cannot act as antecedents for logophors because they cannot hold perspective since they cannot be in a mental state (cf. Charnavel and Sportiche 2016)."

6.5 Accounting for the Data with Collins 2005a

How can such data (in sections 6.3 and 6.4) be explained in terms of the Binding Theory? Consider the following standard formulation of Principle A of the Binding Theory (Sportiche, Koopman, and Stabler 2014:168):

(28) Principle A: An anaphor must be bound in its domain.

Now consider example (9c), with the structure sketched in (29):

(29) *The pictures were painted [$_{PP}$ near [$_{DP}$ the children]$_1$] for [each other]$_1$.

Clearly, the DP *the children* does not c-command the reciprocal (since it is dominated by the PP *near the children*). Therefore, the reciprocal does not satisfy Principle A.

What about the (a) sentences of (8–11)? In the theory of Collins 2005a, *by the children* is not even a constituent (see Angelopoulos 2019a for a similar analysis). The underlying structure of (8a) is as follows (irrelevant details are omitted):

(30)

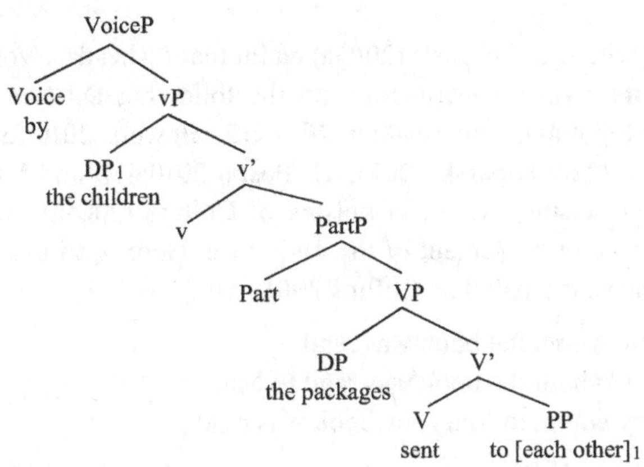

To derive the structure for (8a), the DP *the packages* must move to the subject position, Spec TP, and the participial PartP must move to Spec VoiceP. But it is clear from this structure that the DP *the children* c-commands (and binds) the reciprocal *each other*. Hence, given the structure in (30), there is no violation of Principle A.

This account predicts that if the reflexives in the (b–d) sentences in (8–11) are replaced by pronouns, they should be acceptable:

(31) a. *The packages were sent by the children to them. (predicted *)
b. ?The packages were sent for the children to them. (predicted OK)
c. ?The packages were sent on behalf of the children to them. (predicted OK)
d. ?The packages were sent because of the children to them. (predicted OK)

(32) a. *The pictures were painted by the children for them. (predicted *)
b. ?The pictures were painted with the children for them. (predicted OK)
c. ?The pictures were painted near the children for them. (predicted OK)
d. ?The pictures were painted in spite of the children for them. (predicted OK)

Even though (31a) and (32a) are completely unacceptable, the other sentences in (31) and (32) are much better.

6.6 An Alternative to Collins 2005a

Legate (2014:79–81) criticizes Collins's (2005a) claim that *by* heads a VoiceP, and therefore does not form a constituent with the following DP (see also Alexiadou, Anagnostopoulou, and Schäfer 2018:412; Bowers 2010:52–53; Fábregas and Putnam 2020; Kiparsky 2013, 11; Postal 2010:417; and Müller 2019:96 for related criticisms). These criticisms of Collins (2005a) mostly revolve around the issue of movement of the *by*-phrase. Here is an example that illustrates the issues, modelled on Collins 2005a:110:

(33) a. the person by whom the book was read
b. ?the person by whom the book was read to Mary
c. *the person by whom to Mary the book was read

While (33b) is awkward, (33c) is completely unacceptable. But if VoiceP can move to Spec CP in (33b), VoiceP should be able to pied-pipe [to Mary] in (33c), since the dative PP is internal to VoiceP. Collins tries to address this in terms of economy conditions on pied-piping (see Collins 2005a:examples (70) and (71)). But the paradigm at least raises the possibility that *by whom* is not a VoiceP in (33b), and that is the reason why (33c) is not possible.

I will not review other criticisms of Collins 2005a, but will instead consider how much of the approach in Collins 2005a can be maintained if one assumes that there is a *by*-phrase constituent [by DP]. Therefore suppose, contra Collins 2005a, that *by the children* is a constituent, but it is generated in Spec vP in the passive, as in the following partial diagram of (8a). I label the *by*-phrase as KP instead of PP for reasons that will become clear below.

(34)

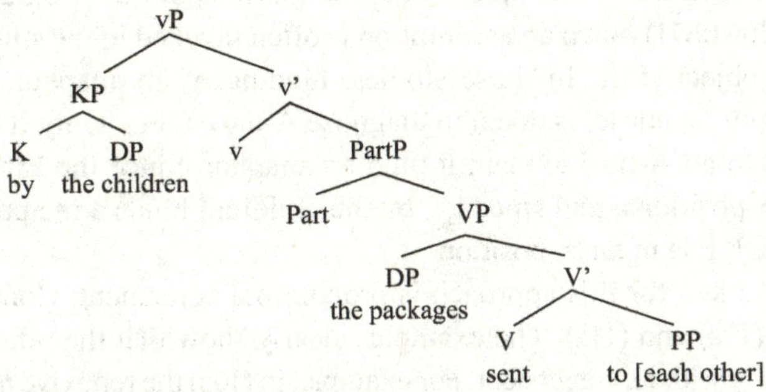

In other words, in (34) the *by*-phrase is an argument (since it occupies Spec vP, an A-position) as opposed to an adjunct. See Watanabe 1993:337, Mahajan 1994:297, Goodall 1997, Borer 1998, Bowers 2010:41, and Hallman 2021:159 for related approaches involving an argument *by*-phrase. See Roberts 2019:433 and Fábregas and Putnam 2020 for KP analyses of the *by*-phrase.

I take it that case markers (heads of KP) are by definition semantically vacuous. If we assume that the *by* is semantically vacuous (denoting an identity function), then the denotation of the KP *by the children* would be identical to that of DP *the children*:

(35) a. ⟦by the children⟧ = ⟦the children⟧
b. ⟦by⟧ = $\lambda x_e.x$

In their discussion of IsiXhosa causatives, Myler and Mali (2021:32) make a similar assumption about the instrumental causee: "We also assume that the apparently instrumental preposition in causative constructions is semantically null, so that the denotation of the PP containing the causee is the same as that of the cause itself." See chapter 10 for a critical discussion of other proposals of Myler and Mali (2021).

Clearly, the DP *the children* does not c-command the reciprocal in (34). And so, in this structure, (8a) should be as bad as (8b–e). But in my analysis, *by* heads a KP (along with the dative *to* and the nominal *of*), which is part of the extended projection of the DP. As such, the *by*-phrase itself can bind the reciprocal (just like any other case-marked DP can bind a reciprocal in the right structural configuration).

(36) The packages were sent [$_{KP}$ by the children]$_1$ to [each other]$_1$.

In this structure, the KP *by the children* is coindexed with the reciprocal *each other.*

I am assuming that the Binding Theory relates A-positions. For example, Chomsky (1981:184) states: "The theory of binding is a theory of A-binding." (See also Barss 2001:671). Such an assumption is often invoked in the study of scrambling and object shift. In those studies, binding of an anaphor (e.g., short scrambling in Japanese) is taken to diagnose A-movement. Only if a DP has been moved to an A-position can it bind an anaphor. Since the Binding Theory relates A-positions, and since [$_{KP}$ by the children] binds a reciprocal, it follows that the KP is in an A-position.

A potential problem for this approach is pronominal agreement. Consider the examples in (10a) and (11a). The examples clearly show that the reflexive agrees syntactically with its antecedent. For example, in (10a) the reflexive *themselves* agrees in phi-features with its antecedent DP *the children.* But if the *by*-phrase were a PP, it would presumably have no phi-features, and so it could not agree with a reflexive that takes it as an antecedent.

In my analysis, *by* heads a KP that is part of the extended projection of a DP. Since it is in the extended projection of the DP, it should have the same phi-features as the DP itself. See Angelopoulos, Collins, and Terzi 2020 for a different solution based on the principles of pronominal agreement in Collins and Postal 2012.

A similar analysis would not rescue examples like the ungrammatical ones in (8–11). PPs headed by prepositions such as *for*, *on behalf of*, *because of*, *via*, *with*, *near*, and *among* would not qualify as KPs, and so PPs headed by them could not function as antecedents. First, none of these PPs are in A-positions, and so they could not bind an anaphor. Second, none of these PPs would have phi-features, which could agree with the pronoun they bind. Third, none of these PPs would have type <e> (the type of individuals), and so presumably would not be the correct type to bind a pronoun.

Therefore, the KP analysis of *by*-phrases neatly explains the asymmetry between *by*-phrases and adjunct PPs illustrated in (8–11) above.

In the analysis sketched in (34), the correct word order would be derived by movement of PartP to Spec VoiceP (see chapter 7). Unlike in Bruening 2013 and Legate 2014, VoiceP does not play a role in projecting the external argument. Rather, VoiceP is a projection that appears with passives to account for word order and the licensing of the participial morphology. See chapter 8 for a comparison of the two different conceptions of VoiceP.

6.7 Responding to Collins 2005a

Perhaps the most compelling reason that Collins (2005a:93) gives for making *by* the head of VoiceP has to do with the distribution of *by*-phrases. Collins puts it as follows:

(37) "Furthermore, the account I presented (see (22)) leaves unexplained the distribution of the *by*-phrase in English. Why is the *by*-phrase restricted to the external argument? Why can't *by*-phrases occur in other syntactic positions? . . . In fact, the problem is more general. What would block *by*-phrases from occurring in all kinds of positions? For example, why couldn't a *by*-phrase appear in nominals such as *the leg of (*by) the table* or *student of (*by) physics*, and in the complement position of an adjective *proud of (*by) his son*, and in certain subject positions *for (*by) John to be happy*? . . . Facts such as these make it clear that on the analysis of the passive proposed in the preceding sections we need to impose a requirement on the *by*-phrase that it appear in Spec,vP: $[_{vP}$ $[_{PP}$ by DP] v']. The question is how such a requirement could be imposed."

The solution Collins (2005a) gives for this distributional problem is to assume that *by* is the head of VoiceP, which has a vP complement. For example, the reason that *the leg by the table* is unacceptable is that there is no vP internal to the DP that VoiceP can take as a complement.

In the KP analysis, there must be some constraint that forces the *by*-phrase to appear in Spec vP, instead of any other position. The generalization is the following:

(38) $[_{KP}$ by DP] appears in Spec vP (and no other position).

I propose that *by* has a c-selectional feature that constrains it to appear in Spec vP. In particular, I propose the following:

(39) *by* has c-selectional feature [__vP].

The technical framework assumed in this account is that of Collins and Stabler 2016:62: "We call the features involved in triggering Merge 'trigger features'. We assume that such features are to be identified with subcategorization features, EPP features and OP features for movement to Spec C. . . ."

Like all trigger features, the feature in (39) is checked under sisterhood (see Collins and Stabler 2016). When *by* is merged with a DP, the resulting syntactic object will have the trigger feature [__vP]. Therefore, it will need to merge with a vP.

The above account also makes sense in terms of the labeling system of Chomsky (2013). Consider the following structure, where Voice c-selects vP as part of its lexical entry.

(40) [$_{VoiceP}$ Voice [$_{vP}$ [by DP] [$_{v'}$ v PartP]]]

In this structure the *by*-phrase stays in situ, since it does not move to Spec TP (unlike the subject in an active). Therefore, vP has two daughter nodes, both of which are complex. This situation raises issues with regard to labeling. Consider the following quote from Chomsky 2013:43:

(41) "The interesting case is SO = {XP, YP}, neither a head . . . Here minimal search is ambiguous, locating the heads X, Y of XP,YP, respectively. There are then two ways in which SO can be labeled: (A) modify SO so there is only one visible head, or (B) X and Y are identical in a relevant respect, providing the same label, which can be taken as the label of SO."

In the structure in (40), neither the *by*-phrase nor the v' phrase undergo movement, so clause (A) is inapplicable. Rather, I propose that clause (B) is applicable. The *by*-phrase and the v'-phrase both share a v-feature, so the [$_{vP}$ [by DP] [$_{v'}$ v PartP]] has a label vP, and this label can be c-selected by VoiceP.

6.8 Other Diagnostics

In this chapter, I have shown that a *by*-phrase can bind a reflexive or a reciprocal. From this I have concluded that the *by*-phrase is in an A-position. In this section, I will show very briefly that *by*-phrases enter into all the other syntactic relations that I have been discussing in this monograph. To the extent that these other syntactic relations require an antecedent in an A-position, they provide additional support for my analysis of *by*-phrases (and against a Bruening-style analysis in which *by*-phrases are adjuncts with a semantically complex preposition):

(42) Helke Expressions
That book was written [by John]$_1$ on his$_1$ own.

(43) *by x-self*
That book was written [by John]$_1$ all by himself$_1$.

(44) Argument Control (control into an argument infinitival clause)
It was decided [by all present]$_1$ [PRO$_1$ to forgo desert].

(45) Adjunct Control
The book was written [by John]$_1$ [PRO$_1$ to impress his wife].

(46) Adjunct Control
That book was written [by John]$_1$ while PRO$_1$ working at a bakery.

Consider argument control in (44). In the theory of this monograph, PRO is controlled by the *by*-phrase (which is externally merged in Spec vP). Presumably, for Bruening (2013) the *by*-phrase (which is a function of functions) would not be a suitable controller. The only remaining possibility would seem to be formulating a semantic theory of control (not needing any syntactically projected antecedent). Similar problems arise for all the cases illustrated in (42–46) above.

Because chapter 3 of the monograph was devoted to secondary predicates, I will spend a little more time discussing *by*-phrases and secondary predicates here. Consider the following examples, which show that secondary predicates can modify the *by*-phrase of a passive.

(47) a. Breakfast is usually eaten [by the campers]$_1$ [PRO$_1$ nude].
b. The book was written [by John]$_1$ [PRO$_1$ drunk].

As noted above, I am arguing that the *by*-phrase is an argumental KP that controls PRO. Hence, in my account, the *by*-phrase is not an adjunct. So, it is useful to compare the distribution of secondary predicates with real adjuncts. Consider the paradigm in (48):

(48) a. The pictures were painted by John drunk.
b. The pictures were painted drunk by John.
c. The pictures were painted near John drunk.
d. The pictures were painted drunk near John.

There is a striking asymmetry between (48a,b) and (48c,d). In (48a,b) John is drunk when he paints the pictures. In (48c,d) *drunk* does not modify *John* at all. Rather, it modifies the implicit argument of the passive. The same contrast is found with adjunct PPs headed by *for*, *on behalf of*, *because of*, and *in spite of*.

How can we explain this data? Consider the structure of (48c):

(49) The pictures were painted [near John$_1$]$_2$ [PRO$_{*1/*2}$ drunk].

The depictive secondary predicate contains PRO. But PRO cannot be controlled by *John* because *John* does not c-command it (because *John* is internal to the *near*-PP). The *near*-PP itself cannot control PRO, because it is of the wrong type (*near John* is presumably a predicative PP of type <e,t>). Furthermore, the *near*-PP is not in an A-position.

So, these examples show a clear distinction between *by*-phrases that can control the PRO of a secondary predicate, and adjuncts where control is not possible. They are completely parallel to the examples in (8–11), which showed that *by*-phrases could bind reflexives, but with true adjunct PPs no reflexive binding is allowed. Similar minimal pairs, showing a clear contrast between *by*-phrases and adjuncts, can be given for all of the diagnostics in (42–46).

6.9 Greek *by*-Phrases

The data concerning *by*-phrases and binding in English can be replicated in Greek, adding strong cross-linguistic support to the conclusions of this chapter. All the data and generalizations in this section come from Angelopoulos, Collins, and Terzi 2020.

The *by*-phrase in a Greek passive has a wide range of possible interpretations, just like in the English passive (see Jaeggli 1986:599 and Collins 2005a:20). In the data below, the *by*-phrase is interpreted as an agent, experiencer, recipient, instrument, and also the subject of an idiomatic expression. Angelopoulos et al. (2020) also show that *by*-phrases can be causers (not shown here).

(50) Ta mallia mu stegno-thikan apo tin komotria.
the hair mine dried-NACT.PAST.3P by the hairdresser
'My hair was dried by the hairdresser.'

(51) I Maria aghapi-thike poli apo ton adra tis.
the Maria love-NACT.PAST.3S a lot by the husband her
'Maria was loved a lot by her husband.'

(52) I tenia pu misi-thike apo ton spudheo skinotheti.
the movie that hate-NACT.PAST.3S by the important director
'The movie that was hated by the important director.'

(53) to ghrama paralif-thike apo ton Emona.
the letter receive-NACT.PAST.3S by the Emona
'The letter was received by Emona.'

(54) I epifania tha kopi ce tha
the surface will cut.NACT.PAST.3S and will
charah-ti apo to laser.
engrave-NACT.PAST.3S by the laser
'The surface will be cut and engraved by the laser.'

(55) Tha enimero-thike apo kapjo pulaci.
must inform-NACT.PAST.3S by some little.bird
'He must have been filled in/informed by some little bird.'

This kind of data indicate that the preposition *by* does not assign its own theta-role. Rather, the interpretation of the external argument in the passive mirrors the interpretation in the active. And just like Chomsky's argument based on selectional restrictions (see chapter 1), such data would be accounted for if external arguments were projected in the passive in exactly the same way as in the active (having the same range of interpretations, depending on the particular verb).

Recall that in English a *by*-phrase can bind a reflexive, which indicates that *by*-phrases are arguments (assuming that the Binding Theory relates DPs in A-positions). In exactly the same way, Greek *by*-phrases can bind a reflexive pronoun:

(56) ena technito skafos pu kataskevas-tike apo tus theus$_1$
an artificial craft that make-NACT.PAST.3S by the Gods
ja tus eaftus tus$_1$.
for the self.ACC.P their.GEN
'an artificial aircraft that was made by the Gods for themselves'

(57) To minima apostel-ete apoklistika apo kathe Learner$_1$
the message send-NACT.PAST.3S exclusively by every Learner
ston eafto tu$_1$.
to.the self.ACC.S his.GEN
'The message is sent by every learner exclusively to himself.'

There is also an argument/adjunct asymmetry in Greek that is very similar to what is found in English. While a *by*-phrase can bind a reflexive, other adjunct PPs fail to do so.

(58) a. Aftes i bluzes epilech-tikan apo ta phedhja$_1$
these the t-shirts select-NACT.PAST.3P by the kids
ja ton eafto tus$_1$.
for the self.ACC.S their.GEN
'These t-shirts were selected by the kids for themselves.'

b. *Aftes i bluzes epilech-tikan brosta/koda s-ta phedhja$_1$
these the t-shirts select-NACT.PAST.3P in front/near at-the kids
ja ton eafto tus$_1$.
for the self.ACC.S their.GEN
'These t-shirts were selected in front/near the kids for themselves.'

c. Aftes i bluzes epilech-tikan brosta/koda s-ta phedhja
these the t-shirts select-NACT.PAST.3P in front/near at-the kids
ja afta ce tis ikojenies tus.
for them and the families their.GEN
'These t-shirts were selected in front of/near the kids for them and their families.'

Why are the Greek data important? First, they show that the relatively subtle effect of binding by *by*-phrases (and the contrast with adjuncts) can be completely replicated in a different language. This gives us confidence that the principles that determine the effect in the first place are principles of UG.

Second, as Angelopoulos, Collins, and Terzi (2020:8) show, Greek differs from English in not having exempt anaphora: "There is a relevant property of *o eaftos mu*, however, which makes it different from the English reflexive, but has received little attention, and this is that it has no usages that do not fall under standard Condition A." But this property of reflexive pronouns in Greek eliminates the possibility of analyzing the Greek data in (56–58) in terms of exempt anaphora. Angelopoulos et al. (2020:8) put the conclusion as follows: "Given that *o eaftos mu* resists logophoric usages . . . it makes sense to assume that in the examples to be discussed in the following section we have clear cases of non-logophoric reflexives that are standardly analyzed as being subject to Condition A."

Third, these facts and the analysis of *by*-phrases they support bear directly on the analysis of nonactive voice in Greek, as discussed in more detail in chapter 8. The data in this section clearly show that nonactive voice is consistent with the syntactic presence of the external argument (in Spec vP). For example, "select" is in the nonactive voice in (58a), but it still has an external argument: [apo ta phedhja]. One popular analysis of nonactive voice (Embick 1998) reduces the presence of nonactive voice to the absence of an external argument. But the data presented in this section show such an analysis does not work.

6.10 Bruening 2013

Now let's reconsider a theory like that of Bruening's (2013) (similar remarks hold for Legate 2014) with respect to the data in (5–8). In Bruening's theory the *by*-phrase is an adjunct, and the preposition *by* has a complex denotation (denoting a function of functions). Like other adjuncts, the DP inside the PP adjunct should be incapable of binding an anaphor.

Furthermore, in Bruening's theory it would not be possible for the *by*-phrase itself to act as an antecedent. First, the *by*-phrase is not in an A-position (it is an adjunct), and the Binding Theory is limited to relations between A-positions. Second, the *by*-phrase does not satisfy equation (35b) in Bruening's theory (rather, it denotes a function of functions). And so, it would make no sense to say that the *by*-phrase itself is the antecedent of a pronoun. Third, the *by*-phrase itself has no phi-features, and so could not bind a pronoun (which agrees in phi-features with its antecedent).

In Bruening's theory, the passive and active are semantically equivalent: "Actives and passives with *by* phrases are truth-conditionally equivalent" (2013:25) Therefore, it might be possible to save Bruening's theory by stating the Binding Theory as a semantic condition of some kind. In other words, it may be possible to save Bruening's theory by giving up the assumption that the Binding Theory is syntactic in nature, a conclusion that I would take as a reductio ad absurdum. Furthermore, given the data in section 6.8, such a semantic approach would necessitate giving a semantic treatment to obligatory control, adjunct control, secondary predicates, and binding of pronouns in Helke expressions. More generally, all of syntactic theory dealing with locally bound reflexives, pronouns and PRO would have to be restated in purely semantic terms.

6.11 Consequences for Implicit Arguments

I have argued above that the *by*-phrase in the passive is not an adjunct (contra Bruening 2013 and Legate 2014). Rather, the *by*-phrase is a KP externally merged into Spec vP in the passive, as outlined in section 6.6. Then the passive and the active are parallel, and both involve an argument in Spec vP. The conclusion is that Spec vP is always filled. The immediate consequence of this proposal is that even in the short passive (where there is no *by*-phrase), Spec vP must be filled.

Consider the following example:

(59) The book was read (by John).

And consider the following argument:

(60) a. When $[_{KP}$ by John] is present, it is in Spec vP.
b. Therefore, Spec vP is a theta-position.
c. The long and short passive have the same v. That is, there are not two different kinds of v, one for long passives and one for short passives.
d. Therefore, in the short passive, Spec vP is also a theta-position.
e. Therefore, in the short passive, Spec vP must be filled.

The only potentially controversial statement is (60c). But it seems like the null hypothesis, unless someone finds evidence from some language that the two kinds of little v (for short and long passives) are morphologically, syntactically, or semantically distinguished.

In other words, our conclusions about the syntax of *by*-phrases in the passive entail that there is a syntactically realized implicit argument in the short passive. Not surprisingly, both Bruening (2013:22) and Legate (2014:41) reject this conclusion.

Therefore, the conclusions reached in this chapter about the syntax of *by*-phrases dovetail nicely with the conclusions reached in chapters 2–5 about the syntactic presence of implicit arguments.

6.12 Optionality

It is commonly claimed that the optionality of the *by*-phrase shows that it is an adjunct or shows that it is not an argument. Consider the following quotes from Grimshaw 1990:145–146:

(61) a. "But regardless of whether *by* phrases are arguments of verbs or of *-en*, a major problem for this view is that the *by* phrase or its counterpart is optional in every language." (pg. 145)
b. "The fact that passive *by* phrases are optional as far as a-structure is concerned cannot be explained under any account in which *by* phrases are arguments." (pg. 146)

In my framework, *by*-phrases are indeed optional, but external arguments are not. Consider again the following paradigm:

(62) a. John wrote the book.
b. The book was written by John.
c. The book was written.

In the passive sentences in (62b,c), the *by*-phrase is optional, but it is also the case that *by*-phrases are arguments (contra Grimshaw 1990). In my framework, the external argument is always required in (62), but it is externally merged in two different ways: either as a *by*-phrase or as an implicit argument pro. So, there is absolutely no contradiction between the optionality of *by*-phrases and their status as arguments, contra Grimshaw 1990.

6.13 Cross-Linguistic Variation

Keenan and Dryer (2010:330) propose the following generalization:

(63) If a language has passives with agent phrases, then it has them without agent phrases.

For Keenan and Dryer, an agent phrase is characterized as follows:

(64) "'agent phrases', such as *by Mary* in *John was slapped by Mary*, most commonly take the position and case marking (including choice of

pre- and postpositions) of some oblique nps in active sentences, most usually an instrumental, locative, or genitive." (pg. 327)

(65) "To say that *by Mary* is the agent phrase of *John was kissed by Mary* is to say that *Mary* functions as the semantic subject but not the syntactic subject of the transitive verb *kiss*, from which the passive vp is derived. In general, an agent phrase is an np (with or without adpositions) which functions as the semantic but not syntactic subject of a verb in an expression derived from that verb (or verb phrase). Note that the term 'agent phrase' is potentially misleading in that its semantic role (agent, experiencer, etc.) is whatever is required by the verb of which it is the understood subject, and need not be specifically agent, as in the example *Money is needed by the church*." (pg. 342)

To illustrate, English has an optional *by*-phrase in the passive, so it conforms to (63). Ewe does not have a passive (with or without an agent-phrase), so it conforms to (63). ǂHoã has a passive (see Collins and Gruber 2014), but the passive does not admit an oblique phrase expressing the agent. So ǂHoã conforms to (63). If a language had a passive that admitted an agent-phrase, but the agent-phrase was obligatory, then it would be a counterexample.

As it turns out, this generalization follows from the theory of passives and implicit arguments outlined in this monograph. The existence of pro as an implicit argument is guaranteed as part of UG. In any language, we expect to see implicit arguments of the kind discussed in chapter 4.

But the existence of an agent-phrase requires two additional assumptions:

(66) a. There needs to be a semantically vacuous preposition (or Case marker).
b. The oblique needs to be able to be externally merged in Spec vP.

For example, in English there is a semantically vacuous preposition *by* that can form a *by*-phrase [by John], and this *by*-phrase can be externally merged into Spec vP. The dative preposition *to* is another semantically vacuous Case marker, but [to John] cannot be externally merged into Spec vP, because [to John] c-selects an ApplP (see chapter 9).

If a language simply lacked semantically vacuous prepositions (or Case markers), or if the semantically vacuous preposition (or Case marker) existed, but had a restricted distribution, then it would result in a passive with no agent phrase. In that language, only short passives would exist.

However, it would be interesting to look into languages that do not have a long passive (that is, languages lacking agent phrases) from the point of view of this monograph. Is it possible to find diagnostics for a syntactically projected implicit external argument in those languages? The clear prediction is that all implicit arguments should be syntactically projected, even in languages that do not possess *by*-phrases.

In fact, Sulemana (2022) claims that Buli is such a language. Buli has a passive that does not allow a *by*-phrase. However, as he shows, there is clear evidence that the implicit argument is syntactically projected (see chapter 5 for discussion).

6.14 Conclusion

In this chapter I have shown that *by*-phrases in passives do not behave like adjuncts with respect to the Binding Theory in either English or Greek (following Angelopoulos et. al. 2020). This difference follows without any further stipulations from the theory of *by*-phrases as arguments, but it remains a complete mystery in such theories as Bruening's (2013) and Legate's (2014).

I have proposed a modification to the theory in Collins 2005a, where the preposition *by* is not the head of VoiceP, but rather heads an argument KP. I have shown that the proposed modification also accounts for the difference between *by*-phrases and adjuncts with respect to the Binding Theory.

The two theories can be summarized as follows:

(67) Bruening (2013) (see also Legate 2014)
  a. Syntactic status of *by*-phrase: adjunct PP
  b. Semantic value of *by*: $[\![\text{by}]\!] = \lambda x \lambda f_{<e,st>} \lambda e.f(e,x)$

(68) This monograph:
  a. Syntactic status of *by*-phrase: argument KP
  b. Semantic value of *by*: $[\![\text{by}]\!] = \lambda x_e.x$

In (67), the complex semantics of the preposition *by* are needed to glue the external argument semantically to the rest of the structure (a VoiceP). In this way, Bruening 2013 and Legate 2014 inherit the problems inherent in the Principles and Parameters view of the passive. As Collins (2005a:83) notes: "The main problem with Jaeggli's analysis is that the external argument in the passive is assigned a theta-role (via theta-role absorption and transmission) in a way that is totally different from how the external argument is assigned a theta-role in the active (in Spec,IP in the principles and parameters framework)." In (68), the semantics of *by* is trivial, because the *by*-phrase is an argument.

More generally, what this section has shown is that there are two different approaches to *by*-phrases in the passive, both of which are compatible with many of the same facts (e.g., range of theta-roles of external arguments, Binding Theory): *by* as head of KP and *by* as head of VoiceP (Collins 2005a). In Collins 2005a (see also Angelopoulos 2019a), I analyze *by* as the head of VoiceP. In this monograph, I am assuming that *by* is the head of KP. But the choice between the two analyses is subtle, and it is unclear what principles of UG would force one analysis over the other. I am hoping that this monograph will stimulate research into this issue, perhaps identifying different groups of languages that make use of each strategy.

I have not discussed *by*-phrases in nominalizations. Simon (2018) provides the following data:

(69) a. the criticism of himself_1 by John_1
b. *the criticism of him_1 by John_1
c. *the criticism of John_1 by him_1

(70) a. the criticism by John_1 of himself_1
b. *the criticism by John_1 of him_1
c. *the criticism by him_1 of John_1

Simon points out that binding in nominalizations obeys Principles A, B, and C of the Binding Theory. On the basis of these data, he gives an analysis of the internal structure of nominalizations very much in the spirit of Collins 2005a.

Recall that in chapter 4, I showed that the implicit argument in nominalizations is syntactically projected. In the Merge-based theory, both the *by*-phrase and the implicit argument in nominalizations are externally merged into Spec vP by the AC/TC.

The next step would be to see if the difference between *by*-phrases and other prepositional phrases discussed above with respect to Principle A of the Binding Theory (see 8–11) could be replicated internal to nominalizations.

7 Derivations

In this chapter, I give the complete derivation of passive sentences, both with and without the *by*-phrase, in order to illustrate the principles discussed in this monograph. Important technical assumptions are discussed, as well as differences from and similarities to Collins 2005a.

Consider the following paradigm from the introduction. We will start with (1b):

(1) a. John wrote the book. (active)
    b. The book was written by John. (passive)
    c. The book was written. (short passive)

I will set aside the issue of whether there are acategorial roots and how they enter into the syntactic derivation, and simply assume that there is a verb *write*. This verb heads a VP, which takes the DP *the book* as a complement. I will also assume that the complement position of the VP headed by *write* is a theta-position (and is therefore obligatorily projected). These simplifying assumptions ignore many issues about the internal structure of the VP (e.g., the position of particles, resultatives, double objects) and the important issue of argument-introducing heads for internal arguments (see section 4.7).

7.1 Passive with *By*-Phrase

Since *write* is in its participial form, I assume that there is a suffix Part that projects a PartP. Unlike in the Principles and Parameters analysis of the passive, I do not assume that the participial suffix *-en* absorbs accusative Case or the external theta-role (see Collins 2005a for discussion). In fact, the arguments are projected in the active in the same way that they are projected in the passive, so there is no room for theta-role absorption.

Furthermore, I assume that Part is merged with VP (not vP). This assumption captures the fact that in a language like French there is sometimes participle agreement with an object, but never with an external argument. Since the external argument is externally merged in Spec vP, and Spec vP is higher than Spec PartP, the external argument does not move through Spec PartP, and there can be no participle agreement with it.

Putting these assumptions together we have:

(2) [$_{\text{PartP}}$ Part [$_{\text{VP}}$ write [$_{\text{DP}}$ the book]]]

Following Collins (2005a:90), I assume that past participles have an uninterpretable feature that can be checked either by moving PartP into Spec VoiceP, or by the c-commanding auxiliary verb *have*.

(3) A participle (PartP) must be licensed by
  a. being c-selected by the auxiliary *have*, or
  b. moving to Spec VoiceP.

Next, the external argument is introduced. I assume that external arguments are introduced in Spec vP. By the Theta-Criterion, Spec vP needs to be filled in the passive (since it is filled in the active, and there is no difference between little v in the passive and the active).

The only two possibilities for filling Spec vP are the DP *John* and the *by*-phrase [by John]. In Collins 2005a, I explored the possibility that the DP *John* itself occupies Spec vP in the passive. In this monograph, I am exploring the possibility that the *by*-phrase occupies Spec vP. See chapter 6 for discussion.

(4)

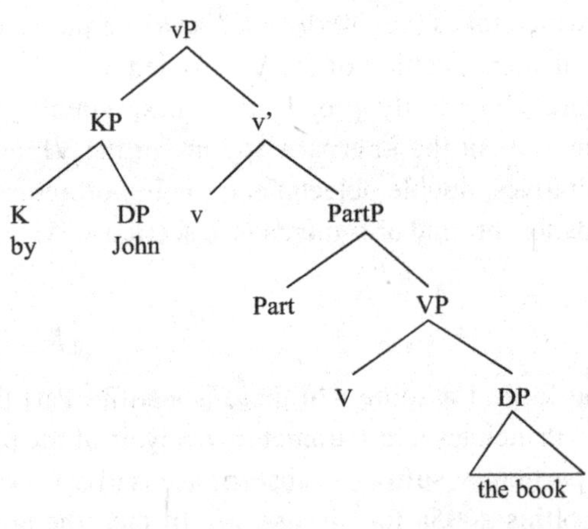

In this structure, I am assuming that the KP is part of the extended projection of the DP *John* (see chapter 6). Since KP is in Spec vP, which is a theta-position, the Theta-Criterion is satisfied.

Recall from chapter 6 that the *by*-phrase has a limited syntactic distribution, appearing only in Spec vP. I proposed there that *by* has a [__vP] c-selectional feature. Such a feature would be checked under sisterhood with v' in (4).

Suppose that the derivation continued from (4) by merging in the copula and T and then raising the KP to Spec TP (with no VoiceP):

(5) a. [$_{TP}$ [$_{KP}$ by John] [$_{T'}$ T [$_{VP}$ was [$_{vP}$ <KP> written the book]]]]
    b. *By John was written the book.

There are a number of problems with the structure in (5a). First, English does not in general have oblique subjects (e.g., dative subjects), so whatever principle blocks oblique subjects in English should also block (5a). Second, since the Case features of *John* are checked in Spec vP (by the KP), it should be frozen in place by the Activity Condition (Chomsky 2000:123), with no possibility of moving to Spec TP. Third, since there is no VoiceP in (5a), the uninterpretable participle feature of PartP will remain unchecked (see (3) above).

Suppose in (5) *was* is replaced by *has* (still with no VoiceP):

(6) a. [$_{TP}$ [$_{KP}$ by John] [$_{T'}$ T [$_{VP}$ has [$_{vP}$ <KP> written the book]]]]
    b. *By John has written the book.

In (6), the participle is now licensed (see (3a)), but the KP in Spec vP still causes problems since it cannot move to Spec TP (because it is frozen in Spec vP by the Activity Condition).

Consider another possible derivation continuing on from the structure in (4). This time, the copula and T are merged (there is still no VoiceP), but the object raises to Spec TP (instead of KP raising):

(7) a. [$_{TP}$ [$_{DP}$ the book] [$_{T'}$ T [$_{VP}$ was [$_{vP}$ [by John] written <[the book]>]]]]
    b. *The book was by John written.

The uninterpretable feature of the participle is unchecked in (7), but replacing *was* by *has* does not result in an improvement, even though according to (3) above *has* should be able to check the uninterpretable participle feature.

(8) a. [$_{TP}$ [$_{DP}$ the book] [$_{T'}$ T [$_{VP}$ has [$_{vP}$ [by John] written <[the book]>]]]]
    b. *The book has by John written.

In (7) and (8), T is separated from the direct object *the book* by a phase boundary. Movement of the direct object to Spec TP violates the PIC (Phase Impenetrability Condition, see Chomsky 2004:108). Suppose that instead of the direct object being moved directly to Spec TP, it was first moved to a second specifier of vP. This movement would avoid violating the PIC. But I am assuming that the second Spec vP position is an A'-position, since it is used in A'-movement out of a vP phase. If Spec vP is an A'-position, such movement would be a case of improper movement (complement of V → second Spec vP → Spec TP). So, there does not appear to be any way to circumvent the PIC in (8).

Another problem with both (7) and (8) is that they involve raising the object DP over the KP in Spec vP. This should result in a violation of Relativized Minimality or the Minimal Link Condition of minimalist syntax.

Consider the classical definition of Relativized Minimality:

(9) Relativized Minimality (Rizzi 1990:7)
X α-governs Y only if there is no Z such that:
(i) Z is a typical potential α-governor for Y.
(ii) Z c-commands Y and does not c-command X.

(10) Z is a typical potential antecedent governor for Y. Y is an A-chain = Z is an A specifier c-commanding Y.

In the example in (7), the KP [by John] is certainly in an A-position (a theta-position), and the object [the book] has undergone A-movement. So, by (9) and (10) the derivations should have been blocked by RM.

Consider now MLC (see Chomsky 1995:311). Suppose that T has unvalued phi-features [uPhi] that need to be valued. When T probes downward in (8a) looking for a matching goal (before movement of [the book]), the search will encounter the KP [by John]. But since the KP is part of the extended projection of *John* (see chapter 6 for more discussion), whatever phi-features are visible at the DP level should also be visible at the KP level (that is why the KP can bind a reflexive pronoun; see chapter 6). But if the probe matches KP, by minimal search, it will be unable to continue probing to find the DP object (a so-called case of defective intervention; see Chomsky 2000:123).

Clearly, the derivations in (5–8) are ruled out, and in all cases it seems that the external argument in Spec vP is causing problems.

Once again continuing from (4), consider the possibility of moving the PartP over the external argument, smuggling the object over the external argument (see Collins 2005a and Belletti and Collins 2020 for works on smuggling). Voice is merged, and PartP moves to Spec VoiceP to check its uninterpretable features (see Collins 2005a on Voice as a strong phase head).

(11) $[_{\text{VoiceP}}$ PartP $[_{\text{Voice'}}$ Voice $[_{\text{vP}}$ KP $[_{\text{v'}}$ v <PartP>]]]]

Lastly, the copula is merged, T is merged, and the object DP raises to Spec TP, yielding the following structure:

(12)

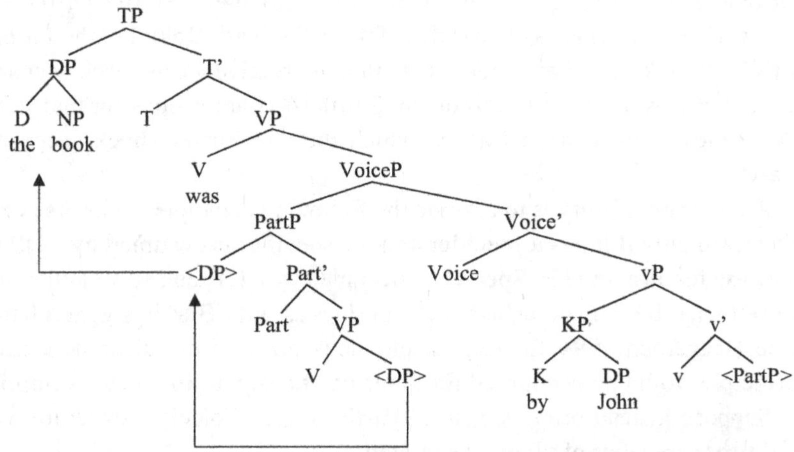

In this structure, T agrees with the object DP in Spec PartP, and then the object DP moves to Spec TP to satisfy the EPP feature of T. The object DP moves through Spec PartP to Spec TP (as can be seen by participle agreement in the passive in languages such as French). On the violation of Freezing in (12), see Bošković 2020. On the range of constructions using smuggling derivations, see Belletti and Collins 2020. On VoiceP as a phase, see Collins 2005a:98.

What about accusative Case? In the Principles and Parameters theory, the passive suffix *-en* absorbed the accusative Case of the verb as well as the external theta-role. I do not make these assumptions about the passive suffix *-en* here (see Collins 2005a for discussion). But that leaves the question of why the object is not assigned accusative Case in (12).

The intuition I will pursue is that movement of the PartP raises the object into a position accessible to T, and so the phi-features of T can agree with DP. In those circumstances, little v does not check the Case feature of any DP.

More precisely, the movement of the PartP in (12) results in five occurrences of the DP *the book* (see Collins and Stabler 2016 the definition of occurrence). The highest occurrence is in Spec TP, but each occurrence of the PartP dominates two occurrences of the DP as well. Consider the occurrence in Spec PartP (itself in Spec VoiceP). This occurrence is c-commanded by the Case-checker T, but not the Case-checker v. Under those conditions, Agree(T, DP) can be formed, and the Case of the DP can be checked (as a reflex of Agree). In this case, the Case-checker v does not check the Case of any DP.

In fact, there are unergative verbs that take an optional cognate object and seem to show that v does not obligatorily check the accusative Case of an object: "John laughed a big laugh/John laughed." Similarly, there are unergative verbs that take so-called fake reflexives: "John laughed himself silly." These kinds of examples show that unergative v can check accusative Case, but it is not required to do so. Similarly, I am proposing that in (12), PartP moves away from little v, which then no longer checks accusative Case.

Another possibility is to assume the following principle: v checks accusative Case only if it has a specifier and the specifier is occupied by a DP with a uCase feature. In (12), Spec vP is occupied by a KP, and so v cannot check Case (since KP has no uCase feature). Just as with Burzio's generalization (see Haegeman 1994 for discussion), it is not entirely clear how such a principle would be accounted for in terms of basic minimalist assumptions.

Suppose instead of movement of PartP to Spec VoiceP, a structure with a rightward specifier of vP was generated:

(13)

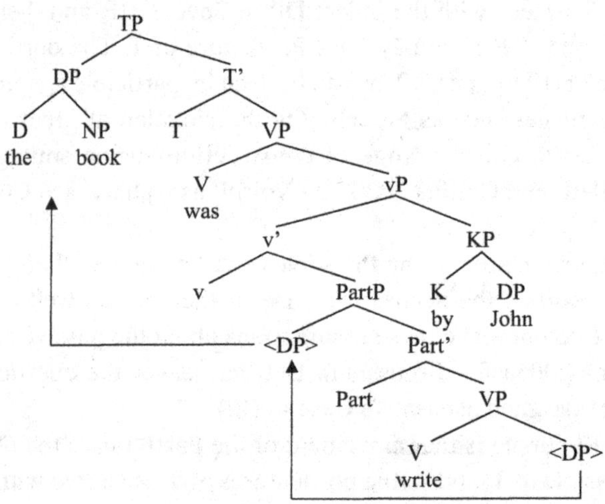

At first sight, this structure is appealing because it yields a rightward position of the *by*-phrase without any smuggling. However, it is not a tenable analysis. The first problem is that clear cases of specifiers (Spec DP, TP, CP) are all leftward in English. So, the rightward specifier of vP would be the odd one out. Second, the rightward specifier in (13) violates Kayne's (1994) Linear Correspondence Axiom (LCA). Third, such an analysis yields incorrect predictions about c-command. It predicts that the *by*-phrase should c-command whatever is found in the preceding VP. But Collins (2005a)

shows in detail that such a prediction does not hold. I repeat some of the core data here:

(14) a. *The book was given to any student by no professor.
 b. *The book was given to the other by each professor.
 c. The book was given by no student to any professor.
 d. The book was given by each professor to the other.

Therefore, for these three reasons, I reject the rightward specifier analysis in (13).

An analysis related to the one in (13) is that the *by*-phrase is right-adjoined to vP (instead of being a rightward specifier). But exactly the same considerations rule out the rightward adjunction analysis. First, it violates the LCA. Second, it yields incorrect predictions about c-command (see also the general remarks about adjunction and Pair-Merge in chapter 1).

Consider lastly a derivation where PartP moves to Spec Voice, but the external argument DP (not KP) merges into Spec vP. The structure is given in (15).

(15)

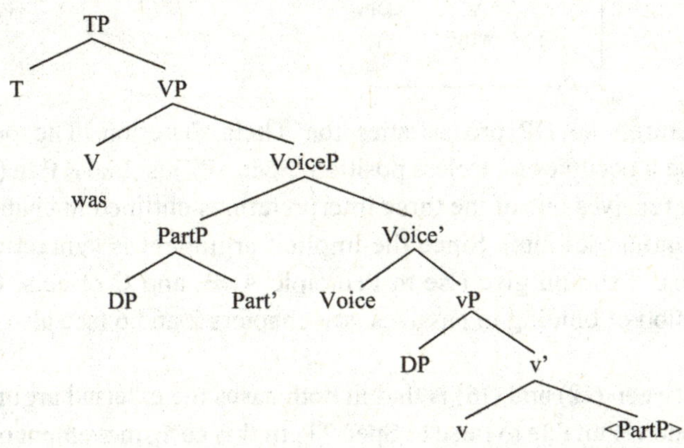

Continuing on from (15), there are two possibilities: either T agrees with and checks the Case of the external argument (EA) or T agrees with and checks the Case of the direct object (DO). Suppose that Agree(T, DO), then the EA will violate the Case Filter (unless it is implicit argument pro). Suppose Agree(T, EA). One possibility is that the Agree relation is blocked by the intervening PartP in Spec VoiceP (an MLC violation). After all, Spec PartP is filled by the object, and that might be enough to block Agree(T, EA).

7.2 Short Passive

Now consider the derivation of the short passive in (1c). Everything about this derivation is identical to (12), except the external argument is now a small pro implicit argument (see chapter 4 for the general theory of implicit arguments):

(16)

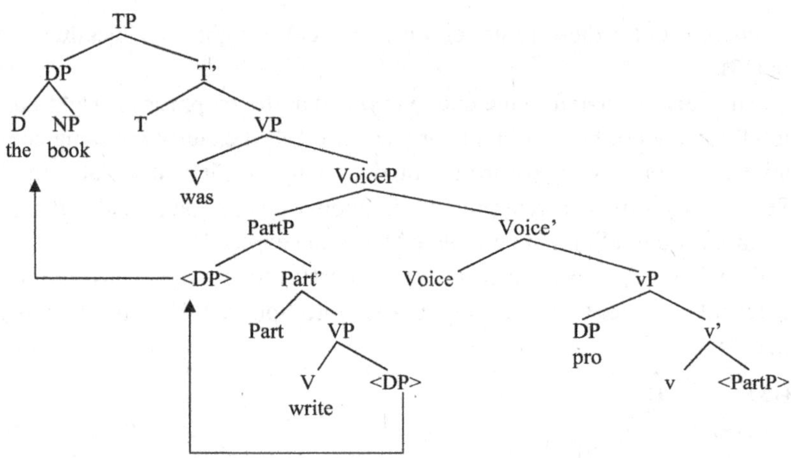

In this structure, the DP pro satisfies the Theta-Criterion. The pro is licensed because it occupies a caseless position, Spec vP (just like KP in (12)). Semantically, it receives one of the three interpretations outlined in chapter 4 (generic, existential, definite). Since the implicit argument is syntactically projected in (16), it should give rise to Principle A, B, and C effects. On a detailed discussion of binding in passives, see chapters 2 and 6 (see also Collins 2005a).

A parallel between (12) and (16) is that in both cases the external argument is trapped in Spec vP, unable to raise to Spec TP. In this case, movement of the PartP to Spec VoiceP smuggles the object over the external argument, rendering it accessible to T.

7.3 Active

Finally, returning to the active, suppose that the DP *John* is merged into Spec vP, but that there is no participle or VoiceP:

(17) [$_{TP}$ John [$_{T'}$ T [$_{vP}$ <John> [$_{v'}$ v [$_{VP}$ write [$_{DP}$ the book]]]]]]

Here, there is no problem. T agrees with the external argument DP, which raises to Spec TP. The Case of the object is checked by v.

Suppose instead that the KP is merged into Spec vP, essentially an active with a *by*-phrase:

(18)

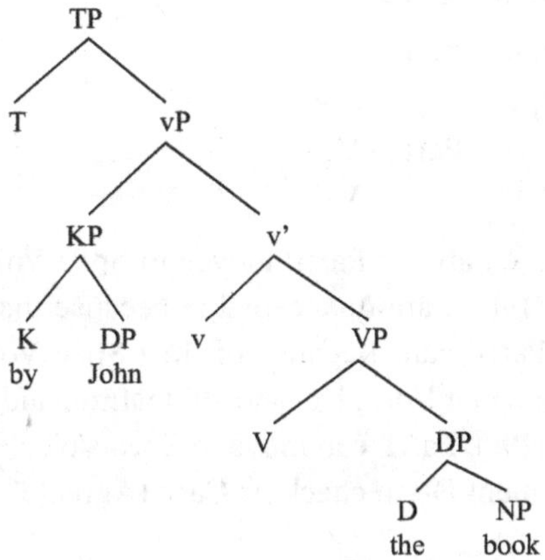

Nothing prevents the *by*-phrase from being merged into Spec vP here. The Theta-Criterion is satisfied, and the syntactic features of *by* are checked. However, there are other problems. First, English does not in general have oblique subjects (e.g., dative subjects), so whatever principle blocks oblique subjects in English should also block (18). Second, since the Case feature of *John* is checked in Spec vP (internal to the KP), it should be frozen in place by the Activity Condition (Chomsky 2000:123), with no possibility of moving to Spec TP, resulting in an unchecked EPP feature for the finite T. Third, the accusative Case of the object is checked by v, and so there is no possibility that the object could raise to Spec TP (the Activity Condition).

7.4 Systematic Presentation of Derivations

In the previous sections, I discussed a few derivations. In this section, I will take a more systematic approach. In the analysis of the passive in this monograph, there is no passive construction. Rather, there are morphemes, each with their own properties, that are merged together but constrained by principles of UG (e.g., the AC/TC), economy principles and interface conditions. Putting aside the issue of implicit arguments for now, there are four choices to make: (a) auxiliary selection: *was*, *has*, or zero; (b) presence or absence of Voice; (c) presence or absence of K; or (d) presence or absence of Part. In total, there are $3 \times 2 \times 2 \times 2 = 24$ combinations. In this section, I will systematically go through all the combinations, and show that only 3 are acceptable (the passive, the active with *has*, and the active without *has*).

I start with sentences that have *was* as the auxiliary and VoiceP. Under these conditions, there are four combinations, depending on the presence or absence of K and the presence or absence of Part:

(19) a. T was Voice [K DP] v Part VP
b. *T was Voice [K DP] v VP
c. *T was Voice DP v Part VP
d. *T was Voice DP v VP

(19a) is just the passive, as discussed above: PartP moves to Spec VoiceP, then the object moves to Spec TP. (19b,d) are unacceptable because the VP cannot raise to Spec VoiceP, only PartP can. Because of this, Spec VoiceP remains unfilled. Concretely, I assume that Voice has an EPP feature, and that feature is not checked in (19b,d). In (19c), PartP can move to Spec VoiceP, but there is no way for the external argument DP to check its Case (Agree(T, EA) being blocked).

In the next set of sentences, *was* is still the auxiliary, but there is no VoiceP:

(20) a. *T was [K DP] v Part VP
b. *T was [K DP] v VP
c. *T was DP v Part VP
d. *T was DP v VP

(20a) and (20c) have a Part but nothing to check it (either *have* or Voice). In (20b), no DP can raise to Spec TP, leaving its EPP feature unchecked. In (20b,d), there is a bare (nonparticiple) verb (v + V) that combines with a copula. Whatever accounts for the contrast between *John will laugh* and **John was laugh* accounts for the unacceptability of (20d). The general constraint is that the bare form of the verb cannot follow the copula, only a participial form can.

In the next set of sentences, the auxiliary is *has* and there is a VoiceP:

(21) a. *T has Voice [K DP] v Part VP
b. *T has Voice [K DP] v VP
c. *T has Voice DP v Part VP
d. *T has Voice DP v VP

All the options in (21) are ruled out because of the combination of *has* and Voice. These can never appear together because they have a similar function (licensing a past participle). PartP moves to Spec VoiceP and is licensed there. It is not possible now for *have* to license the PartP a second time. Concretely, if the Part has an uninterpretable [uPart] feature, once it is deleted by Voice, it cannot be deleted again by *have*.

In the next set of sentences, *has* is still the auxiliary, but there is no VoiceP:

(22)	a.	*T	has	[K DP] v	Part	VP
	b.	*T	has	[K DP] v		VP
	c.	T	has	DP v	Part	VP
	d.	*T	has	DP v		VP

In (22a,b), no DP is available to move to Spec TP, leaving the EPP feature of T unchecked. (22c) is a grammatical sentence, where the external argument (in Spec vP) raises to Spec TP. (22d) is ruled out because *has* requires a participle.

In the next set of sentences, there is no auxiliary, but VoiceP is present:

(23)	a.	*T	Voice	[K DP] v	Part	VP
	b.	*T	Voice	[K DP] v		VP
	c.	*T	Voice	DP v	Part	VP
	d.	*T	Voice	DP v		VP

In (23), VoiceP is the complement of finite T, but VoiceP requires a PartP, and a PartP cannot appear with finite T. In other words, in all cases where VoiceP is present, a copula is also needed. For example, in (23a), PartP moves to Spec VoiceP, but this leaves a sentence where finite T is followed by a participle (and there is no copula). This is bad for whatever reason finite T cannot combine with participles: **John written.*

In the last set of sentences, there is no auxiliary and no VoiceP:

(24)	a.	*T	[K DP] v	Part	VP
	b.	*T	[K DP] v		VP
	c.	*T	DP v	Part	VP
	d.	T	DP v		VP

(24a,c) are ruled out because Part needs to appear with either *have* or Voice. (24b) is ruled out because nothing can raise to Spec TP to check its EPP feature. In particular, the KP cannot move to Spec TP. Nor can the direct object, which is separated from Spec TP by a phase boundary. (24d) is acceptable. It is the active without a participle.

7.5 Conclusion

In this chapter, I have given complete derivations of the passive, the short passive, and the active. Even though I use expressions such as "passive construction," there in fact is no passive construction in minimalist syntax. Rather, there are morphemes that are combined by Merge (internal or external). Some combinations of these morphemes yield acceptable results and some do not. Out of twenty-four possible combinations, only three are acceptable. The combination (19a) involving *was*, Voice, KP, and a participle is called the passive.

(25) a. Passive (19a) ("The book was written by John.")

T	was	Voice	[K DP]	v	Part	VP

b. Active with participle (22c) ("John has written the book.")

T	has		DP	v	Part	VP

c. Active without participle (24d) ("John wrote the book.")

T			DP	v		VP

Such a result provides striking confirmation of the general Merge-based approach to the passive.

8 Two Conceptions of VoiceP

8.1 Introduction

In recent literature on argument structure, the VoiceP projection plays two distinct and incompatible roles. I will call the two theories the *projection theory* and the *realization theory.* In the projection theory, due to Kratzer (1996), VoiceP plays a central role in projecting the external argument of an active clause; see (1). The external argument is externally merged as a specifier of VoiceP.

(1) Projection Theory

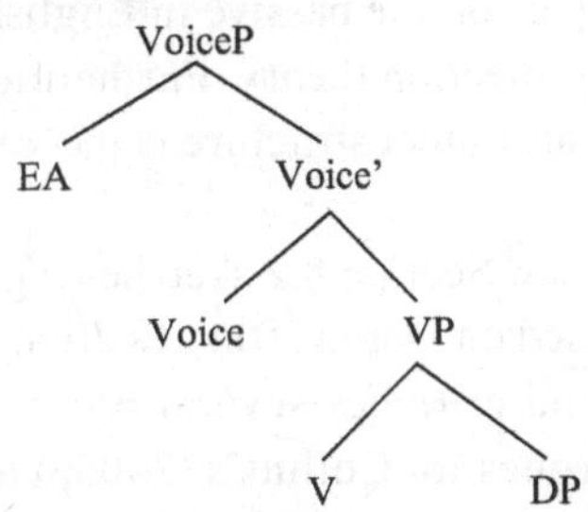

In the realization theory, VoiceP has nothing to do with the external Merge positions of arguments. The external argument is not externally merged into Spec VoiceP, but rather is externally merged into the specifier of vP (see Chomsky 1995 and Collins and Thráinsson 1996). In the realization theory, VoiceP plays a role in how arguments are realized in A-positions (such as Spec TP). For example, in Collins 2005a, the presence of VoiceP makes it possible for the object of the active to move to Spec TP and be realized as the subject of the passive.

The realization theory is illustrated in (2) below:

(2) Realization Theory

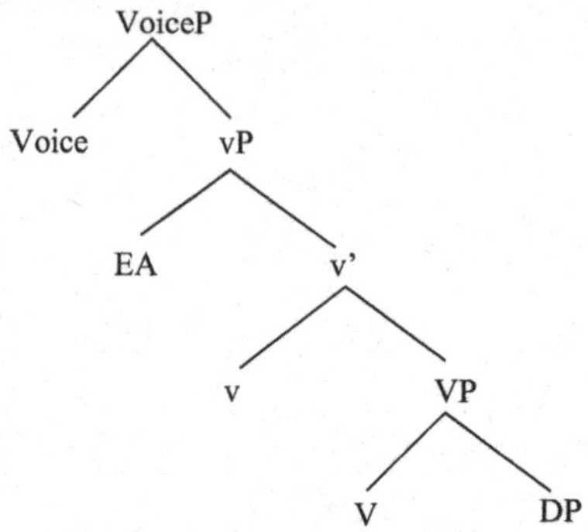

I summarize these two theories below:

(3) a. Projection Theory:
VoiceP plays a role in the projection (external Merge) of arguments. In particular, the external argument of the active is merged into Spec VoiceP.
b. Realization Theory:
VoiceP plays no role in the projection (external Merge) of arguments. Rather, VoiceP determines the A-positions of arguments.

In this chapter, which focuses for the most part on the passive in English, I will argue for the realization theory over the projection theory. Furthermore, I will argue that the Merge-based approach to argument structure is inconsistent with the projection theory.

The rest of the chapter is structured as follows. Section 8.2 sketches a general characterization of grammatical voice (based on Doron 2015). Section 8.3 outlines Kratzer's (1996) theory of VoiceP and critiques several proposals adopting Kratzer's framework. Section 8.4 argues for Collins's (2005a) theory of VoiceP over Kratzer's. Section 8.5 gives some quotes from various authors arguing against Kratzer's conception of VoiceP. Section 8.6 goes deeper into the issue and shows that Kratzer's approach is not consistent with the Merge-based approach to argument structure. Section 8.7 shows that Kratzer's approach to external arguments makes incorrect predictions about binding in nominalizations. Section 8.8 is the conclusion.

8.2 What Is Grammatical Voice?

It is not the purpose of this chapter to give a survey of grammatical voice, or to offer a unified theory of constructions characterized by voice. But as a starting point, I adopt Doron's (2015:749) characterization:

(4) "Voice (diathesis) alternations are particular alternations, typically marked as part of the verb's morphology, in the assignment of grammatical functions to the verb's arguments."

In the Principles and Parameters tradition, grammatical functions are normally characterized in terms of A-positions: Spec TP, complement of the verb, etc. So, I reformulate the characterization of voice alternations as follows:

(5) Voice alternations are typically marked as part of the verb's morphology and determine the realization of the verb's arguments in A-positions.

There are problems with this simple characterization. For example, in ECM (Exceptional Case Marking) constructions, the object is not an argument of the matrix verb but can be passivized: *John was believed to be nice.* I put such problems aside, as (5) is sufficient for the purposes of this chapter.

Under such a characterization are found phenomena like the passive (including impersonal passives), antipassive, inversion (e.g., in Algonquian), and various kinds of middles (see Ackema and Schoorlemmer 2017 for a survey of middles).

The phenomena traditionally characterized as voice phenomena may have very different syntactic analyses. But whatever the analysis, the following terminological assumption should be adhered to:

(6) Terminological Assumption
Any theory of VoiceP must play a crucial role in accounts of voice phenomena (e.g., passive, inversion, middle). Equivalently, if a projection XP plays no role in accounting for voice phenomena, then it should not be called VoiceP.

This is a standard position on terminology in the field of generative syntax. A theory of FocP (focus phrase) plays a role in the accounts of focus. A theory of AspP (aspect phrase) plays a role in accounts of verbal aspect. A theory of NumP (number phrase) plays a role in accounts of number in the DP. If the VoiceP of some theory played no role in voice phenomena, it would not be advisable to label the relevant projection VoiceP.

8.3 Kratzer 1996

Kratzer develops her proposals about VoiceP within the neo-Davidsonian conception of event semantics. In particular, she suggests that the Voice head for agent has the following denotation:

(7) Agent* = $\lambda x_e \lambda e_s$[Agent(x)(e)]

However, Kratzer (1996) presents no arguments at all that the functional head VoiceP has anything to do with voice phenomena, which seems to be explicitly acknowledged on page 120:

(8) "I will call it VOICE. This choice of name is not arbitrary. Kratzer (forthcoming) argues that Voice is truly at the heart of a theory of voice."

In other words, there is no indication in Kratzer 1996 of how the VoiceP plays a role in the passive, middle, inverse, and other voice phenomena. And so Kratzer's paper fails the terminological assumption (6) above.

But later authors do provide analyses that implicate VoiceP in voice phenomena. Perhaps the first such analysis is that of Pylkkänen (2008a:26), who claims that there is an active Voice head as well as a passive Voice head:

(9) "The inability of depictives to modify an implicit external argument is predicted, as long as we assume that passive Voice makes the external argument syntactically unavailable. In (35), I assume that passive Voice existentially closes off the external argument."

Consider the following diagram (based on (35) of Pylkkänen 2008a:26):

(10)

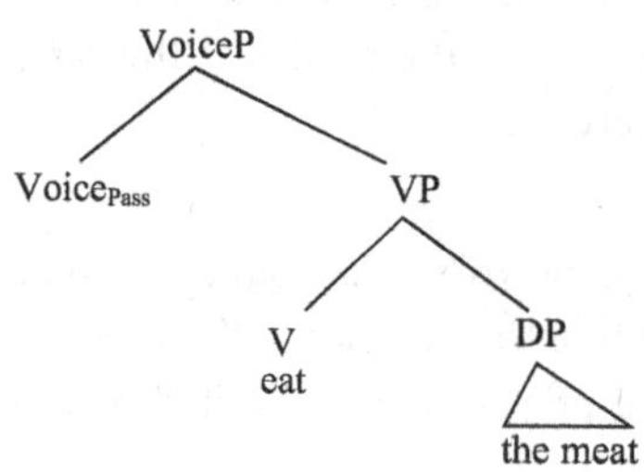

In Pylkkänen's system there are two Voice heads: an active Voice head whose Spec contains the external argument and a passive Voice head that does not project a specifier. If Pylkkänen's analysis is right, it would provide striking confirmation for Kratzer's basic idea that the external argument is projected in Spec VoiceP. It would be exactly the kind of data needed by Kratzer to support her VoiceP analysis. Here is the reasoning: if the external argument is projected in Spec VoiceP, then it could be the case that the projection of the external argument varies with the flavor of the Voice head (active or passive).

However, there are a number of severe empirical problems for Pylkkänen's analysis of the passive. First, it is founded on the generalization that the implicit argument in the passive cannot be modified by a depictive secondary predicate (pg. 22): "if the external argument is implicit, as in a passive, it cannot be modified by a depictive." But I have shown in great detail in chapter 3 that this generalization does not hold. An example from Collins 2005a:101 is given below:

(11) At the commune, breakfast is usually eaten nude.

Furthermore, there are data discussed in chapter 2 (and other sources) that show that the implicit argument of a passive can bind a reflexive pronoun:

(12) a. Such privileges should be kept to oneself.
(Baker, Johnson, and Roberts 1989:228; Roberts 1987:162)
b. Damaging testimony is always given about oneself in secret trials.
(Roberts 1987:162)

These sentences are predicted to be unacceptable by Pylkkänen's theory in (10), because the reflexive pronouns have no antecedents. Rather, it seems that in the short passive there must be a null pro in Spec VoiceP that binds the reflexive, as argued extensively in chapters 2–5.

(13)
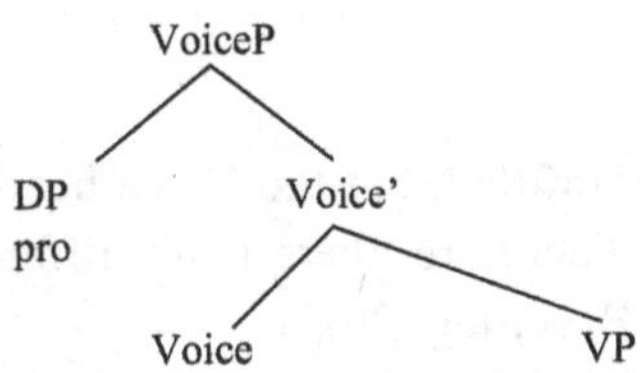

But then the external argument in the passive would be projected in the same way as the external argument in the active; both are projected in Spec VoiceP. In other words, given (13) it is unclear that there is any distinction at all between the active and the passive VoiceP in English. And if there is no distinction, then there is no support from the English passive for the idea that the external argument is projected in Spec VoiceP.

A proposal related to Pylkkänen's is that there is a Voice$_{\text{Pass}}$ that selects for a pro specifier. This appears to be the analysis of Baker and Vinokurova (2009:528): "the primary difference is that active voice typically takes an overt NP in its specifier position and passive voice takes a phonologically null NP, which is interpreted as a free variable." This kind of analysis would be able to handle data like (11) and (12) since there is a syntactically projected external argument. But it is unclear why a distinction between active and passive Voice is needed here. In both cases, Spec VoiceP is filled by the external argument. The distribution of the phonologically null pro falls under the general theory of implicit arguments in chapter 4. Therefore, there is no need to stipulate that there is a distinct passive Voice head that "takes a phonologically null NP" in its specifier position.

One of the best worked-out analyses of the passive in the VoiceP framework is Bruening (2013). In his theory, there is no difference between an active and a passive Voice head; they have exactly the same syntactic and semantic features. Bruening assumes that "passive is a head (Pass) that selects a projection of Voice that has not yet projected its external argument. I notate this [S: Voice(S:N)]. That is, Pass selects for a Voice with an unchecked [S:N] feature. This means that the complement of Pass is an unsaturated Voice projection" (pg. 22).

The analysis is sketched below (modified slightly):

(14)

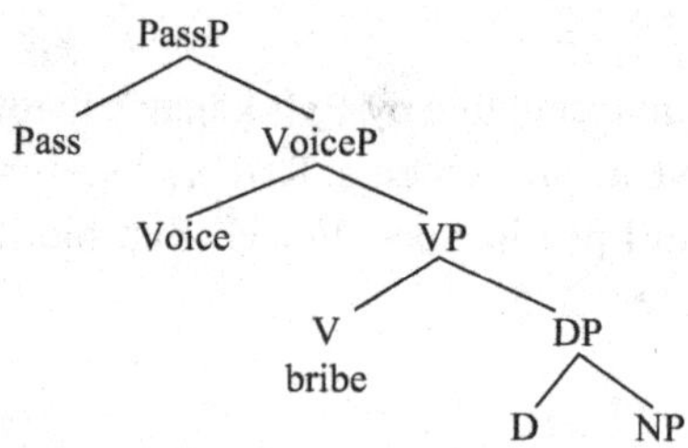

So, in the passive, Spec VoiceP remains unfilled, but the Voice head has exactly the same features as in the active. Therefore, there is no difference between passive and active Voice heads for Bruening (2013).

The surprising consequence of Bruening's analysis is that even though he adopts Kratzer's (1996) VoiceP framework, the VoiceP itself plays no essential role in his analysis of the English passive voice. Rather, all the work is done by PassP, which (pg. 22) "selects for a Voice with an unchecked [S:N] feature." Clearly, this situation represents a failure of the terminological assumption in (6). There is no reason internal to Bruening's analysis of the passive that the head that introduces the external argument should be called Voice.

Consider next Alexiadou, Anagnostopoulou, and Schäfer 2015, which adopts the VoiceP framework to analyze various voice-related phenomena, including the passive and anticausatives in German and Greek. My discussion here closely follows that of Angelopoulos, Collins, and Terzi 2020. Nonactive voice is used in a variety of contexts: passives, reflexives and reciprocals, middles, deponent verbs, and some anticausative verbs. An example with a Greek active and passive (present and past tense) is given below (from Angelopoulos et al. 2020:2, (1)):

(15) a. O kathijitis chirokrot-i tus fitites.
The professor applaud.ACT.PRES-3SG the students
'The professor applauds the students.'

b. I fitites chirokrot-unde apo ton kathijiti.
the students applaud-NACT.PRES.3PL by the professor
'The students are applauded by the professor.'

c. I fitites chirokroti-thik-an apo ton kathijiti.
the students applaud-NACT.PAST-3PL by the professor
'The students were applauded by the professor.'

Alexiadou, Anagnostopoulou, and Schäfer (2015:101) propose that the nonactive voice morphology in Greek marks the absence of Spec VoiceP:

(16) ". . . we propose that a Voice head is spelled out with nonactive morphology in Greek, if it lacks a specifier. In other words, the common property shared by passives and marked anticausatives in languages of this type is the lack of a syntactically projected external argument in Spec VoiceP."

Concretely, they adopt the analysis of Embick (1998, 2004) about the spell-out of Voice:

(17) Voice → Voice[NonAct]/ __ No DP Specifier.

But Angelopoulos, Collins, and Terzi (2020) show that the *by*-phrase in the Greek passive behaves like an external argument in its ability to bind reflexives. Therefore, they conclude that the external argument in the passive and the active are projected in the same position (for them, Spec vP). From this it follows that the presence of nonactive voice is not sensitive to whether or not there is a syntactically projected external argument. But if the distribution of nonactive voice is independent of the projection of an external argument, there can be no support for Kratzer's (1996) theory from Greek.

Yet another influential paper using the VoiceP framework is Harley 2013, which argues that for Hiaki "the external-argument-introducing projection VoiceP . . . must be distinct from the verbalizing head" (34). Harley (2013:50) notes that in applicatives of causatives, the morpheme order is the following:

(18) ni'i-tua-ria
fly-caus-appl

She assumes that the caus head is a flavor of little v. Now if caus itself introduces the causer, then because of the order of suffixes in (18), one would expect the applied DP to be higher than the causer DP, but it is not (as Harley shows). Rather, the causer subject is higher than the applied object. Therefore, it follows that (a) the caus head does not introduce the matrix causer subject and (b) there is another head that introduces the matrix causer subject. As Harley (2013:55) summarizes:

(19) "The Mirror Principle problems posed by the interaction of the applicative and causative in Hiaki require that the head that introduces causative morphology and semantics be distinct from the head that introduces external arguments; that is, vP is not VoiceP."

Harley (2013:52) then claims that "Voice should be the locus of Voice morphology—passive morphemes included." If the proposed head, introducing the causer in examples like (18), was also the locus of passive morphology, that would be strong support for Kratzer's (1996) program. As Harley (2013:53) notes: "If the external argument is introduced separately by Voice, however, then passive Voice morphology can embed a causative v without requiring the presence of an external argument." And in the diagrams (40) and (41) of Harley's paper, passive VoiceP is clearly shown with no specifier.

This logic seems very similar to Pylkkänen's (2008a) account of the English passive presented above. And just as in Pylkkänen's account, one can ask if there really is no syntactically present external argument in the passive in Hiaki. Harley presents no relevant data. But if the relevant tests (e.g., Principles A,B, secondary predicates, Helke expressions, argument control, adjunct control) showed that the external argument was projected in the passive, then both active Voice and passive Voice would involve a projected external argument. Such a conclusion would raise the possibility that the projection of arguments is identical in the active and passive in Hiaki, making Harley's (2013) use of VoiceP to project the external argument suspect (since the projection of the external argument would be independent of voice).

The above short survey of Kratzer 1996; Bruening 2013; Pylkkänen 2008a; Alexiadou, Anagnostopoulou, and Schäfer 2015; and Harley 2013 show that in all cases there is insufficient evidence to warrant an analysis where the external argument is projected in Spec VoiceP. Kratzer (1996) provides no evidence at all. Bruening (2013) gives an analysis using VoiceP, but where VoiceP plays no essential role in accounting for the passive (violating the terminological assumption in (6)). Furthermore, the analyses of Pylkkänen 2008a; Bruening 2013 and Alexiadou, Anagnostopoulou, and Schäfer 2015 all make incorrect empirical predictions about the short passive. Lastly, Harley (2013) does not provide sufficient empirical evidence to support her claim that there is a VoiceP projection lacking an external argument in the passive.

8.4 Collins 2005a

In Collins 2005a, VoiceP is needed in the syntax of passive constructions, but it has nothing to do with the projection of external arguments into theta-positions. Rather, VoiceP allows the direct object of the active to be moved to Spec TP of the passive, which is why I call it the realization theory (as opposed to the projection theory). See chapter 7 for technical details on the derivation of the passive and the role of VoiceP.

In the theory of chapter 6, the *by*-phrase occupies Spec vP in the passive. In the short passive, there is a null pro that occupies Spec vP. Therefore, the structure of the vP in the passive is as follows:

(20)

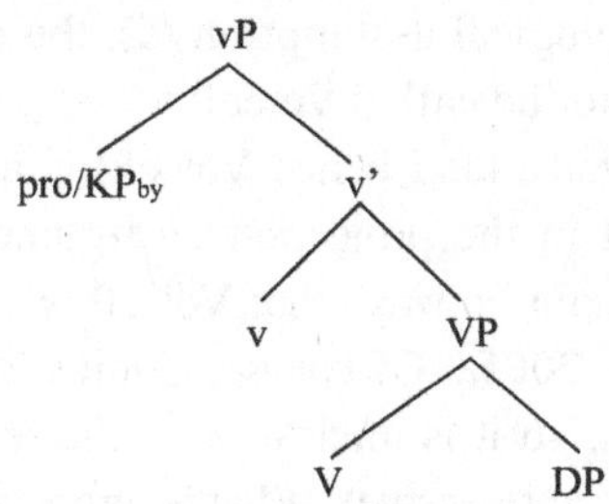

But if this vP were embedded under a finite TP (as the complement of T), there would be no way for the structure to be realized. English does not allow non-nominative subjects, so the *by*-phrase could not move to Spec TP. And English is not a null subject language, which I assume entails that pro cannot appear in Spec TP (although pro may appear in other positions, such as Spec vP in the short passive; see chapter 4 for discussion). Furthermore, the object DP could not raise to Spec TP, since vP is a strong phase (because it has a filled specifier). Furthermore, Spec vP is a filled A-position intervening between the object and Spec TP, and so movement of the object to Spec TP would violate Relativized Minimality. See chapter 7 for details.

Therefore, in the theory of Collins 2005a, the reason VoiceP is projected between TP and vP is to allow the object to move to Spec TP, while the subject stays in Spec vP. Collins assumes that the direct object is smuggled over Spec vP. On smuggling, see Collins 2005a and chapter 7.

The advantage of Collins's (2005a) theory is that the projection of arguments in the passive is identical to the projection of arguments in the active. This accounts for Chomsky's (1957) observation that the selectional restrictions in the active and passive are identical (see discussion in chapter 1). It also accounts for the fact that the range of theta-roles found for the external argument in the passive matches those found for the external argument in the active (see chapter 6 for an illustration of this fact from Greek). Lastly, it accounts for the fact that the *by*-phrase in the passive can bind reflexive and reciprocal pronouns, as shown below (from chapter 6):

(21) a. The packages were sent by the children to each other.
b. The pictures were painted by the children for each other.
c. The packages were sent by the children to themselves.
d. The pictures were painted by the children for themselves.

These properties are hard to account for unless one assumes that the projection of arguments in the passive and active are identical. But if one makes this identity assumption, then the projection of arguments is independent from the passive voice. And by the terminological assumption (6), the category projecting external arguments should not be called VoiceP.

I speculate that the primary function of voice (and hence VoiceP) is in the realization of arguments in A-positions (not in the projection of arguments). However, it is important to note that there might be ways that VoiceP operates differently from the ways outlined in Collins 2005a. Of course, Collins 2005a and this monograph only discuss the passive, so it is unclear what the role of VoiceP is in other voices (e.g., middle, inverse, antipassive). What is important is that VoiceP has nothing to do with projecting the external argument, but is rather implicated in how the argument DPs are realized in (moved to) A-positions.

A more articulated theory of the syntax of various voice phenomena, and the role of VoiceP in those phenomena (under the realization theory) will have to await further research. A restrictive theory would start from the assumption that the arguments in all these constructions are projected in exactly the same way. In other words, if there is an agent (either implicit or overt) in the active, passive, middle, impersonal, or inverse, then that agent should be projected the same way in all the constructions (see chapter 10 on the status of UTAH in the Merge-based theory). But if the agent is projected in the same way across all the different voices, then it is a violation of (6) to claim that the agent is projected in Spec VoiceP.

8.5 Other Authors

I have argued in this chapter that the external argument is not introduced in Spec VoiceP. Many other authors have come to the same conclusion (see also Newman 2020; Roberts 2019; and Zyman 2017 for views compatible with the one I am arguing for). I provide some quotes here.

In discussing ellipsis involving the passive, Merchant (2013:98) states:

(22) "The crucial element involved in these accounts is the separation of the head that determines voice from the head that determines the external valency of the predicate. There is in fact no conceptual reason these two should go together, and the ellipsis facts argue directly against this assumption."

Myler and Mali (2021:3, fn. 3), who otherwise fully adopt Kratzer's (1996) VoiceP framework, echo Merchant's conclusions (see chapter 10 for further discussion of Myler and Mali). Surprisingly, Myler and Mali continue to use the VoiceP notation in their paper.

(23) "Since the head that introduces external arguments is in some languages clearly separate from and lower than the head that encodes passive-active alternations, the label Voice turns out to be something of a misnomer; see especially Merchant 2008, 2013. Nevertheless we retain the usage here for consistency with the works cited in the final paragraph of this section and with other recent literature on causatives that uses the same framework."

Based on morpheme order in the Latin passive, Zyman and Kalivoda (2020:8) explicitly reject Kratzer's (1996) use of VoiceP in favor of the Collins/Merchant conception:

(24) "Fifth, the external argument (EA) originates in [Spec,vP] not [Spec, VoiceP] (Collins 2005; Merchant 2013). This is advantageous for three reasons."

Ramchand (2017:241) notes that the Voice as used by Kratzer does not fit into her framework:

(25) "But if the Voice head (and its different "flavors" or versions) is supposed to track the kind of externalization that varies with traditional voice morphology, then it certainly cannot be equivalent to the head labeled CAUSE, or INIT for that matter. Clearly, VoiceP is not the same thing as the highest head of the Ramchandian decomposition argued for in section 10.2."

These references show that the Kratzerian analysis of external arguments as being introduced in Spec of VoiceP is far from universally accepted. Furthermore, as Merchant (2013) notes, there is no conceptual reason to conflate voice and valency.

8.6 Merge-Based Approach

In this monograph, I have argued that the heads that determine argument structure (v, Appl, V) are distinct from the head that determines voice (Voice). I showed that in the passive (long or short) the external argument is projected in exactly the same way as in the active. In other words, the projection of the external argument is independent of voice. Therefore, there is no reason to externally Merge the external argument into Spec VoiceP.

In this section, I make the stronger claim that the Kratzerian conception of VoiceP introducing the external argument is inconsistent with the Merge-based approach to argument structure.

Kratzerian approaches to the passive have in common that in the active Spec VoiceP is filled, but in the passive it is not. As noted in this monograph, that assumption leads to severe empirical problems, since the implicit argument in the passive in English can bind reflexives, reciprocals, and pronouns in Helke expressions and be modified by secondary predicates.

Not only is the Kratzerian approach problematic empirically, it is also problematic theoretically from the point of view of the Merge-based approach to argument structure. Kratzerian approaches are unified in holding that the external argument in the passive is not projected syntactically (although it is existentially bound semantically). But this is just the kind of analysis that the Merge-based theory blocks, since in one case (the active) the external-argument taking property of Voice is satisfied by external Merge, and in the other (the passive) it is not (it is instead satisfied by some semantic mechanism involving existential closure).

This can be seen by looking carefully at analyses (such as Bruening 2013) that adopt Kratzer's (1996) VoiceP. As noted in chapters 4 and 6, Bruening allows Spec VoiceP to be filled or empty while retaining the same semantics. This is a clear violation of the Theta-Criterion, since it means that a theta-position remains unfilled in the passive.

Consider now Pylkkänen's (2008a) analysis of the passive. She postulates that there is a passive $\text{Voice}_{\text{Pass}}$ head that does not project a specifier, and that head existentially binds the external argument. The two kinds of Voice heads are given below:

(26) a. $[\![\text{Voice}]\!] = \lambda x.\lambda e.\text{agent}(e,x)$
b. $[\![\text{Voice}_{\text{Pass}}]\!] = \lambda e.\exists x.\text{agent}(e,x)$

The structure in (27) is slightly modified from Pylkkänen 2008a:26:

(27)

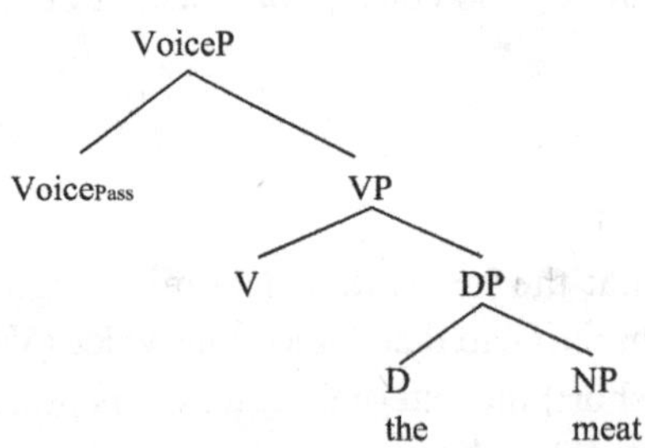

In Pylkkänen's analysis, Spec $\text{Voice}_{\text{Pass}}$ is never filled, since $\text{Voice}_{\text{Pass}}$ is only used in the passive, not the active. Therefore, the Theta-Criterion does not force a filled specifier in (27). Or to put it in different terms, $\text{Voice}_{\text{Pass}}$ is never an argument-introducing head, so it does not need to introduce an argument in (27). Therefore, it seems like Pylkkänen's analysis (unlike Bruening's) does not violate either the Argument Criterion or the Theta-Criterion.

However, there is an issue with Pylkkänen's definition of $\text{Voice}_{\text{Pass}}$. It seems to combine two completely separate kinds of information: (a) the fact that the external argument is an agent, and (b) the fact that the external argument is existentially closed.

To rule this out, one possibility is to invoke the Principle of Decompositionality (Kayne 2005:212):

(28) Principle of Decompositionality
UG imposes a maximum of one interpretable syntactic feature per lexical item.

However, it is not entirely clear that (28) rules out (26b), since $\text{Voice}_{\text{Pass}}$ could count as a single interpretable syntactic feature. In general Kayne's principle suffers from the lack of specification of what a possible interpretable feature is. Or to put it another way, Kayne's principle blocks syntactically complex lexical items, but does not block semantically complex syntactic features and lexical items.

What is needed is an additional constraint that minimizes the semantic complexity of each interpretable syntactic feature. A preliminary attempt is the following (thanks to Phillipe Schlenker and Sam Alxatib for discussing this issue with me):

(29) Principle of Semantic Decompositionality
If ⟦X⟧ = SV1(SV2) (SV1 and SV2 are semantic values)
and ⟦Y⟧ = SV1 or SV2 (where Y is a morpheme in the lexicon)
then X = [. . . Y . . .]

The basic idea of this principle is that if X can be decomposed semantically, then X can also be decomposed syntactically. I assume that SV1 and SV2 do not have trivial (identity function) values.

From this point of view, (26b) bundles together the semantic values of the active Voice head and the existential quantifier *some*, and therefore should be ruled out. The decomposition is shown below:

(30) a. $[\![\text{Voice}]\!] = \lambda x.\lambda e.\text{agent}(e,x)$
b. $[\![\text{Voice}_{\text{Pass}}]\!] = \lambda e.\exists x.\text{agent}(e,x)$
$= [\lambda P.\lambda e.\exists x.P(e,x)]([\![\text{Voice}]\!])$

Of course, we can modify Pylkkänen's analysis in the following way: One head would be active Voice (defined as in (26a)), and the other would existentially bind the external argument (as with the Pass head in Bruening's analysis). But then if Spec VoiceP is empty, the analysis would violate the Theta-Criterion just as it does in Bruening 2013 (see chapter 4 for discussion).

Another analysis violating (29) is Baker and Vinokurova's (2009:531) analysis of agentive nominalizations suffixes such as *-er* in English. They give the following semantic value (the symbol $\frown$ is the nominalization operator):

(31) -er: $\lambda P^\frown \lambda x$ Gen e ((P(e) & agent(e,x))

Baker and Vinokurova (2009) assume the same semantic value for Voice as in (30a). So, (31) contains the semantic value of Voice and should be ruled out by (29). In other words, (29) forces nominalization and the introduction of external arguments to be done by two different syntactic heads.

8.7 Kratzer on Nominalizations

Kratzer (1996: section 5) uses English nominalizations to give additional support for her theory of external arguments: "The discussion of English gerunds confirmed our claim that external arguments are introduced by independent heads that are also responsible for the assignment of accusative Case."

Consider the following minimal pair:

(32) a. Maria enjoyed a reading of *Pride and Prejudice.*
b. Maria enjoyed reading *Pride and Prejudice.*

According to Kratzer, in (32a) there is no external argument (and hence no control) and no accusative Case. In (32b), there is a controlled external argument, and the direct object receives accusative Case. This difference can be explained in terms of the absence of VoiceP in (32a) and the presence of VoiceP in (32b).

The first point to note about this analysis is that it is completely independent of voice. The same exact explanation could have been given in Chomsky's (1995) vP theory, where the external argument is introduced in Spec vP.

But a more serious issue is the generalization that (Kratzer 1996:128) "in of_{ing} gerunds, the absence of accusative Case is accompanied by the absence of the verb's external argument." Consider the following example:

(33) a. The constant promoting of himself_1 at conferences is hurting John_1's career.
b. The constant promoting of him_1 at conferences is hurting John_1's career.

To me, the sentences in (33) sound as good as any other of_{ing} gerund. In (33a), there is a phonologically null implicit argument (the promoter) that binds the reflexive, satisfying Principle A of the Binding Theory. A partial structure is given below (see section 4.4.4 for more discussion of nominalizations):

(34) the pro_1 promoting of $himself_1$

Furthermore, in (33b) the interpretation is that the promoter is distinct from *John*. Such an interpretation is accounted for by Principle B if there is a null implicit argument. Such sentences show that of_{ing} gerunds do not lack external arguments. The fact that control is not possible in (32a) does not have to do with the absence of an external argument, but rather the absence of controlled PRO.

How to represent (33) syntactically and how to account for the lack of accusative Case are questions I will leave to future research (but see chapter 4 for a discussion of implicit arguments in nominalizations).

8.8 Conclusion

In this chapter I compared two conceptions of VoiceP, the projection theory and the realization theory. I discussed a number of analyses using Kratzer's (1996) framework. In each case, they either (a) violate the terminological assumption (6), or (b) are empirically inaccurate or (c) are empirically incomplete.

I suggested the realization theory (e.g., Collins 2005a) as an alternative way to think about voice. Lastly, I argued that the Kratzerian conception of VoiceP as introducing the external argument is actually inconsistent with the Merge-based theory of argument structure outlined in chapter 1.

There is by now a large literature adopting the theoretical assumptions of Kratzer (1996). It is possible that in some paper the smoking gun has been found that crucially links the projection of the external argument to VoiceP. Alternatively, the whole project is doomed to fail, since it conflates two very different syntactic systems: argument structure and voice.

9 The Dative Alternation

9.1 Introduction

A long-standing debate in the syntax literature is the relation between (1a) and (1b), which I call the *dative alternation*. This terminology is neutral between analyses where either (1a) is derived from (1b) (Larson 1988; Baker 1997:91) (*dative shift*) or (1b) is derived from (1a) (Bowers 1981:65; Postal 2010:123), or neither structure is derived from the other (Harley 2002; Harley and Jung 2015; Harley and Miyagawa 2017:21; Holmberg, Sheehan, and van der Wal 2019:685).

(1) a. John gave Mary the car. (double object construction)
b. John gave the car to Mary. (prepositional dative)

Support for the analysis where (1b) is derived from a structure underlying (1a) comes from systematic parallels between the dative alternation and the passive.

(2) a. John wrote the book. (active)
b. The book was written by John. (passive with *by*-phrase)

In (1a), the indirect object and direct object are unmarked DPs, unaccompanied by prepositions. In (2a), the subject and object are unmarked DPs. (1b) involves a word order reversal, changing the order goal-theme to the order theme-goal. (2b) also involves a word order reversal, changing the order agent-theme to the order theme-agent. In (1b), the goal argument is marked by a semantically vacuous preposition *to*. In (2b), the agent argument is marked by a semantically vacuous preposition *by*.

The passive and the active share the same truth conditions (putting aside the issue of quantifier scope), in the same way that (1a) and (1b) share the same truth conditions.

(3) a. John gave Mary the book iff John gave the book to Mary.
b. John wrote the book iff the book was written by John.

Lastly, just like in the passive (see Chomsky 1957:42–43), selectional restrictions are maintained between the orders in (1a) and (1b). For example, (5c) is a violation of selectional restrictions, since the object of *frighten* must be sentient. A similar constraint holds for the passive in (5d). Similarly, (4c) is a violation of selectional restrictions, since the first object must be the receiver. These selectional restrictions are maintained in the prepositional dative variant in (4d).

(4) a. I gave John a lovely gift.
  b. I gave a lovely gift to John.
  c. *I gave a lovely gift John.
  d. *I gave John to a lovely gift.

(5) a. Sincerity frightened John.
  b. John was frightened by sincerity.
  c. *John frightened sincerity.
  d. *Sincerity was frightened by John.

My conclusions about selectional restrictions and truth conditions are supported by Rappaport Hovav and Levin (2008:129), who put their thesis as follows: "We challenge the predominant view of the English dative alternation, which takes all alternating verbs to have two meanings: a caused possession meaning realized by the double object variant and a caused motion meaning realized by the *to* variant. Instead, we argue that verbs like *give* and *sell* only have a caused possession meaning, while verbs like *throw* and *send* have both caused motion and caused possession meanings. We show that the caused possession meaning may be realized by both variants. Concomitantly, we argue that verbs like *give*, even in the *to* variant, lack a conceptual path constituent, and instead have a caused possession meaning which can be understood as the bringing about of a 'have' relation."

Given these five striking parallels, I assume that (1a) is syntactically related to (1b) in a way parallel to the syntactic relation between (2a) and (2b). More specifically, just like the passive is derived by moving the theme over the agent (see chapter 7 for details), I propose that the prepositional dative construction is derived by moving the theme over the goal.

In this chapter, I will give further evidence that (1b) is derived from the structure underlying (1a) by movement of the theme over the goal (a conclusion reached on similar grounds by Aoun and Li (1989) and Kitagawa (1994)). I point out that such a derivation yields a locality problem (a DP moves over a KP) and suggest a solution to this problem in terms of smuggling (on smuggling, see Collins 2005a, 2005b; Belletti and Collins 2020).

The rest of the chapter is structured as follows. Section 9.2 discusses some asymmetries between the double object construction and the prepositional dative construction. Section 9.3 proposes an analysis for double object constructions. Section 9.4 proposes an analysis for the dative alternation parallel to the analysis of the passive given in chapters 6 and 7 of the monograph. Section 9.5 discusses striking supporting data from Hallman 2015. Section 9.6 is the conclusion.

9.2 Asymmetries of Asymmetries

Barss and Lasnik (1986) and Larson (1988) show that there are c-command asymmetries in double object constructions and prepositional dative constructions. But there is also an asymmetry between the double object construction (DOC) and the prepositional dative (see also Kitagawa 1994; Harley and Miyagawa 2017; Takano 1998:824):

(6) a. John gave every man his paycheck.
    b. ?John gave his paycheck to every man.

(7) a. John gave every dog to its owner.
    b. *John gave its owner every dog.

(6a) shows that the goal c-commands the theme in a double object construction (since bound variable anaphora is allowed), and (7a) shows that the theme c-commands the goal in a prepositional dative construction. While (6b) is marginal in the bound variable reading, (7b) is completely unacceptable. Assuming that (7b) violates the c-command condition on bound variable anaphora (Barss and Lasnik 1986:348), the problem is to explain why (6b) does not incur a similarly strong violation.

A contrast similar to the one in (6) and (7) exists for reciprocals (see also Kitagawa 1994; on the marginal status of (8b) see Takano 1998:824):

(8) a. I showed the boys each other's pictures.
    b. ?I showed each other's pictures to the boys.

(9) a. I showed the students to each other's parents.
    b. *I showed each other's parents the students.

Backwards anaphora in (8b) with the prepositional dative is considerably better than backwards anaphora in (9b) with the double object construction.

A similar asymmetry between the DOC and the prepositional dative can be seen in quantifier scope (see Bruening 2001; Kitagawa 1994; Aoun and Li 1989; and Harley and Jung 2015 for an extensive discussion):

(10) a. I gave a student every car.
     b. I gave a car to every student.

In (10a), the only possible interpretation is that there is a single student who receives all the cars. (10a) resists the inverse scope interpretation where every car is given to a different student. On the other hand, (10b) admits the inverse scope interpretation, where every student receives a different car.

Burzio (1986:198–199) points out that there is a c-command constraint on the following use of *each* (although see Safir and Stowell 1987, which coins the term binominal *each*):

(11) a. We met one girl each.
b. *One girl each met us.

In (11a), the plural subject c-commands the structure [one girl each]. But in (11b), the plural object does not c-command [one girl each], and the sentence is unacceptable.

Given this constraint, consider the following data ((13) is from Burzio 1986:199):

(12) a. John assigned [the visitors] one interpreter each.
b. John gave [the kids] one present each.
c. John sent [the students] one letter each.

(13) a. (?) John assigned one interpreter $each_1$ to $[the visitors]_1$.
b. ?John gave one present $each_1$ to $[the kids]_1$.
c. ?John sent one letter $each_1$ to $[the students]_1$.

(14) a. *John assigned one visitor each the interpreters.
b. *John gave one child each the toy cars.
c. *John sent one student each the letters.

(15) a. John assigned the interpreters to one visitor each.
b. John gave the toy cars to one child each.
c. John sent the letters to one student each.

There is a clear contrast between (13) and (14), even though in both cases [DP each] precedes its antecedent.

As argued by Kitagawa (1994), Aoun and Li (1989), and Takano (1998), these kinds of asymmetries between DOCs and the prepositional dative can be explained if the prepositional dative is derived by movement of the theme over the goal.

Focusing on the quantifier data in (6) and (7), consider first the relevant condition from Barss and Lasnik (1986:348):

(16) "in order for a pronoun to be related to a quantificational NP (QNP) as a variable, it must be in the domain of the QNP at S-Structure."

The relative acceptability of (6b) can be accounted for if (6b) is derived by A-movement of the theme over the goal. Under that assumption, the quantifier phrase c-commands one of the occurrences of *his paycheck*, and therefore c-commands the pronoun. This derivation is sketched below:

(17) John gave his paycheck to every man <his paycheck>

Supporting evidence for this analysis is given by the following contrast involving A-movement:

(18) a. His$_1$ mother seems to [every boy]$_1$ to be nice.
b. *His$_1$ mother told [every boy]$_1$ to be nice.

(18a), which involves raising, is acceptable with a bound variable interpretation. (18b) is unacceptable. Since (18a) involves A-movement, *every boy* c-commands one occurrence of the pronoun (on a similar case involving psych-verbs, see Belletti and Rizzi 2012:134).

I assume that the Binding Theory data, quantifier scope data, and binominal *each* data can be explained in a similar way (see Kitagawa 1994; Aoun and Li 1989). On reconstruction effects in A-movement more generally, see Sportiche 2017a, Lebeaux 2009, and Barss 2001.

However, a theoretical problem arises in the putative derivation for (6b) illustrated in (17). Such a derivation should violate Relativized Minimality (see Rizzi 1990) or the Minimal Link Condition (see Chomsky 1995), since the movement of the theme DP crosses over the goal KP [$_{KP}$ to every man]. To overcome this problem, I propose a smuggling analysis, parallel to the smuggling analysis of the passive discussed in chapter 7. In other words, I am proposing that the prepositional dative construction has a passive-like derivation.

9.3 Structure of DOCs

For background, I assume that the double object constructions should be analyzed in terms of VP shells (see Larson 1988; Pylkkänen 2008a), where the VP shells are vP, ApplP, VP, and perhaps others (see the introduction for references). In particular, I assume v takes an ApplP complement, and Appl takes a VP complement (see Collins 1997).

I do not follow Pylkkänen (2008a), who analyzes English as having a low applicative. Pylkkänen argues that the semantics of the low applicative differ from the semantics of the high applicative: "A high applicative head is very much like the external-argument-introducing head: it simply adds another participant to the event described by the verb. In contrast, low applied arguments bear no semantic relation to the verb whatsoever; they only bear a transfer-of-possession relation to the direct object" (14).

Although I will not discuss Pylkkänen's approach in detail (see Larson 2010, 2014 for critical discussion), I briefly note here that it is possible to obtain the semantics attributed to the low applicative syntax (Pylkkänen 2008a, pg. 18) from a high applicative syntax (pg. 12). It is only necessary to define high applicative lexical entry as follows:

(19) $[\![\text{APPL}]\!] = \lambda P.\lambda x.\lambda e.[P(e) \wedge \text{to-the-possession}(e, \text{Theme}(e), x)]$

In this semantic value, Theme(e) is the function yielding the unique theme argument of e. In other words, when Appl is added to the VP, it adds a goal argument and states that the goal argument is related to the theme of the event by the to-the-possession relation.

Since Pylkkänen admits that the high applicative head comes in several semantic flavors (e.g., instrumental, benefactive, malefactive; see pg. 17), I propose that (19) is just one more flavor. This new definition of the semantic value of the high applicative head also captures some of the other properties listed by Pylkkänen (see pg. 18). Since Appl introduces the to-the-possession relation, V must have a theme argument. Pylkkänen also claims that high applicatives and low applicatives differ with respect to secondary predication. For brevity's sake, I do not pursue that issue here (see Harley and Jung 2015 for a recent discussion of depictives and DOCs). For more discussion of Pylkkänen's theory, see chapter 10.

A partial underlying structure of (1a) is given below (I leave out the representation of the movement of the V to Appl and the movement of Appl to v):

(20)

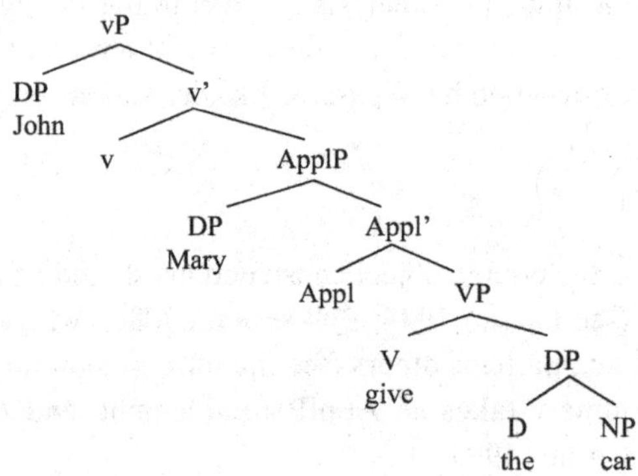

9.4 Analysis

In Collins 2020, I analyzed the dative preposition *to* as the head of VoiceP. However, in this chapter I will analyze *to*-phrases as KPs, just as I did with *by*-phrases in chapter 6. If the *to*-phrase is a KP, the question is what determines its syntactic distribution. For example, why can't the *to*-phrase appear in Spec vP in the passive? I will assume that on the KP analysis, there must be some constraint that forces the dative *to*-phrase to appear in Spec ApplP, instead of any other position. The generalization is the following:

(21) $[_{KP}$ to DP] appears in Spec ApplP (and no other position).

I put aside the relation between the dative *to* and the directional *to* found in sentences like "I went to the store." I assume that the distribution of the directional *to* does not fall under (21). This issue is analogous to the fact that passive *by* is homophonous to a locative *by*.

I propose that dative *to* has a c-selectional feature that constrains it to appear in Spec ApplP. In particular, I propose the following:

(22) *to* has c-selectional feature [__ApplP]

The technical framework assumed in this account is that of Collins and Stabler (2016:62): "We call the features involved in triggering Merge 'trigger features'. We assume that such features are to be identified with subcategorization features, EPP features and OP features for movement to Spec CP."

Recall that the passive *by* has the c-selectional feature [__vP], limiting a KP headed by *by* to Spec vP. The difference between passive *by* and dative *to* is purely syntactic (specified by c-selectional features). They do not differ semantically; both are semantically vacuous.

The underlying structure of the prepositional dative is given below (see also Hallman 2021 for a related analysis):

(23)

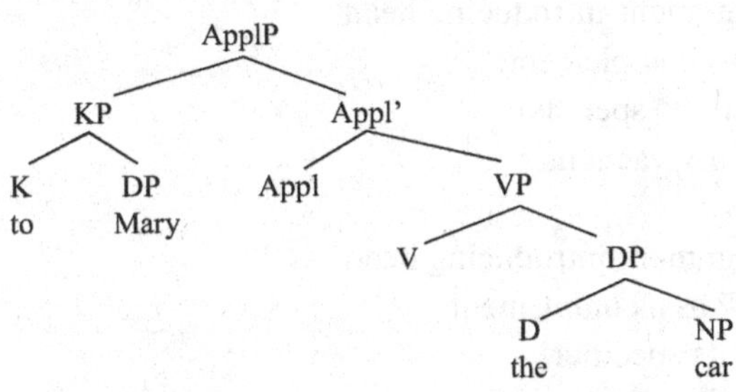

Consider how the Theta-Criterion is satisfied by (23). Because of structure (20), we concluded that Spec ApplP is a theta-position (because an argument DP is externally merged there). Therefore, in (23) Spec ApplP must also be a theta-position because we are assuming there are not different flavors of Appl (at least for the two forms of the dative alternation). Rather, the same kind of Appl is used in both the double object construction and the prepositional dative (exactly like the same little v is used in both the active and the passive). But $[_{KP}$ to Mary] is an argument, so merging it in Spec ApplP satisfies the Theta-Criterion.

Compare this structure to the structure of the vP in the passive (e.g., *the book was written by John*):

(24)

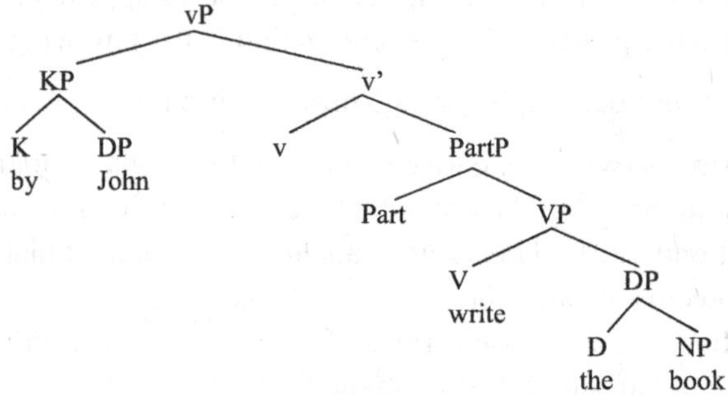

Given this background, I propose that the dative alternation should be analyzed in terms of smuggling, just like the passive (see Collins 2005a, Collins 2005b, and chapter 7). I propose that (1b) is derived from (1a) by VP movement, smuggling the theme past the goal. In particular, there is a VoiceP projection whose specifier the VP moves into. Technically, VP satisfies an EPP feature of Voice. I will refer to this Voice head involved in the dative alternation as *inner Voice*, to distinguish it from the one used in the passive, which I will refer to as *outer Voice.*

Therefore, there are at least two Voice heads in English, with slightly different properties:

(25) a. outer Voice:
 i. It is not an argument-introducing head.
 ii. It takes vP as a complement.
 iii. PartP moves to its specifier.
 iv. It is semantically vacuous.
 b. inner Voice:
 i. It is not an argument-introducing head.
 ii. It takes ApplP as a complement.
 iii. VP moves to its specifier.
 iv. It is semantically vacuous.

It is possible that these two Voice heads (inner Voice and outer Voice) are just two instantiations of the same general head, appearing in two different positions. When Voice is merged high, we get outer Voice. If Voice is merged low, we get inner Voice. But syntactically, there is just one Voice head. Such an analysis predicts that there are correlations between the passive and dative alternation cross-linguistically (because they are triggered by the same Voice head). For example, whereas Ewe lacks both a passive and the dative alternation, English has both. I have not investigated this prediction.

The derivation of the prepositional dative construction is given below:

(26) John gave the car to Mary.

a. $[_{ApplP}$ KP $[_{Appl'}$ Appl $[_{VP}$ V $[_{DP}$ the car]]]] → Merge Voice
b. $[_{VoiceP}$ Voice $[_{ApplP}$ KP$[_{Appl'}$ Appl $[_{VP}$ V $[_{DP}$ the car]]]]] → Move VP
c. $[[_{VP}$ V $[_{DP}$ the car]] $[_{Voice'}$ Voice $[_{ApplP}$ KP $[_{Appl'}$ Appl <VP>]]]]

A problem with the derivation in (26) is that it gives the wrong c-command relations between the theme and goal. As discussed by Larson (1988), the theme DP c-commands the goal DP in prepositional dative constructions.

(27) I showed the students to each other's teachers.

In (27), the DP *the students* c-commands the DP *each other*, and hence is able to bind it. However, in (26c), because of the presence of the fronted VP constituent, the theme does not actually c-command the goal (the theme DP is dominated by VP, which does not dominate the goal DP). Such considerations suggest that the theme DP in (26c) must undergo one subsequent A-movement out of the VP. I assume that Spec AgroP (object agreement phrase) is the relevant position. For an analysis involving raising to object, see Postal 1974. For vP internal functional projections, see Collins 2003, Collins and Thráinsson 1996, and Baker and Collins 2006.

Putting all these steps together yields the following structure (I leave out the movement of the verb to Agro, Agro to v, and other head movements):

(28)

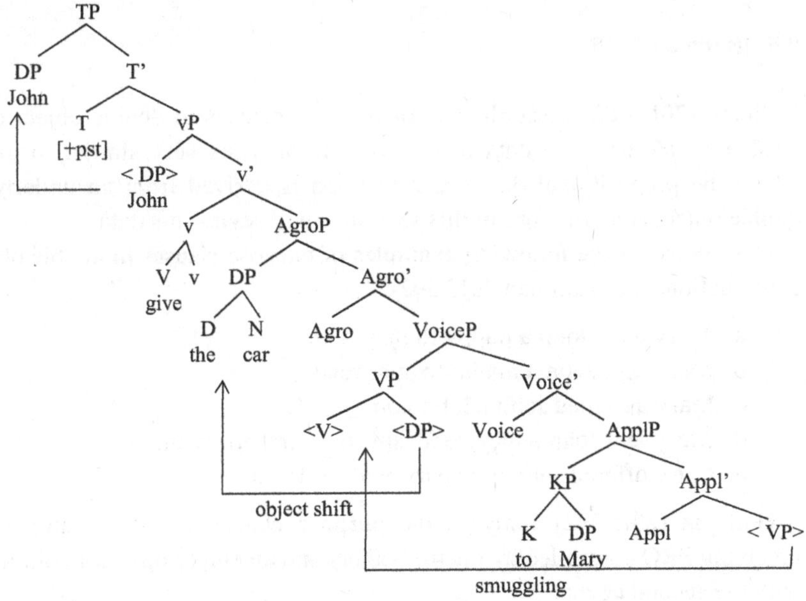

Let's verify that this structure meets all the requirements outlined earlier.

First, since the prepositional dative is derived from a structure underlying the DOC, we can account for the fact that they share identical selectional restrictions (and truth conditions).

Second, the AC/TC is satisfied, since KP *to Mary* is externally merged as the specifier of ApplP.

Third, since VP is moved over the KP *to Mary* in Spec ApplP, there is no violation of Relativized Minimality or the MLC. The theme DP does not directly move over the goal KP, rather the theme DP is smuggled over the goal KP by VP movement.

Fourth, the DP *the car* c-commands the DP *to Mary* (after raising to Spec Agro). Hence the standard c-command facts will hold (see (27)).

Fifth, since the theme DP *the car* originates in a position lower than the goal DP *to Mary*, we can account for the acceptability of the various reconstruction effects.

The analysis in (28) is similar to the analysis of *faire* causatives given in Kayne 2005:chapter 5. And in fact, the parallelism between my analysis and Kayne's analysis strongly supports the assumption I made earlier that the prepositional dative should be the derived structure (and not the underlying structure) in the dative alternation. In the *faire* causative of a transitive verb, the external argument of the causativized verb bears a dative preposition *à*. But the embedded clause corresponds to an underlying SVO structure (with no dative preposition).

9.5 Hallman 2015

Hallman (2015) discusses the use of purpose clauses in double object constructions. He uses the data to motivate an analysis very similar to mine, where the prepositional dative construction is derived from an underlying double object construction. In this section, I will review his data.

First, consider the following examples of purpose clauses in double object constructions (see Hallman 2015:392):

(29) a. Mary gave John a puppy to play with.
b. Mary sent John a manuscript to read.
c. Mary assigned John a job to do.
d. Mary lent John a bicycle to run some errands with.
e. Mary offered John her apartment to stay in.

Hallman (2015:392) analyzes the purpose clause in these examples as involving PRO controlled by the first object and an empty operator coindexed with the second object:

(30) Mary gave John$_1$ a puppy$_2$ [$_{CP}$ Op$_2$ [PRO$_1$ to play with t$_2$]]

The structure of the purpose clause in (29a) [to play with] is given in (31). Following Hallman, I will assume that the subject of the purpose clause is PRO, but there is also an empty operator in Spec CP.

(31)

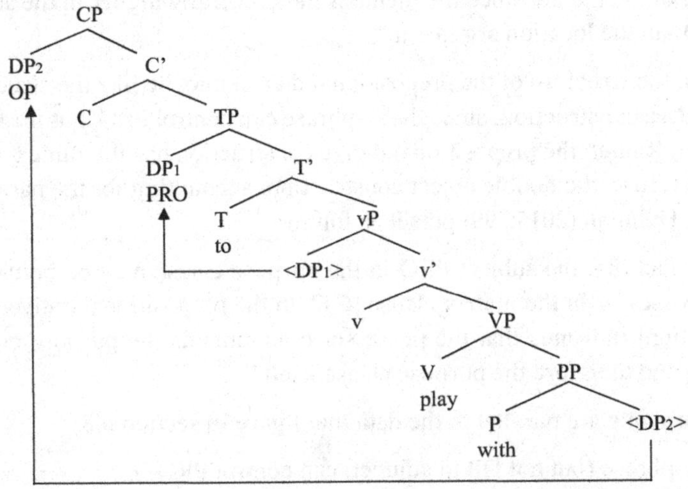

Hallman assumes that PRO is c-commanded by its antecedent (399). He claims that the purpose clause with an empty operator in Spec CP is a derived predicate (392), although he does not clearly state what the structural conditions on predication are.

The prepositional dative shows the same control possibilities as the double object construction in (29):

(32) a. Mary gave a puppy to John to play with.
b. Mary sent a manuscript to John to read.
c. Mary assigned a job to John to do.
d. Mary lent a bicycle to John to run some errands with.
e. Mary offered her apartment to John to stay in.

Locative constructions that select a DP+PP frame do not accept such purpose clauses:

(33) a. *Mary put the child$_2$ on the horse$_1$ [PRO$_1$ to carry e$_2$].
b. *Mary led the horse$_2$ to John$_1$ [PRO to feed e$_2$].
c. *Mary poured honey$_2$ on her little brother$_1$ [PRO$_1$ to lick off e$_2$].
d. *Mary immersed the cloth$_2$ in oil$_1$ [PRO$_1$ to permeate e$_2$].
e. *Mary placed the planting pots$_2$ under the tomato vines$_1$ [PRO$_1$ to grow over e$_2$].

Hallman (2015:399) explains the data as follows:

(34) "Binding of PRO in the purpose clause by the location argument in locative constructions is impossible . . . That argument does not c-command the PRO subject of the purpose clause when the purpose clause is predicated of the theme, since the theme is hierarchically higher in the structure than the location argument."

But then the structure of the prepositional data cannot be like the structure of the locative construction, since the *to*-phrase can control PRO, but the locative cannot. Rather, the prepositional dative construction has the same underlying structure as the double object construction, accounting for the parallels in control. Hallman (2015:399) puts it as follows:

(35) "The fact that the subject PRO in the purpose clause may be bound by the possessor in the matrix clause [C.C. in the prepositional dative construction] indicates that the possessor c-commands the purpose clause PRO, and therefore the purpose clause itself."

Hallman's data are parallel to the data that I gave in section 6.8:

(36) a. *by*-phrase (but not DP in adjunct) can control PRO.
b. *to*-phrase (but not DP in locative phrase) can control PRO.

9.6 Conclusion

In this chapter, I have argued that the dative alternation should be given an analysis parallel to that of the passive construction. I started by outlining five parallels between the passive and the dative alternation. Then I showed how the dative alternation gives rise to asymmetries that are only explicable if the theme moves over the goal in the prepositional dative construction.

Given this background, I gave an analysis of the dative alternation parallel to that of the passive. In the prepositional dative construction, a KP is externally merged into Spec ApplP, and then the VP moves over Spec ApplP into the specifier of an inner Voice head, smuggling the theme over the goal.

Lastly, I showed how my analysis can account for Hallman's (2015) data concerning control of PRO in purpose clauses in the dative alternation versus locatives.

The c-command asymmetries and Hallman's data provide empirical support for the analysis of the dative alternation in this chapter, which rests squarely on the AC/TC of the Merged-based approach to argument structure.

10 On the Tension with Formal Semantics

In this chapter, I will present several recent proposals about argument structure involving various powerful mechanisms of formal semantics (Heim and Kratzer 1998; Pylkkänen 2008a; Jacobson 2014; Myler and Mali 2021). In each case, I argue that the analyses are inconsistent with the Merge-based approach to argument structure. I also briefly consider the place of UTAH (Uniformity of Theta-Assignment Hypothesis) in syntactic theory, arguing that UTAH is not a principle of UG.

10.1 Heim and Kratzer 1998

As noted in the introduction, there are people who deny the existence of the Theta-Criterion. For example, Bruening (2013:23) gives the following statement:

(1) "Because there are no syntactic thematic roles in this system, there is also no θ-Criterion. Elements will either combine semantically, or they will not. If a head is a function that calls for an argument and an argument of the appropriate type combines with it, the semantics will be well-formed. If a predicate calls for an argument and no argument combines with it, it will be ill-formed. If there is an argument that does not serve as the argument of any predicate in the semantics, the result will also be ill-formed. All the work of the θ-Criterion is done by the semantics."

A similar sentiment can be found in Myler and Mali (2021:3):

(2) "Also, the Theta Criterion has no status in this conception: all that is required is that the structure compose successfully in the semantics (Full Interpretation; see also Baker 1997:121–122, Heim and Kratzer 1998:53–58)."

The issue of the Theta-Criterion and formal semantics was first discussed in Heim and Kratzer (1998:51). I give the extended quote below:

(3) "Suppose we have a predicate α with one θ-role to assign. In our terms, suppose that ⟦α⟧ is of the type <e,t>. According to the θ-Criterion, α must appear in the vicinity of something that receives its θ-role. That means α has to have a sister node with a meaning of type e. According to our Interpretability principle, on the other hand, a sister node of type e is not strictly required. It would provide one suitable environment for α, but not the only kind. Imagine instead that α has a sister node whose meaning is *a function with domain* $D_{<e,t>}$. (For instance, it might be of type <<e,t>, e>.) In that case, the next higher node could be interpreted as applying this sister's meaning to ⟦α⟧. So we could have an interpretable structure which does not contain an argument for α! α would not be assigning its θ-role to any phrase, in violation of the θ-Criterion. Yet Interpretability would be fulfilled, in virtue of α being a suitable argument for its sister node."

In this paragraph, they are explicitly arguing against the Theta-Criterion in favor of a weaker Principle of Interpretability, which is stated below (Heim and Kratzer 1998:49):

(4) Principle of Interpretability
All nodes in a phrase structure tree must be in the domain of the interpretation function ⟦ ⟧.

Basically, the interpretation function divides into several cases depending on the structure involved: terminal node, nonbranching node, function application. What the Principle of Interpretability says is that all nodes must fall under one of these cases.

Crucially, Heim and Kratzer (1998:53) note that whether or not the Theta-Criterion exists is an empirical issue: "These two arguments against the θ-criterion are not beyond question, of course. They are only as good as the syntactic and semantic analyses we have sketched."

Heim and Kratzer (1998:51–53) present two empirical arguments against the Theta-Criterion. I discuss these examples at length to bring out the relevant issues. The first issue concerns nouns as predicates:

(5) "In the following chapter, we will propose that common nouns like 'barn' are 1-place predicates (type <e,t>). In other words, they have a θ-role to assign, and thus the θ-Criterion requires the presence of an argument. In certain examples (predicative uses), this is unproblematic:

(6) This is a barn.
The required argument here is the subject NP 'this'. (6) is true if and only if the object referred to by 'this' has the property of being a barn. But consider the following sentence:

(7) The barn burned down.

(7) contains no phrase that receives the θ-role of 'barn'. It thus seems to violate the θ-Criterion. Yet it is perfectly fine, and we will see below how it can be interpreted by assigning 'the' a meaning of type <<e,t>, e> suitable to take ⟦barn⟧ as an argument. So this is the sort of case that we have been looking for. The Interpretability Principle and the θ-Criterion make different predictions here, and if the analysis we will give for (7) is on the right track, then the empirical facts favor the former."

From the point of view of the Theta-Criterion, we have three choices here: (a) The Theta-Criterion is wrong and should be abandoned in favor of weaker principles like the Interpretability Principle. (b) The Theta-Criterion is right, but somehow it does not apply to *barn*. That is, somehow *barn* does not require a syntactically present argument as its sister in the expression *the barn*. (c) The Theta-Criterion is right, but the analysis of the *barn* in the quote is wrong and there is a syntactically represented argument of *barn* in sentences such as "The barn burned down."

Curiously, Heim and Kratzer choose option (c) later on in their book. Based on issues having to do with the interpretation of quantifier phrases internal to DPs, they state (pg. 229): "Once we entertain a subject position not only in VP but also in PP, it is natural to do the same for the remaining categories that were traditionally analyzed as 1-place predicates: namely, APs and NPs."

Consider the following example:

(6) No owner of an expresso machine drinks tea.

The question is how to interpret the quantifier phrase *an espresso machine*, which takes scope internal to the subject DP. They propose the following structure:

(7) $[_{NP}$ PRO $[_{N'}$ owner $[_{PP}$ of an espresso machine]]]

In this structure, the whole NP is of type t, and so the DP *an espresso machine* can undergo QR (quantifier raising) and adjoin to it.

But once one allows this kind of syntactic structure for *owner of an expresso machine*, it is unclear what would block it for *barn* in (5). In other words, I propose *the barn* has the following structure consistent with the Theta-Criterion (for a similar conclusion, see Koopman 2003, 2005):

(8) $[_{DP}$ the $[_{NP}$ ec barn]] (ec = empty category)

Whether ec should be the same as pro, PRO or a copy of some moved element is unclear. But I assume that Spec NP is a theta-position. And so, by the Theta-Criterion, the theta-position associated with *barn* is filled in (8).

The second argument in Heim and Kratzer 1998 is based on VP coordination, which they represent as follows (I number the VPs for exposition purposes):

(9) (=(8) in Heim and Kratzer 1998:52)

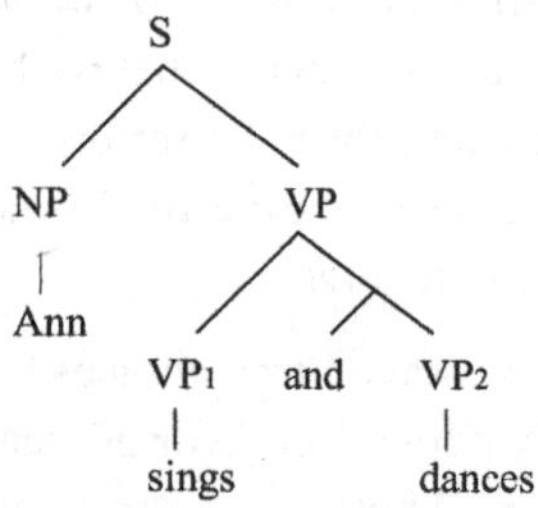

Heim and Kratzer (1998:52) state the following: "What interests us here is that this is another interpretable structure which seems to violate the θ-Criterion, in that there are not enough arguments to go around for all the θ-roles that need to be assigned in (8). 'Sing' and 'dance' each have a θ-role to assign, but only one potential argument (the NP 'Ann') is present. Once more, we tentatively conclude that the weaker requirements imposed by our Interpretability Principle make the better empirical predictions."

But clearly (8) is not a well-formed syntactic structure, since it does not comply with the VP internal subject hypothesis (discussed in Heim and Kratzer, section 8.4). Suppose that the subject *Ann* raises by ATB (across-the-board) movement from Spec VP_1 and Spec VP_2 to Spec TP. The structure is illustrated below:

(10) [$_{S}$ Ann [$_{VP}$ [$_{VP}$ <Ann> sings] and [$_{VP}$ <Ann> dances]]]

Consider the resulting structure from the standpoint of the Theta-Criterion, repeated below (see chapter 1 for discussion of different versions of the Theta-Criterion):

(11) Theta-Criterion
Each argument α appears in a chain containing a unique visible theta-position P, and each theta-position P is visible in a chain containing a unique argument α.
(Chomsky 1986:97)

An important issue is how to interpret the notion of chain formed by ATB movement. Is there one chain or are there two chains? Let us assume for the sake of argument that there are two chains (understood as a sequence of positions; see Collins and Stabler 2016 for a formalization of the notion of chain):

(12) a. <Spec TP, Spec VP_1>
b. <Spec TP, Spec VP_2>

As for the first half of the Theta-Criterion, *Ann* is in a chain containing a unique theta-position (e.g., chain (12a)). As for the second half of the Theta-Criterion, each theta-position P (Spec VP_1 and Spec VP_2) is visible in a chain containing a unique argument α, that is, *Ann*.

In summary, neither of Heim and Kratzer's arguments against the Theta-Criterion is particularly compelling. For the argument based on nouns like *barn*, they change their analysis later in the book. For the argument based on VP coordination, they propose an arguably erroneous syntax for VPs (without the VP internal subject hypothesis) to make their point.

10.2 Jacobson 2014

The function composition and type-shifting mechanisms of Jacobson (2014) allow violations of the Theta-Criterion. In a discussion of relative clauses, Jacobson (2014:229) notes:

(13) "The Direct Compositional version sketched here—which makes no use of traces and no use of indices or assignments—ends up with the same result. Notice that the function composing the lifted (GQ) ⟦Martha⟧ with ⟦refinish⟧ directly results in an expression *Martha refinished* which denotes the set of things that Martha refinished . . . There is no need to assume *refinish* combines in the syntax with an actual NP (such as a trace) and no reason to assume ⟦refinish⟧—of type <e,<e,t>>—needs to actually find an argument of type e to combine with. Indeed, it does not find such an argument, but is composed with the GQ subject."

The combination of ⟦Martha⟧ with ⟦refinish⟧ is made possible by the function composition rules, summarized as follows (see Jacobson 2014:221–222):

(14) "Take a function f from A to B and a function g from B to C (any two of those sets could happen to be the same). Then the two functions can be composed into a new function notated as g∘f which is a function from A to C, where for any x in A, g∘f(x) = g(f(x))."

Jacobson's approach to argument structure is not consistent with the Merge-based approach. For Jacobson, *refinish* is of type <e,<e,t>>, but does not combine with an internal argument in the relative clause. The claim that "There is no need to assume *refinish* combines in the syntax with an actual NP (such as a trace)" contradicts the Theta-Criterion, which imposes exactly such a requirement.

Empirically, it looks like Jacobson is allowing dependencies to be formed using the powerful devices of formal semantics and making syntactic movement unnecessary (internal Merge). It is unclear how under this approach traditional arguments for movement (such as island effects, or morphological reflexes of movement) would be accounted for (see Jacobson 2014:232 for a short remark on island constraints). This issue was recognized by Keine and Bhatt (2016:1467, fn. 16), in a paper otherwise devoted to arguing for function composition as a semantic rule of interpretation: "Function composition is a powerful device. If left unrestricted, it would allow for the formation of syntactic dependencies across island boundaries."

Another line of investigation would be to probe whether there are tests for a syntactically projected direct object in the relative clause *Martha refinished.* There are a very large number of such diagnostics (e.g., anaphora, secondary predicates, control, as well as others discussed in chapters 2,3,4,5 and 6). Jacobson's analysis makes the counterintuitive prediction that all of these will come up negative when looking at the direct object position of *Martha refinished.* Or alternatively, if the tests came up positive, it would need to be argued that all of these tests have to be recast semantically (that is, not diagnosing a syntactically projected direct object, but rather a variable in the semantic value of the relative clause).

For example, consider the relative clause construction *the fish that Martha ate.* We can ask whether or not there is a syntactically projected direct object. But a secondary predicate can appear there: *the fish that Martha ate raw.* On the assumption that a secondary predicate requires a syntactically projected DP to be predicated of (see chapter 3), the fact that a depictive secondary predicate can be predicated of the missing object argues against Jacobson's claim that "There is no need to assume *refinish* combines in the syntax with an actual NP (such as a trace)." Of course, Jacobson could try to give a purely semantic theory of the licensing of secondary predicates, but then similar semantic theories would have to be given for reflexive binding and control as well.

10.3 Pylkkänen 2008a

Pylkkänen (2008a) gives arguments for distinguishing high versus low applicatives. High applicatives involve an applicative head merged with VP. Low applicatives involve the verb merging with the ApplP. I will not review her arguments for this distinction here (for some discussion see chapter 9). Nor will I discuss the structure of high applicatives. The structure of a low applicative (as in English double object constructions) is given below:

(15) Structure of Low Applicative

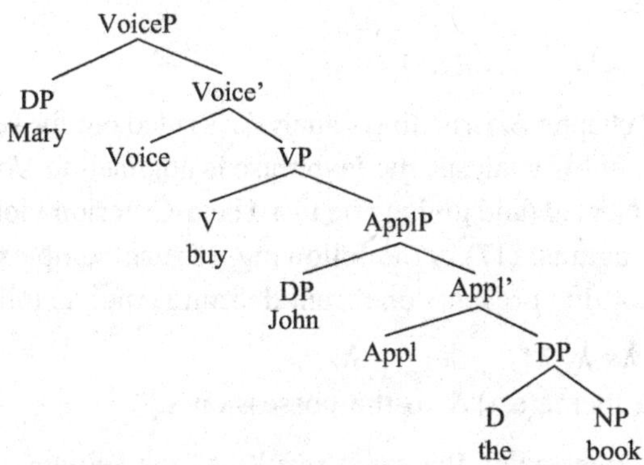

The issue that this tree raises is how to interpret the verb *buy*, for which Pylkkänen (2008a:18) gives the following semantic values:

(16) a. ⟦Voice⟧ = $\lambda x.\lambda e.\text{agent}(e,x)$
  b. ⟦buy⟧ = $\lambda x.\lambda e.\text{buying}(e)\ \&\ \text{theme}(e,x)$

The problem is that the sister of *buy* in (15) is not *the book*, but rather the whole ApplP. Pylkkänen (2008a:17–18) resolves this issue by giving Appl the following semantic value:

(17) ⟦Appl⟧ = $\lambda x.\lambda y.\lambda f_{<e,st>}.\lambda e.f(e,x)\ \&\ \text{theme}(e,x)\ \&\ \text{to-the-possession}(x,y)$

Pylkkänen (2008a:17–18) justifies this analysis as follows: "The structure in (14a) [C.C. (15) above] can, however, be maintained by treating low Appl as a higher-order predicate, so that ApplP actually ends up taking the verb as its argument, rather than vice versa. This may seem counterintuitive, but bear in mind that this is in fact how Generalized Quantifier Theory associates quantifier phrases with their verbs, as well."

Given these semantic values, we have the following semantic value for VP:

(18) ⟦VP⟧ = $\lambda e.\text{buying}(e)\ \&\ \text{theme}(e,\text{the book})\ \&\ \text{to-the-possession}(\text{the book},\text{John})$

But note that the predicate *buy* does not combine with its DP argument by Merge, but rather combines with ApplP (the semantic value of *buy* and the semantic value of the theme DP are combined indirectly), and so this is a violation of the Merged-based theory of argument structure. More concretely, the complement position of *buy* is a theta-position, but it is not filled by an argument in (15).

Pylkkänen's (2008a) approach to the semantic value of ApplP is similar to Bruening's (2013:25) approach to the semantic value of *by* (see chapter 6). Both *by* and Appl take functions as arguments, which are then applied to arguments:

(19) ⟦by⟧ = $\lambda x \lambda f_{<e,st>} \lambda e.f(e,x)$

As we discussed in chapter 6, Bruening's analysis is ruled out for very similar reasons. In particular, in his analysis, the *by*-phrase is adjoined to VoiceP, leaving Spec VoiceP unprojected (and giving rise to a Theta-Criterion violation).

Another argument against (17) is the following. If such complex semantic values are allowed, nothing prevents one from defining Appl as follows:

(20) ⟦Appl⟧ = $\lambda x.\lambda y.\lambda f_{<e,st>}.\lambda g_{<e,st>}.\lambda z.\lambda e.$
g(e,z) & f(e,x) & theme(e,x) & to-the-possession(x,y)

Such a semantic value yields the same results as the semantic value for Appl that Pylkkänen gave, λg introduces the agent function (found in Voice), and λz introduces the agent. But given (20), it is possible to define numerous other semantic values that do not seem to exist in the world's languages:

(21) ⟦Appl⟧ = $\lambda x.\lambda y.\lambda f_{<e,st>}.\lambda g_{<e,st>}.\lambda z.\lambda e.$
g(e,z) & f(e,x) & theme(e,x) & to-the-possession(z,y)

The difference between (20) and (21) is in the variables of the to-the-possession function. In (20), the variables are (x,y), but in (21) the variables are (z,y). This has the effect of making the agent be possessed by the goal.

Applied to (15), this yields the following interpretation:

(22) Mary bought the book and Mary is to-the-possession of John.

In fact, one can also get a kind of inverse reading:

(23) ⟦Appl⟧ = $\lambda x.\lambda y.\lambda f_{<e,st>}.\lambda g_{<e,st>}.\lambda z.\lambda e.$
g(e,y) & f(e,x) & theme(e,x) & to-the-possession(x,z)

In this semantic value, both the variables of the function g and the to-the-possession function change. The effect is that the subject comes to possess the theme, and the agent is projected as the indirect object (first object). Applied to (15), this yields the inverse interpretation, where *John* is the agent:

(24) John bought Mary the book.

In fact, adopting the kind of technology that Pylkkänen uses implies that there are no constraints at all on how arguments are projected into the syntax. The complex semantic values (involving functions applying to functions) can yield any hierarchical order of the arguments. Clearly, such powerful devices raise the issue of restrictiveness, and must be either completely eliminated or constrained in some manner.

10.4 Myler and Mali 2021

Myler and Mali (2021) present an analysis of isiXhosa causatives that aims to analyze an alternation in the expression of the causee: the causee is either an unmarked DP or an instrumental DP (examples are from Myler and Mali 2021:8–9).

(25) a. uSarah w-ong-is-e uDallas abantwana.
1Sarah 1SBJ-look.after-CAUS-PRF 1Dallas 2children
'Sarah made/helped Dallas look after the children.'
b. uSarah w-ong-is-e abantwana ngo-Dallas.
1Sarah 1SBJ-look.after-CAUS-PRF 2children INS-1Dallas
'Sarah made Dallas look after the children.'

In (25a), there is both a causative and a sociative (helping) interpretation, whereas in (25b) there is only a causative interpretation. In other words, the sociative interpretation is not possible with instrumental causees. Myler and Mali attempt to explain both the alternation between unmarked and instrumental causees, and the fact that only unmarked causees can have the sociative interpretation.

According to Myler and Mali, external arguments can be introduced (externally merged) in three completely different positions: Spec VoiceP (matrix clauses), Spec CauseP (causee in causative) and adjoined to vP (instrumental cause in causative). Myler and Mali claim that this analysis "adds to the growing body of evidence that the same thematic roles are not always assigned in the same syntactic positions." In other words, Myler and Mali claim to have found a counterexample to UTAH. They put the general issue as follows (pg. 7, fn. 4): "It follows as a consequence of this approach to the nature of thematic roles that the Uniformity-of-Theta-Assignment Hypothesis (Baker 1988:46) is false, although linking regularities are still predicted for the general case, because the extended verb phrase is rigidly structured and is interpreted compositionally."

When causees are not introduced in Spec VoiceP, Myler and Mali propose a rule of coercion that inserts the thematic role predicate into vP at LF:

(26) "vP Coercion
$\lambda e_S.[P(e) \ldots] \Rightarrow \lambda x_e.\lambda e_S.[P(e) \wedge \theta_{Ex}(e,x) \ldots]$

where θ_{Ex} is a thematic role drawn from the set of roles that can be introduced by Voice and vP denotes an eventuality compatible with such a role."

Myler and Mali (2021:27) specify the derivational timing of the vP coercion as follows: "We will assume that vP Coercion applies to the denotation of vP when it is selected by Cause whenever failure to do so would result in the cause being unable to be integrated into the composition." From this, it can be seen that vP coercion modifies a semantic value by adding in a predicate θ_{Ex}(e,x).

Such an operation raises immediate and serious questions of restrictiveness. The possibility of coercion rules inserting semantic material into semantic values in a derivation is a powerful device, raising at least the following questions:

(27) a. Should rules that directly manipulate semantic values be allowed in UG?
b. What are the possible coercion rules made available by UG?
c. What kinds of semantic values can be inserted?
d. What kinds of semantic values can be inserted into?
e. What kinds of conditions can coercion rules have on them (e.g., in (26) "can be introduced by Voice")?

Myler and Mali (2021) do not comment on any of these restrictiveness issues in their paper.

vP coercion is incompatible with the spirit of the Merge-based theory of argument structure: the only way to build argument structure is by Merge. The predicate θ_{Ex}(e,x), which is normally introduced by Voice, is now being directly inserted (without Merge) into the semantic value of little v during the derivation. A derivation compliant with the Merge-based approach would be to merge a head (such as Voice) bearing θ_{Ex}(e,x) as part of its semantic value into the syntactic structure.

The alternation between an unmarked cause and an instrumental cause is reminiscent of the active-passive alternation in English, where in the passive the external argument appears in a *by*-phrase. Myler and Mali (2021:8, fn. 7) directly address this parallel as follows:

(28) "Another approach to such alternations is the smuggling approach, which Collins 2005 applies to passives in English and Kayne 2004 applies to transitive causes in Romance. The main reason we do not adopt such an approach to the instrumental-causee construction here is that it will not explain the disappearance of the sociative reading in this construction (see section 5.2), since the starting assumption of such analyses is that the argument in both alternants starts off in the same structural position and bears the same thematic role."

I cannot offer an alternative analysis of the interesting Zulu facts here. But a possible avenue to explore is that the difference between the causative with and without the sociative interpretation is similar to a difference between control and raising-to-object constructions in English. Myler and Mali (2021:26) note that "the sociative reading does not appear to be allowed with inanimate causees in isiXhosa (whereas the plain causative reading of the unmarked cause is)." They further note that idioms are possible in causatives, but not with the sociative interpretation (38). These distinctions recall the distinction between raising to object and object control in English:

(29) a. John expected it to rain. (raising to object)
b. *John persuaded it to rain. (object control)

(30) a. John expected the shit to hit the fan. (raising to object)
b. *John persuaded the shit to hit the fan. (object control)

In (29a), *expect* is a raising-to-object verb, and in (29b) *persuade* is an object control verb. Suppose the causative/sociative distinction worked in a similar manner. In the causative interpretation, the causative construction is a case of raising to object. In the sociative interpretation, the causative construction is a case of object control. In this analysis (which is different from Myler and Mali's), it is unsurprising that the instrumental marked *causee* cannot take a sociative interpretation: if the causee is an instrument, it is then excluded from being a controller in an object control construction. I am unable to develop these ideas any further here.

10.5 Whither UTAH?

In the discussions in chapters 1–9, no reference was made to UTAH in constraining the possibilities of projecting the external argument in the passive. Rather, all the work was done by the AC/TC. This suggests the possibility that UTAH could be eliminated altogether and reduced to other principles. UTAH is repeated below (see Baker 1988):

(31) The Uniformity of Theta Assignment Hypothesis (UTAH)
Identical thematic relationships between items are represented by identical structural relationships between those items at the level of D-structure.

There are many reasons why UTAH does not fit easily into minimalist syntax (see Collins 2005a:83). First, it explicitly invokes D-structure, and there is no such level of representation in minimalist syntax. Second, it references thematic relationships, raising the tricky question of how they are differentiated. Third, (31) references "items" (meaning lexical items), but syntactic representations have become much more ramified in the last thirty years, including VP shells of various kinds. It is not clear how (31) is meant to apply to these more complex structures. Lastly, it was never exactly clear how UTAH applied to the external argument in the passive, which is the main topic of discussion of this monograph.

As Baker (1997:127, fn. 127) notes: "Larson correctly points out that Baker (1988) does not adopt the strictest imaginable sense of UTAH in his analysis of the passive. Rather, Baker claimed that the agent role was assigned to the specifier of IP in normal active sentences, but to the head of I containing the morpheme -EN in corresponding passive sentences. These are not identical structural relationships, but they were held to be equivalent positions inasmuch as both are 'maximally external' to the VP (outside VP but inside the next highest maximal projection)." This quote raises the vexing question of what count as equivalent positions. The informal description "outside VP" does little to narrow down the possibilities.

In light of these considerations, I propose that UTAH is not a principle of UG, and I speculate that UTAH-like effects are the result of the following:

(32) a. the universal existence of various VP shells such as vP and ApplP
  b. a universal hierarchical order of such shells (vP > ApplP > VP)
  c. the AC/TC

This kind of analysis has already been proposed in Baker 1997:125–126:

(33) "The basic function of the original UTAH was to regulate where the various arguments of a predicate are expressed. This is a nontrivial task if predicates have multiple arguments of the same type, because one must keep track of which NP is associated with which argument position. If, however, syntactic structure is built from the lexical decomposition of a verb, such that each predicate in the decomposition takes a single NP argument, the UTAH becomes trivial. All that remains is a simple convention that an argument must be in a local configuration with its argument-taker; the rest follows from compositional semantics."

Baker states: "All that remains is a simple convention that an argument must be in a local configuration with its argument taker." This convention is a weaker version of the Argument Criterion/Theta-Criterion in chapter 1.

One problem with this deconstruction of UTAH is that there must be some way to restrict the structural relations between the heads in the verbal extended projection. For example, assuming v, Appl, and V as the relevant heads, what determines that (a) is projected and not (b)?

(34) a. $[_{vP}$ DP $[_{v'}$ v $[_{ApplP}$ DP $[_{Appl'}$ Appl VP]]]]
  b. $[_{ApplP}$ DP $[_{Appl'}$ Appl $[_{vP}$ DP $[_{v'}$ v VP]]]]

Of course, one can stipulate that v takes ApplP as a complement, and not vice versa, but such a stipulation lacks restrictiveness. What would prevent another language from having the opposite stipulation where Appl selects vP? Putting aside the lexical verb, if there are *n* argument-introducing heads, there will be *n*! (*n* factorial) possible orders of those heads. In the general case, only one of them will be grammatical. This is the ordering/selection problem that is familiar from works on the cartography of the left periphery.

A related hierarchy problem is the following: Why couldn't there be two light verbs v_1 and v_2, each of which introduces agents, but which have a different place in the hierarchy of light verbs? Some sort of nonsynonymy principle may be needed to block this sort of possibility. In addition, the way that the semantic properties of an argument-introducing head determine its syntactic position needs to be better understood.

At the end of the quote, Baker adds "the rest follows from compositional semantics." But if I am right, nothing about where arguments are projected in a syntactic structure really follows from the mechanisms of formal semantics (see sections 10.1–10.4).

In spite of these issues, I will assume that UTAH can be eliminated, reduced to the principles in (32).

10.6 What Is the Problem with Formal Semantics?

The discussion above raises the question of where formal semantics goes wrong as a theory of argument structure. The basic problem is that formal semantics (as presented in standard textbooks) is far too unrestricted to serve as theory of anything, even natural language semantics. As Chomsky notes (quoted in Collins 2021:5):

(35) "Work in formal semantics has been some of the most exciting parts of the field in recent years, but it hasn't been treated with the kind of critical analysis that other parts of syntax (including generative phonology) have been within generative grammar since its origins. Questions about explanatory power, simplicity, learnability, generality, evolvability, and so. More as a descriptive technology. That raises questions."

Formal semantics of the kind discussed in Heim and Kratzer 1998 employs powerful and unrestricted mechanisms of semantic composition based on the lambda calculus. And even though the lambda calculus is used to formulate semantic values in Heim and Kratzer 1998, it is itself a very powerful syntactic system. For example, single morphemes (lexical items) can be of type <e>, <e,e>, <e,t>, <<e,t>, t> or any of an unlimited number of other alternative types, including functions of functions, functions of functions of functions, functions of functions of functions of functions, and so on (see Heim and Kratzer 1998:28).

In addition to the unlimited number of lexical types, there is also the unrestricted mechanism of type-shifting that makes it so that a single syntactic object can have many different alternative types. Such rules are defined in Heim and Kratzer 1998:68 as follows "general recipes that map arbitrary denotations of the basic type to secondary denotations of the appropriate non-basic type. Rules of this kind are called 'type-shifting rules'." See Pylkkänen 2008b for references and for an overview of accounting for syntax-semantics mismatches in terms of type-shifting.

Lastly, it is possible to define powerful interpretational rules (e.g., function composition) in such a framework (see the discussion of Jacobson above). As noted there, function composition gives rise to the possibility of creating dependencies between syntactic positions without invoking internal Merge.

The relevant properties are summarized here:

(36) a. the ability to define lexical items of arbitrary semantic complexity (and arbitrary complex types)
b. the ability to formulate rules (such as type-shifting and coercion) that modify semantic values
c. the ability to define different kinds of interpretation rules (e.g., function composition)

Such powerful mechanisms present learnability issues for a child learning a language. How is the child supposed to assign semantic values to X and Y in a simple phrase like [X Y]? Of course, it might be possible to make semantic theory more restrictive by either eliminating some of these options or limiting them in some way. I am not aware of any systematic discussion of this nature.

A theory including (36) is essentially a descriptive framework for semantic analysis, and not a restrictive theory in the standard sense of *restrictive* used for syntactic theory.

(37) "The theory of UG must meet two obvious conditions. On the one hand, it must be compatible with the diversity of existing (indeed, possible) grammars. At the same time, UG must be sufficiently constrained and restrictive in the options it permits so as to account for the fact that each of these grammars develops in the mind on the basis of quite limited evidence. In many cases that have been carefully studied in recent work, it is a near certainty that fundamental properties of the attained grammars are radically underdetermined by evidence available to the language learner and must therefore be attributed to UG itself."
(Chomsky 1981:5)

The Merge-based theory of argument structure is not, in principle, incompatible with formal semantics of the kind presented in Heim and Kratzer 1998. That is, it is possible to interpret the syntactic structures generated by the theory presented in this monograph (see Kratzer 1996 for some suggestions). But the semantic rules of interpretation should be tightly constrained by the syntactic structures.

To move toward this goal, consider the following principle (see also the related discussion at the end of chapter 8):

(38) Minimize Semantic Values
  a. Minimize the number of semantic arguments (lambda expressions) of the semantic value of a morpheme. Equivalently, minimize the semantic type of a morpheme.
  b. The number of semantic arguments (lambda expressions) of the semantic value of a morpheme cannot exceed three (one for the head, specifier, and complement of the projection of the morpheme).

The purpose of (38a) is to rule out overly complex semantic values such as the one that permits inversion in (23) above (partly addressing (36a)). The problem with the constraint is that it seems to involve a comparison of two structures (one structure involving one set of morphemes with their semantic values versus another structure involving a different set of morphemes). A simpler way to limit semantic complexity might be to let it be directly constrained by syntax, as in (38b). A crude first-pass attempt would be that the number of lambda expressions of a morpheme cannot exceed three (one for the head, specifier, and complement of a projection). This constraint also rules out (23).

The principle in (38) goes with the Principle of Decompositionality of chapter 8 in limiting the power of formal semantics, thereby shifting the work to Merge and the syntactic component.

10.7 Conclusion

In this chapter, I have considered a number of issues that arise when we think about argument structure in relation to theories of formal semantics. I have argued that it is not possible to eliminate the Theta-Criterion in favor of interpretability. I have discussed a few concrete proposals, including Heim and Kratzer 1998, Jacobson 2014, Pylkkänen 2008a, and Myler and Mali 2021. I have shown how these approaches are all inconsistent with the Merge-based theory of argument structure. On the basis of these examples, I have tried to clarify what, exactly, it is about formal semantics that makes it unsuitable as a theory of argument structure.

11 Conclusion

The goal of this monograph is to argue for a theory of argument structure based on the syntactic operation Merge.

Although the monograph is titled *Principles of Argument Structure*, I discuss only a very few topics in depth, focusing on the implicit argument in the passive, implicit arguments more generally, *by*-phrases and the dative alternation. For the following topics, I either did not discuss them, or only mentioned them in passing: idiom chunks, expletives, unaccusatives, unergatives, middles (see Gotah 2022), psych verbs, syntactic causatives (e.g., *faire à* versus *faire par*), morphological causatives (e.g., in Bantu), object control versus raising to object, particle verbs, resultative secondary predicates, the spray-load alternation, verbal possession (e.g., *have* versus *be*), conflation (in the Hale and Keyser 1993 sense), action nominalizations (e.g., process versus result interpretations; see Grimshaw 1990), agent nominalizations (on a strongly Merge-based theory, see Collins 2006; Fábregas 2012; Ntelitheos 2012; Gotah and Lee 2022), nominal compounds, serial verb constructions (e.g., in Ewe), locative versus directional uses of PPs (see Collins 2007) and *-able* constructions (see Ishizuka and Koopman 2014).

For each such phenomenon, one could try to formulate a Merge-based analysis within the restrictive framework outlined in this monograph. There are other topics that I have discussed briefly but that still need much more work (e.g., the implicit arguments with evaluative adjectives, middles, and nominalizations; see chapter 4).

In this chapter, I will summarize the principles of argument structure proposed in the monograph and the empirical consequences of those principles.

11.1 Summary

The principles of argument structure are meant to hold for any system that uses a dedicated set of verbal heads to introduce arguments (so-called "argument-introducing heads"). Even though the system of Kratzer (1996) (and similarly Pylkkänen 2008a) differs greatly from that of Ramchand (2008), both systems would fall under these principles.

The most important principle is the Argument Criterion:

(1) Argument Criterion
  a. Each argument is introduced by a single argument-introducing head.
  b. Each argument-introducing head introduces a single argument.

In chapter 1, I pointed out that the Argument Criterion is largely equivalent to the following version of the Theta-Criterion (Chomsky 1986:97):

(2) Theta-Criterion
  Each argument α appears in a chain containing a unique visible theta-position P, and each theta-position P is visible in a chain containing a unique argument α.

From the AC/TC, the following principle concerning implicit arguments follows:

(3) The implicit argument in the English short passive is syntactically projected.

I gave empirical support for (3) in chapters 2 and 3. Then in chapter 4, I generalized (3) to a wide variety of constructions and all languages in (4) (using the wedge argument):

(4) Implicit arguments are syntactically projected.

For cross-linguistic support for (4), see chapter 5 discussing implicit arguments in three African languages.

If implicit arguments are syntactically projected, then what are their syntactic properties? I provide a sketch of a theory in chapter 4:

(5) a. Implicit arguments are syntactically projected as pro.
  b. Implicit argument pro lacks a structural Case feature [uCase].
  c. Implicit argument pro has the same range of interpretations as other pronouns.

Although the fine details of the general theory in (4) do not follow directly from the Argument Criterion, they are consistent with it. For example, (5b) does not follow directly from (4) but is consistent with it. That raises the question of what the relation between (5) and UG is, and whether (5) allows any cross-linguistic variation. One possibility that I have not considered, but which would be consistent with AC/TC, is that some implicit arguments could be null R-expressions (the equivalent of a logical constant, instead of a logical variable). However, I adopt the strongest possible position that the theory in (5) is part of UG: the existence of a pronoun lacking [uCase] is an immediate consequence of UG allowing for pronouns defined by various sets of features.

Another direct consequence of the AC/TC is the projection of *by*-phrases in the passive:

(6) The external argument of the passive is projected in exactly the same way as the external argument of the active.

Concretely, this principle entails the following analysis of *by*-phrases:

(7) The *by*-phrase is externally merged in Spec vP (the position of the external argument).

Empirical support for this prediction was given in chapter 6 based on the binding of reflexives in both English and Greek.

I give a similar analysis of the dative alternation in chapter 9. Based on parallels with the passive, and the c-command asymmetries, I argue:

(8) The goal argument in the prepositional dative construction is projected in exactly the same way as the goal argument in the double object construction.

Concretely, this principle entails the following analysis of *to*-phrases, parallel to (7) for *by*-phrases:

(9) The *to*-phrase is externally merged in Spec ApplP (the position of goals).

(7) and (9) can be generalized in the following way:

(10) KPs are arguments (and hence obey the AC/TC).

The head of KP (e.g., passive *by*, dative *to*) is by definition semantically vacuous, and is part of the extended projection of the DP.

The last consequence of the AC/TC is the independence of voice and argument structure (discussed in chapter 8):

(11) Voice is independent of the projection of arguments.

Concretely, (11) entails the following (contra Kratzer 1996 and many others):

(12) The external argument is not externally merged in Spec VoiceP.

If (11) is correct, it has far-reaching implications for the analysis of various voice phenomena (e.g., passive, active, nonactive, middles, inverse, antipassives, *-able* constructions, various *se* constructions in Romance).

Lastly, in chapter 10, I discussed the tension between the Merge-based approach to argument structure and approaches such as that of Kratzer (1996) and Heim and Kratzer (1998) that are based on formal semantics. I noted that adopting the full strength of formal semantic frameworks such as that presented in Heim and Kratzer 1998 implies that there are no constraints at all on how arguments are projected into the syntax. The complex semantic values (involving functions applying to functions) can yield any hierarchical order of the arguments. Clearly, such powerful devices must be constrained.

In response to that tension, I proposed the following principle in chapter 8 (partly modeled on the Principle of Decompositionality of Kayne 2005:212):

(13) Principle of Semantic Decompositionality
If ⟦X⟧ = SV1(SV2) (SV1 and SV2 are semantic values)
and ⟦Y⟧ = SV1 or SV2 (where Y is a morpheme in the lexicon)
then X = [. . . Y . . .].

(13) says that if an expression is semantically complex, then it is also syntactically complex.

A different principle that also has the effect of constraining complex semantic values is given below:

(14) Minimize Semantic Values
a. Minimize the number semantic arguments (lambda expressions) of the semantic value of a morpheme. Equivalently, minimize the semantic type of a morpheme.
b. The number of semantic arguments (lambda expressions) of the semantic value of a morpheme cannot exceed three (one for the head, one for the specifier, and one for the complement of the projection of the morpheme).

The effect of these principles is to limit the semantic complexity of morphemes, forcing the need for Merge-based analyses. I have not investigated the relation between these two principles in (13) and (14). It is possible that the decomposition principle will ultimately entail the minimization principle. To the extent that semantic values are decomposed, they become less complex and the burden shifts to Merge to build up argument structure.

Here, I pull together the core principles and summarize:

(15) Merge-Based Theory of Argument Structure
a. AC/TC
b. Implicit arguments are syntactically projected.
c. KPs are arguments (and hence obey the AC/TC).
d. Voice is independent of the projection of arguments.

I have argued that (15b,c,d) are all entailed by (15a).

11.2 Parallel to Morphology as Syntax (MaS)

It is worthwhile to point out that there is a parallel between the research program outlined in this monograph and the research program outlined in Collins and Kayne 2023, "Towards a Theory of Morphology as Syntax." In that paper, Collins and Kayne discuss the relationship between syntax and morphology and ask the question: To what extent can morphological generalizations be accounted for in terms of syntactic operations and principles? The thesis they defend is this:

(16) Morphology as Syntax (MaS)
Morphological generalizations are accounted for in terms of syntactic operations and principles. There is no morphological component in UG. There are no postsyntactic morphological operations.

Similarly, in this monograph I have tried to sketch a Merge-based approach to argument structure, where the only way to build argument structure is by Merge. This means that arguments and argument-introducing heads (predicates) should be combined by Merge. There is no other way to satisfy the lexical properties of argument-introducing heads.

Whereas Collins and Kayne (2023) argue for eliminating the morphological component entirely, in this monograph I have not argued for eliminating formal semantics. Rather, I argue that generalizations concerning argument structure should be explained in terms of Merge, and not in terms of complex semantic values and complex semantic operations (see chapter 10 for an overview). For example, in the passive, the *by*-phrase is merged in Spec vP. There is no need to rely on a theory where *by* denotes a function of functions that is combined with an unsaturated VoiceP.

Restating the results of this monograph in a way maximally parallel to (16) yields the following:

(17) Merge-Based Theory of Argument Structure
Argument structure generalizations are accounted for in terms of syntactic operations and principles (in conformity with 1–14 above).

In both cases, there is a tension between syntax (Merge) and some other system. For (16) the tension is between syntax and the morphological component. For (17), the tension is between syntax and formal semantics. In both cases, I argue that the tension is theoretically resolved in favor of Merge-based approaches.

Appendix: Internet Searches as a Tool in Syntactic Research

Collins and Postal 2012, 2014 contain lots of data obtained from Internet searches. Such data are also cited extensively in chapters 2 and 3 of this monograph. In this section, I will briefly go over the methodology.

A.1 Motivation

Internet searches have turned out to be a revolutionary tool in syntactic research. There are a few reasons for this. First, if the domain you are looking at is controversial, Internet searches afford a way of finding nonelicited English examples that might help resolve the issue. For example, chapter 3 claims that secondary predicates can modify the implicit argument of the short passive. That is controversial since various authors have claimed that secondary predicates cannot do so. However, it is quite easy to find relevant examples on the Internet that I find completely acceptable.

More generally, Internet searches are a tool that can give the syntactician confidence in their claimed empirical results. Suppose that I propose a particular generalization that has not been investigated before. If I am able to easily find examples on the Internet conforming to the generalization (and crucially, I find those examples to be acceptable) then I will have increased confidence in my generalization.

Second, if you are looking at a relatively unexplored data domain, Internet searches can help to fill out the range of combinatorial possibilities. For example, in chapter two of this monograph, such searches helped me to figure out the range of possible phi-feature values of the implicit argument in the short passive. Once you have dissected the combinatorial nature of any particular problem, you can run searches on all the various possibilities, greatly expanding your knowledge of an empirical domain in a short period of time. Furthermore, tracking down and documenting the combinatorial possibilities will often lead to surprising empirical discoveries.

A.2 Searching

The basic technique is to search for phrase types that are being investigated. For example, in chapter 2, I investigate the use of Helke expressions like *on my own* in short passives. So, I would search the following, where the quotes ensure that a string, not just a set of words, is the target:

(1) Google: "was done on my own"

In this example, I included "was done" to make sure that the search includes a passive participle, not an active participle. However, I have left out the subject, because examples would be relevant no matter what their subject is. Some of the hits may be completely irrelevant so you may have to scroll through several screens to find good examples.

One of the hits of the search in (1) is:

(2) None of this was done on my own. To me success always takes collaboration.

This example is useful to my research. My hypothesis is that the implicit argument in the passive is syntactically active. (2) supports that hypothesis since the antecedent of *my* is the implicit argument (the doer). (2) is also helpful because the second sentence clarifies the meaning of the first.

Follow-up searches based on (1) can be done, yielding further information. For example, to investigate the phi-features of the implicit argument, *my* in (1) can be replaced by a whole range of possessive pronouns: *your, his, her, our, their.* Alternatively, the main verb could be changed from *done* to *written, created,* or *built.* Lastly, to vary the syntactic context, the copula could be changed from *was* to *were, is, are, to be, will be,* or *been.* Just these choices would yield $5 \times 3 \times 6 = 90$ additional searches, any of which could yield interesting example sentences and interesting follow-up questions.

A.3 Verify with Target

I use the Internet as a tool for looking into the properties of a particular dialect, usually my own I-language (the target of investigation). In doing Internet searches, I am looking for data that I myself find acceptable. For example, after doing the search in (1), I found (2). Crucially, (2) is acceptable for me as a native speaker of English. If I find a relevant sentence and I judge it as acceptable, then I save it to a list for future use in a paper or book. If I judge the sentence as unacceptable, I put it aside for further consideration (see below).

Of course, I could even do further verification of the sentence with other people. It is common to do an informal judgment survey with a small group of speakers to see what kind of variation there is. But the crucial point of this section is that any examples found on the Internet need to be verified with at least one native speaker.

Suppose that you do a search and come across a sentence S that you find unacceptable. Furthermore, S is relevant to the theoretical issues you are looking into. What then? There are two routes to take at this point. First, you can do further searches to make sure that S was not just an error of some kind. If there are many such examples, and they look like they were produced by native speakers of English, then that is evidence that S is acceptable for some native speakers. Second, you can try to find a native speaker of the dialect in question. Any serious investigation of S will have to involve native speakers who find S acceptable.

A.4 Controls

Of course, there is no guarantee that the data on the Internet will be of high quality for syntactic research. It is completely uncontrolled, so caution needs to be exercised. I propose the following guidelines:

(a) Compare the string searched to actual hits. For example, for (1) above, the hits included the example "Today's work *was done on my own* fingernails." Although the hit contains the search string, it is not the kind of example I am interested in (because it does not use the expression *on my own*).

(b) Immediately after finding an example in the search result list, you should check to see that the URL is active and that the sentence actually appears on the accompanying website.

(c) Examine the sentence to make sure that it does not represent any of the following: (i) a clear grammatical error, (ii) humorous writing (which plays with language), (iii) poetic license (again playing with language), (iv) an AI-generated text (not produced by a human), or (iv) a Google translation (again not produced by a human). Examples of this sort should be excluded from further consideration.

(d) A related concern is whether the sentence is being used as an example in a linguistics paper published online. If so, it might be elicited data constructed by a linguist, and not nonelicted Internet data.

(e) While at the website, you can try to see if there is anything that might indicate that the example was created by non-native speakers of English. If there are red flags, you should discard the example. For example, does the text on the website generally show signs of being written by a non-native speaker?

(f) Look at the context of the example, in the preceding and following text. Such context might shed light on the interpretation and might be useful to include in your work. For example, in (2), the second sentence explains the first sentence.

A.5 Number of Hits

The number of hits that result from a particular search can be significant. If I search for S and I find scores of high-quality hits (satisfying all the controls above), that is significant. Furthermore, if I search for S and do not find any hits (or only one or two suspicious hits), that is also significant. But other than this basic dichotomy (many versus zero/few), it is not recommended to rely on actual counts. For example, what would I make of the fact that when I search for Sl I find 67 hits, but when I search for S2 I find 112 hits?

Here is the way we put such frequency results in Collins and Postal 2012:

(pg. 1) "And there are many instances of English speakers referring to themselves as *yours truly.*"

(pg. 18) "Naturally occurring examples of 1st person plural reflexives anteceded by plural imposters are frequent on the Web."

(pg. 20) "However, even though (11) accurately represents our dialect, the Web provides numerous examples that arguably illustrate a different variant of English."

(pg. 21) "Many other such examples are found on the Web."

(pg. 158) "Instances of this pattern are easily found on the Web."

(pg. 241) "We have also found one occurrence of this kind of sentence on the Web."

David Pesetsky points out a technical issue in counting hits (personal communication): "On a more technical note, if you ever care about the number of attestations—even informally to make a claim like 'has more than 7,000 Google hits', click through at least 30 screenfuls before believing the number of hits Google lists initially. There is a weird longstanding bug where Google will initially list a very high number of hits, but if you keep clicking through the pages, it actually turns out to be much much less. I read somewhere that the bug has something to do with how the webcrawler identifies duplicates. In any case, I've seen numbers in the thousands winnowed down to numbers like 40 once you get to page 5, for example. It's very very common. And I have seen syntax papers fall into the error of believing the initial hit number and citing it."

To give an example illustrating the issues involved, consider again the search in (1). When I did the search on Google, Google noted "About 1,360,000 results" (March 6, 2023, but the number varied each time I did the search). After counting the actual hits by hand, I found only 73. Of the 73, many of them contained a result that was longer than the string I was looking for, such as "was done on my own time." Excluding those yielded 41 hits. Four of those were duplicates (from the exact same website). Excluding the duplicates gave me 37 hits. I then manually looked through each of the remaining hits (opening the URL and locating the example on the website). For three of the hits, I could not find the string on the website. Excluding those gave me 34 hits. The remaining examples were of very high quality (conforming to the quality controls above).

The number of hits, and the quality of the hits, in addition to the fact that all the examples are perfectly acceptable to me, gives me confidence in the descriptive generalization: the pronoun *my* in the expression *on my own* can refer back to the implicit argument in a passive formed with the participle *done*. Further searches would broaden this generalization in various ways.

I am not suggesting that the reader go through such a long counting process for their own research. For example, making sure there are no duplicates is quite painstaking work. There is really no need for such a detailed count. There is no need at all to cite specific numbers.

A.6 Discussion

In order to further clarify the method, I ask some possible questions about it and answer them here.

Is the goal of the Internet searches to describe the English data found on the Internet?

No. The goal is definitely not to give a description of the English data found on the Internet. That task is hopelessly obscure. First, there are many different dialects of English represented there (e.g., varieties of American, Canadian, British, South African, Indian, Australian, and Ghanaian English, to name just a few). Second, the people using English are from very different ages and backgrounds (e.g., socioeconomic and cultural). Third, the English found on the Internet is of all kinds of registers and styles. Fourth, there may be citations from earlier stages of English. Fifth, as noted above, a lot of the English on the Internet has been produced by non-native speakers. There are just way too many dimensions to think that a coherent description of that data could ever be given.

If you find a construction attested on the Internet, can you immediately conclude that it is part of the dialect of some speaker?

No, you cannot. There are all kinds of reasons that a construction may appear on the Internet. In fact, it is not unlikely that it was written by a nonnative speaker. This is the reason for "Verify with Target" above. If the construction that you find is relevant to your research, you need to find native speakers who accept it.

My response here supports Jason Merchant's dictate: "Beware the fetishization of attestation!" Jason explains the phrase as follows (personal communication): "I've used it in various talks and handouts to warn people against taking attested sentences as direct input to theorizing. Particularly when a speaker might actually classify that sentence as unacceptable . . . The broader point is really about corpus linguistics, and why data from corpora still need to be checked with speakers, and some of it should be rejected."

If you search for a particular construction and do not find it, can you use this as evidence that the construction is unacceptable?

No, you cannot. There are endless reasons why a particular sentence may not yield any hits in a search. To determine if a sentence is acceptable or not, a native speaker needs to judge it for acceptability.

References

Aarts, Bas. 1995. Secondary Predicates in English. In *The Verb in Contemporary English*, edited by Bas Aarts and Charles F. Meyer, 75–101. Cambridge: Cambridge University Press.

Ackema, Peter, and Maaike Schoorlemmer. 2017. Middles. In *The Wiley Blackwell Companion to Syntax*, Second Edition, edited by Martin Everaert and Henk C. van Riemsdijk, 131–203. Oxford: Wiley-Blackwell.

Alexiadou, Artemis, Elena Anagnostopoulou, and Florian Schäfer. 2015. *External Arguments in Transitivity Alternations: A Layering Approach.* Oxford: Oxford University Press.

Alexiadou, Artemis, Elena Anagnostopoulou, and Florian Schäfer. 2018. Passive. In *Syntactic Structures after 60 Years: The Impact of the Chomskyan Revolution in Linguistics*, edited by Norbert Hornstein, Howard Lasnik, Pritty Patel-Grosz, and Charles Yang, 403–426. Berlin: De Gruyter Mouton.

Andrews, Avery. 1982. A Note on the Constituent Structure of Adverbials and Auxiliaries. *Linguistic Inquiry* 13: 313–317.

Angelopoulos, Nikos. 2019a. *Complementizers and Prepositions as Probes: Insights from Greek.* PhD Dissertation, UCLA.

Angelopoulos, Nikos, Chris Collins, and Arhonto Terzi. 2020. Greek and English Passives and the Role of *by*-Phrases. *Glossa* 5(1): 90, 1–29.

Angelopoulos, Nikos, Chris Collins, Dimitris Michelioudakis, and Arhonto Terzi. 2023. On the Syntactic Status of Implicit Arguments in UG: Greek as a Case Study. Talk given at WCCFL 41, University of Santa Cruz, California.

Aoun, Joseph, and Yen-hui Audrey Li. 1989. Scope and Constituency. *Linguistic Inquiry* 20: 141–172.

Baker, Mark. 1988. *Incorporation.* Chicago: The University of Chicago Press.

Baker, Mark. 1997. Thematic Roles and Syntactic Structures. In *Elements of Grammar*, edited by Liliane Haegeman, 73–137. Dordrecht: Kluwer.

Baker, Mark. 2014. On Dependent Ergative Case (in Shipibo) and Its Derivation by Phase. *Linguistic Inquiry* 45: 341–379.

Baker, Mark. 2015. *Case: Its Principles and Parameters*. Cambridge, UK: Cambridge University Press.

Baker, Mark, Kyle Johnson, and Ian Roberts. 1989. Passive Arguments Raised. *Linguistic Inquiry* 20: 219–251.

Baker, Mark, and Chris Collins. 2006. Linkers and the Internal Structure of the vP. *Natural Language and Linguistic Theory* 24: 307–354.

Baker, Mark, and Nadya Vinokurova. 2009. On Agent Nominalizations and Why They Are Not Like Event Nominalizations. *Language* 85: 517–556.

Barss, Andrew. 2001. Syntactic Reconstruction Effects. In *The Handbook of Contemporary Syntactic Theory*, edited by Mark Baltin and Chris Collins, 670–696. Oxford: Blackwell.

Barss, Andrew, and Howard Lasnik. 1986. A Note on Anaphors and Double Objects. *Linguistic Inquiry* 17: 347–354.

Belletti, Adriana, and Chris Collins. 2020. *Smuggling in Syntax*. Oxford: Oxford University Press.

Belletti, Adriana, and Luigi Rizzi. 2012. Moving Verbal Chunks in the Low Functional Field. In *Functional Heads: The Cartography of Syntactic Structures*, edited by Laura Burgè, Anna Cardinaletti, Giuliana Giusti, Nicola Munaro, and Cecilia Poletto, vol. 7, 129–137. Oxford: Oxford University Press.

Bhatt, Rajesh and Rouyana Pancheva. 2006. Implicit Arguments. In *Blackwell Companion to Syntax*, edited by Martin Everaert and Henk van Riemsdijk, 558–588. Oxford: Wiley-Blackwell.

Bhatt, Rajesh, and Rouyana Pancheva. 2017. Implicit Arguments. In *Blackwell Companion to Syntax*, Second Edition, edited by Martin Everaert and Henk van Riemsdijk, 1–25. Oxford: Wiley-Blackwell.

Bianchi, Valentina. 2015. Italian Arbitrary External Arguments in Active and Passive Clauses. *Rivista di Grammatica Generativa* 37: 1–16.

Borer, Hagit. 1998. Deriving Passive without Theta Roles. In *Morphology and Its Relation to Phonology and Syntax*, edited by Steven G. Lapointe, Diane K. Brentari, and Patrick M. Farrell, 60–99. Stanford: CLSI Publications.

Borer, Hagit. 2020. Nominalizing Verbal Passive: PROs and Cons. In *Nominalization: 50 Years on from Chomsky's Remarks*, edited by Artemis Alexiadou and Hagit Borer, 111–137. Oxford: Oxford University Press.

Bošković, Željko. 2020. On Smuggling, the Freezing Ban, Labels, and *Tough*-Constructions. In *Smuggling in Syntax*, edited by Adriana Belletti and Chris Collins, 53–95. Oxford: Oxford University Press.

Bowers, John. 1981. *The Theory of Grammatical Relations*. Ithaca: Cornell University Press.

Bowers, John. 1993. The Syntax of Predication. *Linguistic Inquiry* 24: 591–656.

Bowers, John. 1997. A Binary Analysis of Resultatives. *Proceedings of the 1997 Linguistics Society Conference, Texas Linguistic Forum* 38: 43–58.

Bowers, John. 2010. *Arguments as Relations*. Cambridge, MA: MIT Press.

Bruening, Benjamin. 2001. QR Obeys Superiority: Frozen Scope and ACD. *Linguistic Inquiry* 32: 233–273.

Bruening, Benjamin. 2013. *By* Phrases in Passives and Nominals. *Syntax* 16: 1–41.

Bruening, Benjamin. 2018. Word Formation Is Syntactic: Raising in Nominalizations. *Glossa* 3(1): 102, 1–25.

Büring, Daniel. 2005. *Binding Theory*. Cambridge: Cambridge University Press.

Burzio, Luigi. 1986. *Italian Syntax*. Dordrecht: Reidel.

Campos, Héctor. 1986. Indefinite Object Drop. *Linguistic Inquiry* 17: 354–359.

Carnie, Andrew. 2013. *Syntax: A Generative Introduction, 3rd ed.* Oxford: Wiley-Blackwell.

Charnavel, Isabelle, and Shannon Bryant. 2022. The Whole Picture: Disentangling Locality, Logophoricity and Subjecthood in English Picture Noun Anaphora. In *Natural Language and Linguistic Theory* 41: 547–610.

Charnavel, Isabelle, and Dominique Sportiche. 2016. Anaphor Binding: What French Inanimate Anaphors Show. *Linguistic Inquiry* 47(1): 35–87.

Charnavel, Isabelle, and Chrissy Zlogar. 2015. English Reflexive Logophors. *Proceedings of CLS* 51: 83–97.

Chomsky, Noam. 1957. *Syntactic Structures*. The Hague: Mouton.

Chomsky, Noam. 1981. *Lectures on Government and Binding*. Dordrecht: Foris Publications.

Chomsky, Noam. 1986. *Knowledge of Language*. New York: Praeger.

Chomsky, Noam. 1995. *The Minimalist Program*. Cambridge, MA: MIT Press.

Chomsky, Noam. 2000. Minimalist Inquiries. In *Step by Step*, edited by Roger Martin, David Michaels, and Juan Uriagereka, 89–155. Cambridge, MA: MIT Press.

Chomsky, Noam. 2004. Beyond Explanatory Adequacy. In *Structures and Beyond*, edited by Adriana Belletti, 104–131. Oxford: Oxford University Press.

Chomsky, Noam. 2005. Three Factors in Language Design. *Linguistic Inquiry* 36: 1–22.

Chomsky, Noam. 2013. Problems of Projection. *Lingua* 130: 33–49.

Chomsky, Noam. 2021. Minimalism: Where Are We Now, and Where Can We Hope to Go? *GengoKenkyu* 160: 1–41.

Chomsky, Noam, Ángel J. Gallego, and Dennis Ott. 2019. Generative Grammar and the Faculty of Language: Insights, Questions and Challenges. *Catalan Journal of Linguistics* (Special Issue): 229–261.

Collins, Chris. 1997. *Local Economy*. Cambridge, MA: MIT Press.

Collins, Chris. 2002. Eliminating Labels. In *Derivation and Explanation in the Minimalist Program*, edited by Samuel David Epstein and T. Daniel Seely, 42–64. Oxford: Blackwell.

Collins, Chris. 2003. The Internal Structure of vP in Ju|'hoan and ǂHoan. *Studia Linguistica* 57: 1–25.

Collins, Chris. 2005a. A Smuggling Approach to the Passive in English. *Syntax* 8: 81–120.

Collins, Chris. 2005b. A Smuggling Approach to Raising in English. *Linguistic Inquiry* 36: 289–298.

Collins, Chris. 2006. A Note on Derivational Morphology. Manuscript, NYU.

Collins, Chris. 2007. Home Sweet Home. In *NYU Working Papers in Linguistics* 1, edited by Lisa Levinson and Oana Savescu-Ciucivara, 1–34.

Collins, Chris. 2017. Merge(X,Y) = {X,Y}. In *Labels and Roots*, edited by Leah Bauke, Andreas Blümel, and Erich Groat, 47–68. Berlin: De Gruyter Mouton.

Collins, Chris. 2018. History of the *By*-Phrase in Generative Syntax (1957 to 2005). *Ordinary Working Grammarian* [Blog].

Collins, Chris. 2021. A Conversation with Noam Chomsky about Formal Semantics. *Ordinary Working Grammarian* [Blog].

Collins, Chris. 2022. The Complexity of Trees, Universal Grammar and Economy Conditions. Biolinguistics 16: 1–13.

Collins, Chris, and Jeffrey S. Gruber. 2014. *A Grammar of ǂHöã*. Köln: Rüdiger Köppe Verlag.

Collins, Chris, and Richard Kayne. 2023. Towards a Theory of Morphology as Syntax. *Studies in Chinese Linguistics* 44: 1–32.

Collins, Chris, and Paul Postal. 2012. *Imposters*. Cambridge, MA: MIT Press.

Collins, Chris, and Paul Postal 2014. *Classical NEG Raising*. Cambridge, MA: MIT Press.

Collins, Chris, and Edward Stabler. 2016. A Formalization of Minimalist Syntax. *Syntax* 19: 43–78.

Collins, Chris, and Höskuldur Thráinsson. 1996. VP Internal Structure and Object Shift in Icelandic. *Linguistic Inquiry* 27: 391–444.

Creissels, Dennis. 2008. Impersonal Pronouns and Coreference: The Case of French *on*. Manuscript, Universite Lumier (Lyon 2).

Demonte, Violeta. 1986. Predication and Passive. In *Generative Studies in Spanish Syntax*, edited by Ivonne Bordelois, Heles Contreras, and Karen Zagona, 51–66. Dordrecht: Foris.

Diesing, Molly. 1992. *Indefinites*. Cambridge, MA: MIT Press.

Doron, Edit. 2015. Voice and Valence Change. In *Syntax—Theory and Analysis*, edited by Tibor Kiss and Artemis Alexiadou, vol. 1, 749–776. Berlin: De Gruyter.

Elbourne, Paul. 2021. Literal vs Enriched Meaning: It's Raining. In *The Wiley Companion to Semantics*, edited by Daniel Gutzmann, Lisa Matthewson, Cécile Meier, Hotze Rullmann, and Thomas Ede Zimmermann, 1–37. Oxford: Wiley-Blackwell.

Embick, David. 1998. Voice Systems and the Syntax/Morphology Interface. *MIT Working Papers in Linguistics* 32: 41–72.

Embick, David. 2004. Unaccusative Syntax and Verbal Alternations. In *The Unaccusativity Puzzle: Explorations of the Syntax–Lexicon Interface*, edited by Artemis

Alexiadou, Elena Anagnostopoulou, and Martin Everaert (eds), 137–158. Oxford: Oxford University Press.

Epstein, Samuel David. 1984. Quantifier-Pro and the LF Representation of PROarb. *Linguistic Inquiry* 15: 499–505.

Fábregas, Antonio. 2012. Evidence for Multidominance in Spanish Agentive Nominalizations. In *Ways of Structure Building*, edited by Myriam Uribe-Etxebarria and Vidal Valmala, 66–92. Oxford: Oxford University Press.

Fábregas, Antonio, and Michael Putnam. 2020. *Passives and Middles in Mainland Scandinavian*. Berlin: De Gruyter Mouton.

Fenger, Paula. 2018. How Impersonal Does One Get? *Journal of Comparative German Linguistics* 21: 291–325.

Fillmore, Charles J. 1986. Pragmatically Controlled Zero Anaphora. In *Proceedings of the Twelfth Annual Meeting of the Berkeley Linguistics Society*, 95–107.

Fodor, Jerry A., and Janet Dean Fodor. 1980. Functional Structure, Quantifiers, and Meaning Postulates. *Linguistic Inquiry* 11: 759–770.

Fu, Jingqi, Hagit Borer, and Tom Roeper. 2001. The VP within Nominalizations: Evidence from Adverbs and the VP Anaphor *do so*. *Natural Language and Linguistic Theory* 19: 549–582.

Gambarage, Joash, and Lisa Matthewson. 2022. The Bantu-Salish Connection in Determiner Semantics. *Glossa* 7(1): 1–35.

Goodall, Grant. 1997. Theta-Alignment and the *By*-Phrase. In *Chicago Linguistic Society* 33: 129–139.

Gotah, Selikem. 2022. The Syntax of Tongugbe (Ewe) *Nyá*-Constructions. Manuscript, NYU.

Gotah, Selikem, and Soo-Hwan Lee. 2022. Negation in Ewe (Tongugbe) Agent Nominalization. Manuscript, NYU.

Grimshaw, Jane. 1990. *Argument Structure*. Cambridge, MA: MIT Press.

Grinder, John. 1971. Chains of Coreference. *Linguistic Inquiry* 2: 182–202.

Gruber, Jeffrey. 2001. Thematic Relations in Syntax. In *The Handbook of Contemporary Syntactic Theory*, edited by Mark Baltin and Chris Collins, 257–298. Oxford: Blackwell.

Haegeman, Liliane. 1994. *Introduction to Government and Binding Theory*, 2nd ed. Oxford: Blackwell.

Hale, Kenneth and Samuel Jay Keyser. 1993. On Argument Structure and the Lexical Expression of Syntactic Relations. In *The View from Building 20: Essays in Linguistics in Honor of Sylvain Bromberger*, edited by Kenneth Hale and Samuel Jay Keyser, 53–109. Cambridge, MA: MIT Press.

Hale, Ken and Samuel Jay Keyser. 2002. *A Prolegomenon to a Theory of Argument Structure*. Cambridge, MA: MIT Press.

Hallman, Peter. 2015. Syntactic Neutralization in Double Object Constructions. *Linguistic Inquiry* 46: 389–424.

Hallman, Peter. 2021. Explaining Siewierska's Generalization. *The Journal of Comparative Germanic* 24: 145–184.

Harley, Heidi. 2002. Possession and the Double Object Construction. *Linguistic Variation Yearbook* 2: 31–70.

Harley, Heidi. 2011. A Minimalist Approach to Argument Structure. In *Linguistic Minimalism*, edited by Cedric Boeckx, 427–448. Oxford: Oxford University Press.

Harley, Heidi. 2013. External Arguments and the Mirror Principle: On the Distinctness of Voice and v. *Lingua* 125: 34–57.

Harley, Heidi, and Hyun Kyoung Jung. 2015. In Support of the P_{HAVE} Analysis of the Double Object Construction. *Linguistic Inquiry* 46: 703–703.

Harley, Heidi, and Shigeru Miyagawa. 2017. Syntax of Ditransitives. *Oxford Research Encyclopedia of Linguistics.*

Heim, Irene. 2011. Definiteness and Indefiniteness. In *Semantics: An International Handbook of Natural Language Meaning (HSK 33.2)*, edited by Claudia Maienborn, Klaus von Heusinger, and Paul Portner, 996–1025. Berlin: De Gruyter Mouton.

Heim, Irene, and Angelik Kratzer. 1998. *Semantics in Generative Grammar.* Oxford: Blackwell.

Helke, Michael. 1973. On Reflexives in English. *Linguistics* 11: 5–23.

Hoekstra, Teun, and Ian Roberts. 1993. Middle Constructions in Dutch and English. In *Knowledge and Language Volume II: Lexical and Conceptual Structure*, edited by Eric Reuland and Werner Abraham, 183–220. Dordrecht: Springer.

Holmberg, Anders. 2005. Is There a Little Pro? Evidence from Finnish. *Linguistic Inquiry* 36: 533–564.

Holmberg, Anders. 2010. Null Subject Parameters. In *Parametric Variation: Null Subjects in Minimalist Theory*, edited by Theresa Biberauer, Anders Holmberg, Ian Roberts, and Michelle Sheehan, 88–124. Cambridge, UK: Cambridge University Press.

Holmberg, Anders, Aarti Nayudu, and Michelle Sheehan. 2009. Three Partial Null-Subject Languages: A Comparison of Brazillian Portuguese, Finnish and Marathi. *Studia Linguistica* 63: 59–97.

Holmberg, Anders, and On-Usa Phimsawat. 2017. Truly Minimal Pronouns. *Diadorim*, Rio de Janeiro, Revista 19.

Holmberg, Anders, Michelle Sheehan, and Jenneke van der Wal. 2019. Movement from the Double Object Construction Is Not Fully Symmetrical. *Linguistic Inquiry* 50: 677–721.

Hornstein, Norbert. 1999. Movement and Control. *Linguistic Inquiry* 30: 69–96.

Ishizuka, Tomoko, and Hilda Koopman. 2014. On the Importance of Being Silent or Pronounced: English *-able* and Japanese *-rare* Potentials Compared. Poster for GLOW 37, Brussels.

Jacobson, Pauline. 2014. *Compositional Semantics.* Oxford: Oxford University Press.

Jaeggli, Osvaldo A. 1986. Passive. *Linguistic Inquiry* 17(4): 587–622.

Johnson, David, and Paul Postal. 1980. *Arc-Pair Grammar*. Princeton: Princeton University Press.

Kayne, Richard. 1975. *French Syntax: The Transformational Cycle*. Cambridge, MA: MIT Press.

Kayne, Richard. 1994. *The Antisymmetry of Syntax*. Cambridge, MA: MIT Press.

Kayne, Richard. 2004. Prepositions as Probes. In *Structures and Beyond*, edited by Adriana Belletti, 192–212. Oxford: Oxford University Press.

Kayne, Richard. 2005. *Movement and Silence*. Oxford: Oxford University Press.

Keenan, Edward L., and Matthew S. Dryer. 2010. Passive in the World's Languages. In *Language Typology and Syntactic Description, Volume 1: Clause Structure*, 2nd ed., edited by Timothy Shopen, 325–361. Cambridge: Cambridge University Press.

Keine, Stefan, and Rajesh Bhatt. 2016. Interpreting Verb Clusters. *Natural Language and Linguistic Theory* 34: 1445–1492.

Kimball, John P. 1971. Super Equi-NP Deletion as Dative Deletion. In *Papers from the Seventh Regional Meeting of the Chicago Linguistics Society*, 142–148.

Kiparsky, Paul. 2013. Towards a Null Theory of the Passive. *Lingua* 125: 7–33.

Kitagawa, Yoshihisa. 1994. Shells, Yolks and Scrambled E.g.s. In *NELS* 24, edited by Mercè Gazàlez, 221–239.

Koenig, Jean-Pierre.1998. On a tué le président! The Nature of Passives and Ultra-Indefinites. In *Cognition and Function in Language*, edited by Barbara Fox, Dan Jurafsky, and Laura Michaelis, 235–251. Stanford: CSLI.

Koenig, Jean-Pierre, and Gail Mauner. 2000. A-Definites and the Discourse Status of Implicit Arguments. *Journal of Semantics* 16: 207–236.

Koopman, Hilda. 2003. The Locality of Agreement and the Structure of the DP in Maasai. In *The Role of Agreement in Natural Language: TLS 5 Proceedings*, edited by William E. Griffin, 207–227.

Koopman, Hilda. 2005. On the Parallelism of DPs and Clauses: Evidence from Kisongo Maasai. In *Verb First, On the Syntax of Verb-initial Languages*, edited by A. Carnie, 281–302. Amsterdam: John Benjamins.

Kratzer, Angelika. 1996. Severing the External Argument from Its Verb. In *Phrase Structure and the Lexicon*, 109–137. Dordrecht: Springer.

Landau, Idan. 2010. The Explicit Syntax of Implicit Arguments. *Linguistic Inquiry* 41: 357–388.

Landau, Idan. 2013. *Control in Generative Grammar: A Research Companion*. Cambridge, UK: Cambridge University Press.

Lappin, Shalom, and Ur Shlonsky. 1993. Impersonal Passives. *Linguistics* 31: 5–24.

Larson, Richard K. 1988. On the Double Object Construction. *Linguistic Inquiry* 19: 335–391.

Larson, Richard K. 2010. On Pylkkänen's Semantics for Low Applicatives. *Linguistic Inquiry* 41: 701–704.

Larson, Richard K. 2014. *On Shell Structure*. New York: Routledge.

Lebeaux, David. 1984. Locality and Anaphoric Binding. *The Linguistic Review* 4: 343–363.

Lebeaux, David. 2009. *Where Does the Binding Theory Apply?* Cambridge, MA: MIT Press.

Legate, Julie. 2014. *Voice and v: Lessons from Achenese*. Cambridge, MA: MIT Press.

Legendre, Geraldine. 1997. Secondary Predicates and Functional Projections in French. *Natural Language and Linguistic Theory* 15: 43–87.

Levin, Beth. 1993. *English Verb Classes and Alternations*. Chicago: The University of Chicago Press.

Levin, Beth, and Malka Rappaport Hovav. 1995. *Unaccusativity: At the Syntax-Lexical Semantics Interface*. Cambridge, MA: MIT Press.

Mahajan, Anoop. 1994. ACTIVE Passives. In *The Proceedings of the Thirteenth West Coast Conference on Formal Linguistics*, edited by Raul Aranovich, William Byrne, Susanne Preuss, and Martha Senturia, 286–301.

Marantz, Alec. 1993. Implications of Asymmetries in Double Object Constructions. In *Theoretical Aspects of Bantu Grammar*, edited by Sam Mchombo, 113–150. Stanford: CSLI.

McCawley, James. 1988. *The Syntactic Phenomena of English*, vol. 1. Chicago: The University of Chicago Press.

Meltzer-Asscher, Aya. 2012. Verbal Passives in English and Hebrew: A Comparative Study. In *The Theta System: Argument Structure at the Interface*, edited by Martin Everaert, Marijana Marelj, and Tal Siloni, 280–307. Oxford: Oxford University Press.

Merchant, Jason. 2013. Voice and Ellipsis. *Linguistic Inquiry* 44: 77–108.

Moltmann, Friederike. 2006. Generic *one*, Arbitrary PRO, and the First Person. *Natural Language Semantics* 14: 257–281.

Müller, Gereon. 2019. The Short Life Cycle of External Arguments in German Passive Derivations. In *Linguistische Arbeits Berichte* 94, edited by Andrew Murphy, 55–112. Leipzig University.

Müller, Stefan. 2008. Depictive Predicates in German and English. In *Secondary Predicates in Eastern European Languages and Beyond, Studia Slavica Oldenburgensia* 16, edited by Christoph Schroeder, Gerd Hentschel, und Winfried Boeder, 255–273. Oldenburg: BIS-Verlag.

Murphy, Andy. 2015. Double Passivization in Turkish: A Structure Removal Approach. *Proceedings of ConSOLE* XXIII, 316–339.

Myler, Neil, and Zoliswa O. Mali. 2021. Two Places for Causees in Productive IsiXhosa Morphological Causatives. *Syntax* 24: 1–43.

Ndapo, Olivia. 2022. Oshigandjera (Oshiwambo) Passive: A Case on Implicit Argument. Manuscript, NYU.

Newman, Elise. 2020. Facilitator Effects in Middles and More. *Glossa: A Journal of General Linguistics*, 5(1): 62.

Ntelitheos, Dimitrios. 2012. *Deriving Nominals: A Syntactic Account of Malagasy Nominalizations*, vol. 3. The Netherlands: Brill.

Postal, Paul. 1974. *On Raising*. Cambridge, MA: MIT Press.

Postal, Paul. 2010. *Edge-Based Clausal Syntax*. Cambridge, MA: MIT Press.

Pylkkänen, Liina. 2008a. *Introducing Arguments*. Cambridge, MA: MIT Press.

Pylkkänen, Liina. 2008b. Mismatching Meanings in Brain and Behavior. *Language and Linguistics Compass* 2/4: 712–738.

Ramchand, Gillian Catriona. 2008. *Verb Meaning and the Lexicon: A First-Phase Syntax*. Cambridge University Press.

Ramchand, Gillian Catriona. 2017. The Event Domain. In *The Verbal Domain*, edited by Roberta D'Alessandro and Irene Franco, 233–254. Oxford: Oxford University Press.

Rappaport Hovav, Malka, and Beth Levin. 2008. The English Dative Alternation: The Case for Verb Sensitivity. *Journal of Linguistics* 44: 129–167.

Reed, Lisa. 2011. *Get*-Passives. *The Linguistic Review* 28: 41–78.

Reinhart, Tanya, and Eric Reuland. 1993. Reflexivity. *Linguistic Inquiry* 24: 657–720.

Rizzi, Luigi. 1986. Null Objects in Italian and the Theory of *pro*. *Linguistic Inquiry* 17: 501–557.

Rizzi, Luigi. 1990. *Relativized Minimality*. Cambridge, MA: MIT Press.

Roberts, Ian. 1987. *The Representation of Implicit and Dethematized Subjects*. Dordrecht: Foris.

Roberts, Ian. 1988. Predicative APs. *Linguistic Inquiry* 19: 703–710.

Roberts, Ian. 2019. *Parameter Hierarchies and Universal Grammar*. Oxford: Oxford University Press.

Roeper, Thomas. 1987. Implicit Arguments and the Head-Complement Relation. *Linguistic Inquiry* 18: 267–310.

Roeper, Thomas. 1993. Explicit Syntax in the Lexicon: The Representation of Nominalizations. In *Semantics in the Lexicon*, edited by James Pustejovsky, 185–220. Dordrecht: Springer.

Roeper, Thomas. 2020. Where Are Thematic Roles? Building the Micro-Syntax of Implicit Arguments in Nominalizations. In *Nominalization: 50 Years on from Chomsky's Remarks*, edited by Artemis Alexiadou and Hagit Borer, 277–308. Oxford: Oxford University Press.

Roeper, Thomas. 2022. Biolinguistic Economy and the Representation of Implicit Arguments. Manuscript, University of Massachussetts.

Ross, John Robert. 1969. On the Cyclic Nature of English Pronominalization. In *Modern Studies in English. Readings in Transformational Grammar*, edited by David A. Reibel and Sanford A. Schane, 187–201. Englewood Cliffs, NJ: Prentice-Hall.

Safir, Ken. 1987. The Syntactic Projection of Lexical Thematic Structure. *Natural Language and Linguistic Theory* 5: 561–601.

Safir, Ken, and Timothy Stowell. 1987. Binominal each. In *Proceedings of the North East Linguistic Society* 18, edited by James Blevins and Juli Carter, 246–250. Amherst, MA: GLSA Publications.

Schäfer, Florian. 2012. The Passive of Reflexive Verbs and Its Implications for Theories of Binding and Case. *The Journal of Comparative Germanic Linguistics* 15: 213–268.

Schultze-Berndt, Eva, and Nikolaus P. Himmelmann. 2004. Depictive Secondary Predicates in Crosslinguistic Perspective. *Linguistic Typology* 8: 59–131.

Sichel, Ivy. 2009. New Evidence for the Structural Realization of the Implicit External Argument in Nominalizations. *Linguistic Inquiry* 40: 712–723.

Sigurðsson, Einar Freyr, and Jim Wood. 2021. On the Implicit Argument of Icelandic Indirect Causatives. *Linguistic Inquiry* 52: 579–625.

Simon, Dan. 2018. Internal Structure of Nominals. Manuscript, NYU.

Simpson, Jane. 2005. Depictives in English and Walpiri. In *Secondary Predication and Adverbial Modification*, edited by Nikolaus P. Himmelmann and Eva F. Schultze-Berndt, 69–106. Oxford: Oxford University Press.

Sportiche, Dominque. 2017a. Reconstruction, Binding, and Scope. In *Blackwell Companion to Syntax*, edited by Martin Everaert and Henk van Riemsdijk, 1–58. Oxford: Wiley-Blackwell.

Sportiche, Dominique. 2017b. Fewer Adjuncts: More Relatives. In A Schrift to Fest Kyle Johnson. *Linguistics Open Access Publications*, edited by Nicholas LaCara, Keir Moulton, and Anne-Michelle Tessier, 1. https://scholarworks.umass.edu/linguist_oapubs/1/.

Sportiche, Dominique, Hilda Koopman, and Edward Stabler. 2014. *An Introduction to Syntactic Analysis and Theory*. Oxford: Wiley-Blackwell.

Storment, John David. 2022. Two Is Better Than One: Implicit Arguments and the EPP in Spanish. Manuscript, SUNY Stony Brook.

Stroik, Thomas. 1992. Middles and Movement. *Linguistic Inquiry* 23: 127–137.

Stroik, Thomas. 1995. On Middle Formation: A Reply to Zribi-Hertz. *Linguistic Inquiry* 26: 165–171.

Stroik, Thomas. 1999. Middles and Reflexivity. *Linguistic Inquiry* 30: 119–131.

Stroik, Thomas. 2000. *Syntactic Controversies*. Munich: LINCOM EUROPA.

Stroik, Thomas. 2005. Review of *Middle Voice: A Comparative Study in the Syntax-Semantics Interface of German*, by Markus Steinbach. *Journal of Comparative Germanic Linguistics* 8: 225–241.

Stroik, Thomas. 2006. Arguments in Middles. In *Demoting the Agent: Passive, Middle and Other Voice Phenomena*, edited by Benjamin Lyngfelt and Torgrim Solstad, 301–326. Amsterdam: John Benjamins Publishing Company.

Sulemana, Abdul-Razak. 2022. Passive without Morphology: A Case for Implicit Arguments. Manuscript, University of Ghana, Legon-Accra.

Takano, Yuji. 1998. Object Shift and Scrambling. *Natural Language and Linguistic Theory* 16: 817–889.

Travis, Lisa. 2000. Event Structure in Syntax. In *Events as Grammatical Objects: The Converging Perspectives of Lexical Semantics and Syntax*, edited by Carol Tenny and James Pustejovsky, 145–185. Stanford: CSLI Publications.

Vinet, Marie-Thérèse. 1987. Implict Arguments and Control in Middles and Passives. In *Advances in Romance Linguistics*, edited by David Birdsong and Jean-Pierre Montreuil, 427–437. Dordrecht: Foris Publications.

Watanabe, Akira. 1993. AGR-Based Case Theory and Its Interaction with the A-Bar System. Doctoral Dissertation, MIT.

Williams, Alexander. 2015. *Arguments in Syntax and Semantics*. Cambridge, UK: Cambridge University Press.

Williams, Edwin. 1985. PRO and Subject of NP. *Natural Language and Linguistic Theory* 3: 297–315.

Williams, Edwin. 1987. Implicit Arguments, the Binding Theory and Control. *Natural Language and Linguistic Theory* 5: 151–180.

Zimmermann, Malte. 2007. Overt Existential Closure in Bura (Central Chadic). In *SALT XVII*, edited by T. Friedman and M. Gibson, 333–350. Ithaca: Cornell University Press.

Zyman, Erik. 2017. P'urhepecha Hyperraising to Object: An Argument for Purely Altruistic Movement. In *Proceedings of the Linguistic Society of America*, vol. 2, edited by Patrick Farrell, 1–15.

Zyman, Erik, and Nick Kalivoda. 2020. XP- and X^0- movement in the Latin Verb: Evidence from Mirroring and Anti-Mirroring. *Glossa* 5(1): 20, 1–38.

Author Index

Subject Index

Linguistic Inquiry Monographs
Samuel Jay Keyser, general editor

1. *Word Formation in Generative Grammar*, Mark Aronoff
2. *$\bar{X}$ Syntax: A Study of Phrase Structure*, Ray Jackendoff
3. *Recent Transformational Studies in European Languages*, Samuel Jay Keyser, editor
4. *Studies in Abstract Phonology*, Edmund Gussmann
5. *An Encyclopedia of AUX: A Study of Cross-Linguistic Equivalence*, Susan Steele
6. *Some Concepts and Consequences of the Theory of Government and Binding*, Noam Chomsky
7. *The Syntax of Words*, Elisabeth O. Selkirk
8. *Syllable Structure and Stress in Spanish: A Nonlinear Analysis*, James W. Harris
9. *CV Phonology: A Generative Theory of the Syllable*, George N. Clements and Samuel Jay Keyser
10. *On the Nature of Grammatical Relations*, Alec P. Marantz
11. *A Grammar of Anaphora*, Joseph Aoun
12. *Logical Form: Its Structure and Derivation*, Robert May
13. *Barriers*, Noam Chomsky
14. *On the Definition of Word*, Anna-Maria Di Sciullo and Edwin Williams
15. *Japanese Tone Structure*, Janet Pierrehumbert and Mary E. Beckman
16. *Relativized Minimality*, Luigi Rizzi
17. *Types of Ā-Dependencies*, Guglielmo Cinque
18. *Argument Structure*, Jane Grimshaw
19. *Locality: A Theory and Some of Its Empirical Consequences*, Maria Rita Manzini
20. *Indefinites*, Molly Diesing
21. *Syntax of Scope*, Joseph Aoun and Yen-hui Audrey Li
22. *Morphology by Itself: Stems and Inflectional Classes*, Mark Aronoff
23. *Thematic Structure in Syntax*, Edwin Williams
24. *Indices and Identity*, Robert Fiengo and Robert May
25. *The Antisymmetry of Syntax*, Richard S. Kayne
26. *Unaccusativity: At the Syntax–Lexical Semantics Interface*, Beth Levin and Malka Rappaport Hovav
27. *Lexico-Logical Form: A Radically Minimalist Theory*, Michael Brody
28. *The Architecture of the Language Faculty*, Ray Jackendoff
29. *Local Economy*, Chris Collins
30. *Surface Structure and Interpretation*, Mark Steedman
31. *Elementary Operations and Optimal Derivations*, Hisatsugu Kitahara
32. *The Syntax of Nonfinite Complementation: An Economy Approach*, Željko Bošković

33. *Prosody, Focus, and Word Order*, Maria Luisa Zubizarreta

34. *The Dependencies of Objects*, Esther Torrego

35. *Economy and Semantic Interpretation*, Danny Fox

36. *What Counts: Focus and Quantification*, Elena Herburger

37. *Phrasal Movement and Its Kin*, David Pesetsky

38. *Dynamic Antisymmetry*, Andrea Moro

39. *Prolegomenon to a Theory of Argument Structure*, Ken Hale and Samuel Jay Keyser

40. *Essays on the Representational and Derivational Nature of Grammar: The Diversity of* Wh-*Constructions*, Joseph Aoun and Yen-hui Audrey Li

41. *Japanese Morphophonemics: Markedness and Word Structure*, Junko Ito and Armin Mester

42. *Restriction and Saturation*, Sandra Chung and William A. Ladusaw

43. *Linearization of Chains and Sideward Movement*, Jairo Nunes

44. *The Syntax of (In)dependence*, Ken Safir

45. *Interface Strategies: Optimal and Costly Computations*, Tanya Reinhart

46. *Asymmetry in Morphology*, Anna Maria Di Sciullo

47. *Relators and Linkers: The Syntax of Predication, Predicate Inversion, and Copulas*, Marcel den Dikken

48. *On the Syntactic Composition of Manner and Motion*, Maria Luisa Zubizarreta and Eunjeong Oh

49. *Introducing Arguments*, Liina Pylkkänen

50. *Where Does Binding Theory Apply?*, David Lebeaux

51. *Locality in Minimalist Syntax*, Thomas S. Stroik

52. *Distributed Reduplication*, John Frampton

53. *The Locative Syntax of Experiencers*, Idan Landau

54. *Why Agree? Why Move?: Unifying Agreement-Based and Discourse-Configurational Languages*, Shigeru Miyagawa

55. *Locality in Vowel Harmony*, Andrew Nevins

56. *Uttering Trees*, Norvin Richards

57. *The Syntax of Adjectives*, Guglielmo Cinque

58. *Arguments as Relations*, John Bowers

59. *Agreement and Head Movement*, Ian Roberts

60. *Localism versus Globalism in Morphology and Phonology*, David Embick

61. *Provocative Syntax*, Phil Branigan

62. *Anaphora and Language Design*, Eric J. Reuland

63. *Indefinite Objects: Scrambling, Choice Functions, and Differential Marking*, Luis López

64. *A Syntax of Substance*, David Adger

65. *Subjunctive Conditionals*, Michela Ippolito

66. *Russian Case Morphology and the Syntactic Categories*, David Pesetsky

67. *Classical NEG Raising: An Essay on the Syntax of Negation*, Chris Collins and Paul M. Postal

68. *Agreement and Its Failures*, Omer Preminger

69. *Voice and v: Lessons from Acehnese*, Julie Anne Legate

70. *(Re)labeling*, Carlo Cecchetto and Caterina Donati

71. *A Two-Tiered Theory of Control*, Idan Landau

72. *Concepts, Syntax, and Their Interface: Tanya Reinhart's Theta System*, Martin Everaert, Marijana Marelj, and Eric Reuland, editors

73. *Contiguity Theory*, Norvin Richards

74. *Impossible Persons*, Daniel Harbour

75. *Agreement Beyond Phi*, Shigeru Miyagawa

76. *The Final-Over-Final Condition: A Syntactic Universal*, Michelle Sheehan, Theresa Biberauer, Ian Roberts, and Anders Holmberg

77. *Situations and Syntactic Structures: Rethinking Auxiliaries and Order in English*, Gillian Ramchand

78. *Features of Person: From the Inventory of Persons to their Morphological Realization*, Peter Ackema and Ad Neeleman

79. *Cardinals: The Syntax and Semantics of Cardinal-Containing Expressions*, Tania Ionin and Ora Matushansky

80. *Composing Questions*, Hadas Kotek

81. *Probes and Their Horizons*, Stefan Keine

82. *A Theory of Indexical Shift: Meaning, Grammar, and Crosslinguistic Variation*, Amy Rose Deal

83. *Merge: Binarity in (Multidominant) Syntax*, Barbara Citko and Martina Gračanin-Yüksek

84. *A Selectional Theory of Adjunct Control*, Idan Landau

85. *Syntax in the Treetops*, Shigeru Miyagawa

86. *On Linearization*, Guglielmo Cinque

87. *Principles of Argument Structure: A Merge-Based Approach*, Chris Collins